NON-BUSINESS ACTORS IN A BUSINESS NETWORK

INTERNATIONAL BUSINESS AND MANAGEMENT SERIES

Series Editor: **Pervez N. Ghauri**

Published

GHAURI & OXELHEIM
European Union and the Race for Foreign Direct Investment in Europe

HYDER & ABRAHA
Strategic Alliances in Eastern and Central Europe

CONTRACTOR & LORANGE
Alliances and Co-operative Strategies

GEMÜNDEN, RITTER & WALTER
Relationships and Networks in International Markets

GHAURI & USUNIER
International Business Negotiations

HAVILA, FORSGREN & HÅKANSSON
Critical Perspectives on Internationalisation

MOROSINI
Managing Cultural Differences

NAUDE & TURNBULL
Network Dynamics in International Marketing

BUCKLEY & GHAURI
The Global Challenge for Multinational Enterprises

HÅKANSSON & JOHANSON
Business Network Learning

LI
Managing International Business Ventures in China

YANG
Intellectual Property and Doing Business in China

Forthcoming titles

HENNART & THOMAS
Global Competitive Strategies

Other titles of interest

FATEMI
International Trade in the 21st Century

DUNNING
Globalization, Trade and Foreign Direct Investment

MONCARZ
International Trade and the New Economic Order

KREININ
Contemporary Issues in Commercial Policy

Related journals – sample copies available on request

European Management Journal
International Business Review
International Journal of Research in Marketing
Long Range Planning
Scandinavian Journal of Management

For full details of all IBM titles published under the Elsevier imprint please go to:
http://www.elsevier.com/locate/series/ibm

NON-BUSINESS ACTORS IN A BUSINESS NETWORK

A COMPARATIVE CASE ON FIRMS' ACTIONS IN DEVELOPING AND DEVELOPED COUNTRIES

BY

AMJAD HADJIKHANI

Uppsala University, Sweden

and

PETER THILENIUS

Mälardalen University, Sweden

2005

ELSEVIER

Amsterdam – Boston – Heidelberg – London – New York – Oxford
Paris – San Diego – San Francisco – Singapore – Sydney – Tokyo

ELSEVIER B.V.
Sara Burgerhartstraat 25
P.O. Box 211
1000 AE Amsterdam
The Netherlands

ELSEVIER Inc.
525 B Street, Suite 1900
San Diego
CA 92101-4495
USA

ELSEVIER Ltd
The Boulevard, Langford
Lane, Kidlington
Oxford OX5 1GB
UK

ELSEVIER Ltd
84 Theobalds Road
London
WC1X 8RR
UK

First edition 2005

Library of Congress Cataloging in Publication Data
A catalog record is available from the Library of Congress.

British Library Cataloguing in Publication Data
A catalogue record is available from the British Library.

ISBN: 0-08-044615-9

⊗The paper used in this publication meets the requirements of ANSI/NISO Z39.48-1992 (Permanence of Paper). Printed in The Netherlands.

Working together to grow libraries in developing countries

www.elsevier.com | www.bookaid.org | www.sabre.org

ELSEVIER   BOOK AID
International   Sabre Foundation

Contents

Preface

Although we are the authors of this text, we cannot claim autonomy in its creation. We have received contributions from various sources, and without these, the work would have been impossible to accomplish. The research would not have been possible without the support received from the Swedish Research Council. The group engaged in the research on the Middle East has given their wholehearted support and assistance during the years needed to complete this task. We are also indebted to other groups that have assisted our work and without whose help the research could not have been undertaken. We are grateful for the enormous assistance received from the Industrial Management Institute (IMI) in Iran. The former Managing Director, Dr. Ja'far Mara'shi,' and the researchers, Dr. Mortezah Emadzadeh, Ali Ayari, Mansour Mojaddam, and Firozeh Saber, worked tirelessly when conducting the survey in Iran. It was only through the input of the IMI research group that the data collection in Iran became possible. The empirical part of the study also received a great deal of help from researcher Francesco Ciabuschi. His input was to assist in the systemization of the statistical measures obtained in the Iranian study and in the Industrial Marketing and Purchasing (IMP2) study. Throughout the writing of this book, Professor Jan Johanson provided a constant stream of encouragement and constructive suggestions. The support of Professors Bo Utas and Annika Rabo sustained our spirits and expanded our thinking. We are also in great debt to Dr. Javad Amid, whose reflections and insights appear in different parts of this book.

Amjad Hadjikhani and Peter Thilenius
Uppsala, September 2004

Part 1

Theoretical and Empirical Fields

The authors of the book "Managing Business Relationships" (Ford *et al.* 1998), which discusses the business network, begin with the statement that "No business exists in isolation. Each business is dependent for its survival on customers and suppliers of products and services, finance and advice . . . they cooperate to receive or supply products; . . . lobby the government for better trading conditions." So far, so good: The statement acknowledges the existence of other actors, such as governments, that interact with the commercial actors. The authors have made a great job of developing concepts and presenting managerial implications, but when the book was studied more closely, it was realized that the statement above on government loses its significance if the factor of non-business actors is left untouched. Except for a few later studies, this is a common omission among studies that apply industrial network theory or other marketing disciplines. Earlier researchers tended to analyze marketing as a single buying or selling transaction. The marketing mix model initially directed its focus at suppliers, and later at the industrial relationship (see, for example, Kotler *et al.* 1996). As with Ford *et al.*'s research on industrial networks, these studies leave the non-business actors in the context of "the environment" and treat them as though constraining factors have some influence.

This brief review shows that there is a gap in marketing research that calls for new studies which pay attention to the interaction between business and non-business actors. The aim of this study has been to develop a conceptual framework for use in analyzing the empirical facts. This model is constructed on the theory of industrial networks, which identifies actors, activities, and resources.

There is a large amount of research that studies marketing from the point of the view of multinational companies (MNCs). Based on empirical evidence about the behavior of MNCs, conclusions are drawn without any reference to the behavior of their local partners. The behavior of the MNCs is not coupled with opportunities open to the local firms. In reaction to this shortcoming, this study goes against the stream and focuses its attention on the behavior of local customers when they interact with foreign MNCs. In addition, and unlike the studies prevailing in industrial networks, this study selects a less industrialized country, namely Iran. The Iranian case study is composed of interviews with 60 large Iranian firms. The aim has been to study the Iranian customers' relationships with their suppliers, which are international enterprises. There are two main reasons for the selection of Iran. First, international firms, through their globalization policies, are expanding increasingly into less industrialized countries. Experience from this study may contribute some knowledge which is significant for the MNCs in their expansion into similar countries. Second, the comparison of the Iranian case with a study that focuses on the experience in industrialized countries can be both fruitful and interesting. The IMP2 (industrial marketing and purchasing) research study that was conducted several years ago is also presented here. Some major outcomes from the IMP2 study are compared with the Iranian case to enrich the discussions and final outcomes.

This research, in contrast to the earlier study, considers the behavior of the customer firms and aims at understanding why they behave in a specific way when interacting with foreign MNCs. Understanding this behavior can help MNCs to undertake strategic measures that would assist in reducing the uncertainty in the interaction. As the study develops a new conceptual and theoretical framework that includes the government, the results can contribute knowledge to governments and assist them in understanding the consequence of their political actions. Whilst it is true that the empirical study in the first instance considers the case of Iran, the conceptual tools and empirical findings are applicable to other studies and contexts.

Finally, the empirical study adds new knowledge on the behavior of firms with their origins in countries similar to Iran. Although these firms interact with international companies, understanding the behavior of these firms is essential for the international companies. Hopefully, this research may open doors for a new research arena that focuses on the behavior of firms with their origins in countries which are in different states of development.

Chapter 1

Business Firms' Interaction with the Environment

Following the construction of industrial network theory, this study develops a new perspective by extending the industrial network boundary. The ultimate purpose of this chapter is to present a model that was developed to include not only business, but also non-business actors within the context. The approach is constructed on the assumption that focal business relationships are embedded in a context infused with business and non-business actors. This construct will be followed in the empirical study, which is presented in Part 2. The chapter begins with the objectives of the study and broadly presents different views on traditional, dyadic, and network studies. The chapter finally turns to the principles exercised when collecting the facts.

1. Consideration of the Book

In international marketing studies, the main attention is reserved for the business behavior of the MNCs. The business competency of the MNCs is seen as sufficient to explain market entry and expansion in foreign markets. The political competency of MNCs or their partners in foreign markets is excluded, and their actions may be viewed as homogeneous.

This tendency has resulted in later studies expressing the need for further research on the interaction between business and non-business organizations (see for example, Boddewyn 1988; Hadjikhani & Sharma 1999; Ring *et al.* 1990). These researchers contend that the earlier studies ignore that firms accumulate resources to raise political competency and influence non-business actors, although, in fact, few researchers have been attracted to the interactions between business and non-business actors.

There are a large number of studies in international marketing that indicate the homogenous impact of government. Studies on risk theories, such as those of Blance (1980), Boddewyn & Brewer (1994), Campa (1994), Korbin (1982), and

Simon (1983) are a few examples of the efforts made to elaborate views on the influence of the government. In other studies, the researchers have emphasized the diverse ways in which host governments restrict foreign firms (e.g. Doz 1986). The homogeneous influence is often measured by adaptive actions. Political activity is indicated by the various strategies used to cope with the environment. Portions of the international marketing literature also include a bargaining focus, whereby governments gain leverage, and MNCs lose leverage over time. Attention has not been given to such questions as how the firm/government relationship is structured or to the eventual content of the political activities of the firms. The literature ignores the essential fact that political uncertainty mainly affects MNCs through local firms and has not paid attention to what political uncertainty means for the local firms and how it transfers to the MNCs. Thus, the question of how the partners of these MNCs experience political uncertainty and what kinds of problems and opportunities they generate has been neglected. The one-dimensional view in the earlier studies discloses no information about the partners of the MNCs and their complex world. These studies always portray the business world from the perspective of the MNCs, as though the local firms do not exist. Even in internationalization cases, such as joint ventures, the local partners are left out of the domain of the study.

Recent researchers, such as Boddewyn (1988) and Ring *et al.* (1990) argue that the MNCs' political behavior affects their market position. Their basis is that the MNCs do not merely passively react to a given condition in their environment but, rather, that they try to shape their political environment. In further considering the view, there has been an increasing amount of research studying how MNCs can exercise influence on government. These include studies on the lobbying and influence of business firms on political actors (Andersen & Eliasson 1996; Austen-Smith 1987), creating bargaining competency to convince the political actors (Ballam 1994; Bolton 1991; Crawford 1982), and on pressure groups, and bribery and lobbying (Rose-Ackerman 1978). Andersen & Eliasson (1996) and Boddewyn & Brewer (1994) extended an understanding of the topic by observing the influence from an interdependence point of view. According to this view, relationships between business firms and government are an outcome of the fact that they need each other. Governments need both local firms and MNCs for economic development, and business firms need government to gain support and stability in the market. However, the view is still dominated by a dyadic perspective in the interaction (i.e. on the interaction between only the business and political actors). The triadic view is an extension of the dyadic business-to-business view and integrates the political actors (Boddewyn 1988; Hadjikhani & Sharma 1999). Despite the efforts of these researchers, the focal attention in these studies is still on the behavior of the MNCs.

The above studies contribute insightful knowledge on the behavior of MNCs in their interaction with non-business actors. However, they contain two fundamental shortcomings, which this study tries to avoid. The first is their point of departure. No matter what their theoretical framework, the focus of these studies is on the behavior of MNCs. An interesting question is how governments can influence only MNCs when they always have to act together with local partners. Together, they make mutual commitments for joint ventures or licensing, or carry on other business activities. One can go even further and explain that government action strongly affects the local partners and thereafter affects MNCs. It lies in the interests of the local partners to reduce or eliminate uncertainty before it reaches the relationships with the MNCs. The influence of governments on MNCs, however, can be: (1) through the local partners; or (2) directly on both MNCs and their local partners. Hence, it becomes difficult to understand how the above studies can ignore the local business actors that actually interact directly with the governments. One reason may be related to the actual research effort: collecting data can be costly and in some countries may be impossible.

The second area reflects the conceptual framework in international marketing studies. The traditional dyadic or triadic views developed by some of the researchers lose their significance, as MNCs and local partners are acting within a network context consisting of a number of different actors. A conceptual framework with a limited boundary may lead a study to draw conclusions with a low level of significance.

There remains a gap in knowledge, and further research can enhance our understanding of the interactions between business and non-business actors. This study pinpoints two different types of competencies. The first considers the management of industrial relationships with business actors. This field is well developed and has been covered in a large number of relationship and network studies. The second is the political competency, and this supports the management of the relationship with non-business actors. This field has attracted fewer researchers. These two competencies are interwoven and complement each other. This research is not a study of competency but recognizes it as a significant issue for the analysis of the empirical facts. The main consideration of this study, however, is to develop a conceptual framework by elaborating a network model evolved through different kinds of political and business relationships and connections. This business network is constructed on the industrial network principle. The complexity is created by the fact that the network involves actors from both the business and non-business sides. The study integrates the two problematic issues of: (1) business to business; and (2) business to non-business, and unifies them into one conceptual tool. The point of departure is that any firm interacts with several business and non-business actors, and that their relationships are interwoven. Instead of limiting the context towards only business or non-business actors, it extends the boundary of the industrial network context to include areas that have a significant influence. In this construction, the two focal business actors, local firms and the firms of their foreign international partners, are prone to be embedded in a context with several business and non-business actors. The study concentrates on the structure of the network, constituted by the content of relationships between different types of actors.

Another focus of the study is the examination of the theoretical view of an empirical case — the case of 60 firms from Iran. The focal actors are the Iranian customers and foreign international suppliers, which have had rather long business relationships. When operationalizing the concepts, in contrast to the earlier research that studied the behavior of the MNCs, this study has altered the focus of attention. It examines the behavior of the Iranian firms when interacting with foreign international companies. Earlier studies treated the partners of MNCs from developing countries as anonymous units, and marketing was explored as a unidirectional activity of the MNCs. In contrast, this study gives identity to these firms and studies their business and political opportunities and limitations. Even studies operationalizing industrial network theory have mainly considered MNCs in industrialized countries. Studies are seldom carried out that explore the interaction between MNCs and firms from developing countries. Such an examination can enhance our understanding of the utility of the theoretical notions evolved in this study but also, hopefully, assist MNCs and local firms in improving their understanding of their business and political environments.

Selecting network theory as the theoretical approach, the study attempts to employ a broad perspective from two points of view. First, it considers the four major concepts of network theory (relationship, adaptation, social interaction, and embeddedness) rather than focusing on one specific concept of the theory. Second, the empirical field covers facts about all five concepts and does not try to formulate a deep analysis based on a few statistical measures.

Such a broad perspective can be criticized for its generality. It is true that the study may ignore a number of interesting points that might have been explored with attention to only a few variables, but such a study would not have been able to provide conclusions on the adaptability of the theory in another business society. One aim of this text is to test network theory in the Iranian business environment rather than confining itself to a narrow concept. The study also develops the theoretical notion of non-business actors and links this to the selected theory. In order to understand how this element is interrelated with the other elements (relationships, adaptation, social interaction, and business embeddedness) in network theory, of necessity, the study presents facts about all these notions. Studying the content of each concept and the connections between them increases our knowledge about the role of each concept and the function of the theory. It is only through this method that the study can evaluate the theory in the context of another empirical world.

2. The Empirical Study

The aim of the empirical study was to gain an understanding of the structure of the relationships between Iranian suppliers and foreign customers, and to draw appropriate conclusions. A survey method was selected here. A case study method, which could have given in-depth information about a few specific cases, could have been chosen. But the method was insufficient for understanding the structure of the network and for drawing general conclusions. It was also the aim of the study to examine a theory that had already been tested in industrialized countries. As there were already a number of studies that employed network theory and analyzed the facts by using the survey method, this led to the selection of network theory and the survey method in the initial stage of this research. Fortunately, analyzing two different conditions, or cases, with the same survey and model, can provide an opportunity for comparison. The questionnaire used in this study has its origin in the IMP2 (European International Marketing and Purchasing) study, which was also designed on the basis of network theory.

2.1. IMP2

The original IMP2 study started in the 1980s, and the questionnaire contained several hundred questions examining different aspects of the network. One specific demand in the IMP2 survey was for personal interviews. The object of these was to discuss and describe the questions when meeting the managers. The purpose was mainly to increase the reliability of the collected data.

The main focus of the IMP2 research project was on international business relationships between companies located in France, Germany, Italy, Japan, Sweden, the U.K. and the U.S.A. Researchers from those countries carried out interviews with several hundred firms located in those countries, and results have been published in the form of scientific articles, books, and doctoral dissertations. The project contains three types of related questionnaires designed to study behavior from three perspectives: those of a purchaser, a customer, and the firms of intermediaries. The general objectives of the IMP2 project were as follows (Havila 1996):

(1) To further develop and understand the relationships between producers, users, and intermediaries (IMP2 was in this respect a logical follow-up of IMP1).

(2) To explore, describe, and analyze how single relationships are connected to each other and thereby constitute networks (The IMP2 differed here from the IMP1, which studied an isolated single relationship).
(3) To involve different firms in order to create an international character and to ensure its international application.

In the IMP2 study, the aim of the standardized questionnaire was to examine each business relationship from three different perspectives. Thus, questionnaires for suppliers, customers, and intermediaries were designed separately. The questions, designed with cooperation between researchers from the various universities involved, were originally framed in English and were then translated into the languages of the researchers.

2.2. Survey Study

The survey conducted in this research has its origin in the IMP2 questionnaire for purchasers. Experience from the IMP2 study showed that the survey contained some questions that the interviewees did not answer and others where there was a low frequency of responses. These questions were omitted in constructing the questionnaire for this study. The aim of this study was to further develop industrial network theory and to extend the boundary by including non-business actors. This affected the construct of the questionnaire. Besides the questions in the IMP2, the survey also contains questions examining the suppliers' connections to such actors as the government, unions, and bureaucrats.

The use of networks as the theoretical basis for the survey required the researchers to conduct interviews with both of the focal actors. Thus, interviews had to be undertaken not only with the customers but also with the suppliers. Unfortunately, it was not possible to do so in this study because the MNCs in interaction with the Iranian firms come from many countries. Such a demand also requires additional time and increases costs. For these reasons, the interviews were conducted only with the Iranian purchasing firms.

2.3. Presentation of Facts; a Comparison IR-Material and IMP2

The statistical analyses in the book are generally limited to a presentation of descriptive statistics, mainly tables of frequency and histograms. To some extent, other statistical methods are also used. In each area where a comparison between the IR-material and the IMP2-material was possible, the information presented and discussed was subjected to an analysis in order to disclose any statistically significant differences between the two groups. This approach must be seen as appropriate for the purpose at hand. With the measures obtained from the questionnaire, the study could analyze the relationships of customers and suppliers, and their connections to the business and non-business actors. The survey contained several questions that measured a specific factor from different angles. This was important for the verification of the results. Furthermore, the comparisons of the Iranian study with some of the IMP2 measurements also increased the validity of the conclusions.

The research did not aim to study one relationship or a limited number of relationships in the network, but rather the generalized patterns occurring in the business which was taking place. The main concern was thus with the structure of the network and the relationships which built that structure. This required the examination of all the relationships on an aggregate level. On the other hand, evaluating a large number of relationships and connections does not permit a deep penetration of the single relationship. This is the price paid for the benefits of the study, namely, an understanding of the network and its structure.

Following the questionnaire in the IMP2 study, the constructs that the study considered were relationship, adaptation, and social relationship. These three constructs reflect the focal interaction. The fourth construct included was that of business connections; the fifth was connections to non-business actors. The measures in the first three constructs (i.e. the focal interaction) are presented in Chapters 3–6. When presenting the measures from the study on the behavior of Iranian firms, some of the results are compared with the IMP2 study. The measures on the last two constructs that deal with the connections to business and non-business actors are discussed in Chapter 7.

2.4. Characteristics of the Firms

In order to build a reliable foundation for analyzing the business relationship and network structure in Iran, some characteristics (which were applied in the original IMP2 study) to be used in selecting the Iranian firms were decided upon. The firms were to be large, to be in manufacturing and engineering industries, and to have relationships with MNCs. The firms that could fulfill these requirements were to be included. If the study had been restricted to only one industry, it would have been impossible to find a large enough number of Iranian firms to include in the survey. Before the initiation of the interviews, the managers were specifically required to concentrate on only one of their most important foreign partners. The Iranian customers were required to select a focal relationship that was ranked on the basis of its importance to the final products of the Iranian firm. The IMP2 study used a similar principle.

2.5. Data Collection

The data were collected on location in Iran. To obtain reliable information, the Industrial Management Institute (IMI), which usually conducts market research in Iran, was contacted and asked to assist in the collection of data. In the beginning, the aim was to collect information about the Iranian suppliers' interaction with foreign customers. The main reason for this choice was that the survey in the IMP2 study contains results from a large number of suppliers' firms, more than 150 MNCs, although the number of firms engaged in the customer survey investigation (IMP2) was less, i.e. 67 firms. However, after several discussions with the IMI group in charge of this project, we realized the difficulty in finding a large enough number of suppliers in Iran. The most fruitful option was, therefore, to focus on the customer side and employ the customer survey of the IMP2-project in the Iranian case.

In early 1998, the first and most difficult task was to translate the questionnaire into the Persian language. In this first period of the research project, several critical problems were identified which had to be overcome:

(1) There is a different research tradition in Iran.
(2) The theoretical framework of the study was unfamiliar for the IMI and for the Iranian firms.
(3) It is difficult to find theoretical terminology concerning industrial networks in the Persian language.
(4) There were a large number of questions.
(5) Several personal interviews with employees from each firm were necessary.
(6) Organizing interviews was complex.
(7) It was difficult to find enough Iranian firms willing to give interviews.
(8) It was difficult to organize and structure the answers in the IMP2.
(9) It was difficult to find a system for comparing answers from IMP2 and the Iranian study.

At the beginning of the study, it became obvious that without the assistance of the IMI in Iran, it would be almost impossible to collect reliable data. It was important for the study that the research group at the IMI understood both the theoretical foundation of the survey and the questions. At the meetings with the researchers at the IMI, we discussed the content of the questions. We realized that the crucial issue was to find out whether or not the interviewees could really understand the questions. After checking and rechecking the questions several times, the decision was made to conduct preliminary interviews with some of the firms. After five preliminary interviews were conducted, questions were modified, and the process of data collection eventually began in June 1998. The last set of planned interviews was finalized at the beginning of 1999, although some complementary interviews became necessary at a later stage.

The questions used in this study, similar to the IMP2 project, were directed at the individual relationships between Iranian firms and their foreign business partners. For this project, we also needed to include questions relating to the relationships between political and business actors, which is a sensitive area. The subject of politics is not only delicate in the case of Iran. Similar studies in industrialized countries have been faced with similar problems (Boddewyn & Brewer 1994; Hadjikhani & Sharma 1999).

The survey document consisted of more than 250 questions on 25 pages. The survey was first distributed to the managers, who were then interviewed personally to discuss and explain each question. This ensured that questions were properly understood and that the information received from the interviewees was reliable. Personal interviews were necessary because there were so many questions, and because many of them were different from what the firms were used to being asked. As it required several hours to cover all the questions in the survey, the questions were split up, and each firm was interviewed a number of times. The interviews mainly involved purchasing managers, as the questions examined purchasing behavior.

After completion of the data collection in Iran, the first task was to translate the answers into English and to find the equivalent questions in the IMP2. The questionnaire was kept within the bounds of the statistical construct in the IMP2. To facilitate comparison, all the questions were measured separately and then linked with the answers given in the IMP2. The major attempt in 1998 was to construct a statistical system that allowed for a simple comparison of each answer. The effort in 1999 was to provide a statistical structure for the answers in the Iranian study, which was similar to the IMP2.

The next critical problem was the presentation of the facts. The Iranian survey, as mentioned, included more than 250 questions. Each question had at least five options, thus creating tens of thousands of combination possibilities. Although the purpose of the research was to conduct a study of the networks, it was impossible to explore a large number of relationships. Therefore, a selective method was chosen.

In the Iranian survey, after 10 questions relating to background, the variables followed the IMP2 construction. Questions began with the focal relationships and continued with adaptations, social interaction, and embeddedness. The survey contained more questions than those presented in this book. The questions selected

Table 1.1: Survey presentation.

Section	Iranian Study		IMP2 Study		Compared
	Surveyed	Presented	Surveyed	Presented	
Exchange relationship	53	18	59	13	20
Adaptation	44	18	44	5	18
Social interaction	60	18	60	7	18
Embeddedness	77	39	24	3	–

here are intended to help clarify the content by following the above constructs. Table 1.1 shows a comparison between the IMP2 and the Iranian study. The "surveyed" column shows the number of questions in the surveys, the "presented" column indicates the number of those questions that are presented in Part 2 of this book, and the last column shows the number of questions used in comparisons between the two studies.

In Part 2, when presenting the facts as shown above, those questions considered pertinent to the topic of this book are analyzed and presented. In the Iranian study, there were many more questions on embeddedness than in the IMP2, principally because the Iranian study contained 59 questions that dealt with non-business actors. The variable of political embeddedness is not measured at all by the IMP2. More information is presented for the Iranian case than for the IMP2. This was based on the research problem in the Iranian case, and also because there were more questions in the former than in the latter. The aim of the research was to study the behavior of the Iranian purchasing firms. There was no attempt at an equal consideration of the two studies. The IMP2 study has a complementary mission in this study. Its role is to assist in comparing those relationship areas that are important for analytical purposes.

3. Brief Notes about Earlier Studies

The theoretical framework used by the business management discipline with respect to business activity appears to be composed of a wide range of theories and models. In previous decades, there has been a proliferation of alternative theories and frameworks in many areas of market and management. Some are built on specific theories; others are constructed by the integration of different concepts from a number of disciplines (e.g. economics and sociology). One of the reasons for the development of these integrated views could be that business activity affects many spheres of social and economic activities. However, in reflecting on the historical development, two distinct groups of principles emerge. In one, the principle of "economy" is used for explanation; in the other, theories of "business behavior" dominate. Some loosely defined tracks of conceptual development are listed below, not because of some absolute value, but simply to make these developments explicit for the theme of this study. The discussion fundamentally covers two criteria that encompass the objects of this study. One is the relationship between the business firms, and the other is the relationship between firms and governments (specifically, the role of the government's trade policy in this relationship).

In the first track, there have been numerous attempts to amend the neoclassical microeconomic theory of the firm, or to propose alternative conceptions of the firm and market. A common trait has been a concern with information processing and knowledge development in an enterprise, and their impact on overall behavior. Directly or indirectly, the assumptions of market equilibrium and homogeneity and the perfect knowledge of market participants have been under question. In this traditional path, the basis of the behavior is a belief in the rationality in the functioning of the market and that government has a neutral role. When introducing the exchange model at the firm level, the voluntary nature of the exchange, economic efficiency, and the maximization of profit are stressed. In these studies, appropriate information from the environment is collected on which to base the strategies. Risk theories challenge the environment, which includes actors such as sub-contractors, customers, consumers, and governments. While firms are assumed to have a high capability in managing their business environment, their political environment acts as a constraining and pre-determined factor.

In another track, business strategy and development has been a growing concern in a number of studies (Kagono *et al.* 1985; Norman 1977; Porter 1986). The firm as the unit of analysis is studied, with more attention being paid to the environment and its business and political components. The more holistic perspective directs greater attention to the external aspect and its connection with the firm's strategy. As a reflection of this externality, the assumption of the hierarchical power of governments has been presented in many studies of business and marketing (Doz 1986; Jacobson *et al.* 1993; Poynter 1985). When firms lose the power to structure a strategy that can maintain their autonomy in relation to the political environment, the political environment becomes unidirectional with given outcomes.

In an extension of the "strategy track" described above, several other researchers in business and marketing have put a clear boundary around the firm and have instead studied the management of business environments. There are a number of different areas of research that have dealt with how business organizations influence or adapt to their environment (e.g. Burns & Stalker 1961; Galbraith 1973; Kagono *et al*. 1985; Thompson 1967). Management in this conceptualization relies on the control dimension of the environmental sources. A change in business organization presents a strategic response to the potentially impeding force of these environmental factors. The political environment reinforces the enterprises in their adaptive actions. In further analyzing the control exercised by governments, some studies, such as that by Albaum *et al*. (1989), categorize the intervention activities into those that promote the firm's market activities, those that impede them, and finally those that are competitive and aim, for example, to replace foreign products with local products to the benefit of the society. The business and market research conducted in this track presents environmental factors as sources of uncertainty affecting the structure of the firms. As a necessity, these researchers limit the boundary of the concept, with the firm as the unit of observation and everything else presented as environmental factors. This approach has led to a decline in the use of system theory, which utilizes an open view on boundaries.

Studies that specifically consider the interplay between business and political actors are also affected by a similar development to that described above. One of the predominant approaches used in many studies of business and marketing (Doz 1986; Jacobson *et al*. 1993; Poynter 1985) has presented a unidirectional view of the assumption of the hierarchical power of governments. In taking this unidirectional view into account, some theories have introduced coping strategies for the management of the political environment. The groundwork for such theories is in industrial organization economics (Caves 1982) or in transaction-cost economics (Rugman *et al*. 1985; Teece 1985). The explicit assumption in the studies of Egelhoff (1988) and Porter (1986) was that extra-organizational constraints are determinants of a firm's success (Jemison 1981). Others followed Ghoshal's reasoning (1987) with regard to political risk and discussed the unidirectional dimension of political influence, thereby interrelating the political aspect with the types of firms and risks. Bradley (1977), Korbin (1982), Phillips-Patrick (1989), and Ting (1988) discussed patterns of political risk in connection with types of industries and firms. For these studies, categorization is a means of explaining homogeneity in the behavior of firms, and consequently, the matter of political uncertainties is treated as a given condition; little attention is paid to the interactive relationships or to the influence of MNCs on local governments.

In order to overcome the interaction between the economic and political systems with the use of behavioral models, Stern & Reve (1979) developed a political economy approach. They claim that political economy views the social system as comprising interacting sets of major economic and socio-political systems (Tunisini 1997). They employ a dyadic approach, and their focal actors are economic actors. They explain that environmental factors, like political factors, affect this socio-economic interaction. This approach has become a point of reference for other researchers to develop further (Dwyer & Welsh 1985; John & Reve 1982), and implies a complementary approach of microeconomic and behavioral perspectives. Later studies, such as that of Achrol, Reve & Stern (1983), explain that interorganizational relationships in marketing take the network instead of dyadic form. This approach captures more completely the interaction between the interested parties.

Recent studies, building on institutional theory, have explicitly rejected the hierarchical view and presented a wider perspective. Yarbough & Yarbough (1987) suggested employing a dyadic view in analyzing the roles of political and business actors. The main contribution of their concept is that both sides are seen as active in influencing each other. The model recognizes an interaction between the two sides. The interactions constitute a market functioning in parallel to the business market (Boddewyn 1988). Boddewyn's model uses Dunning's (1988) analysis of ownership, internalization, and location advantages, and is structured to deal with the mutual influence of political and business actors. For example, Moran's (1985) basic tactic (namely, vertical integration of risk-sharing financial networks) tends to be couched in economic terms and underlies truly political responses of the business actors. The dyadic approach presented by these authors is different from that of Doz (1986) and Poynter (1985), in which governmental policies toward foreign investors must be responded to by absorbing the cost of governmental intervention, either by avoiding it or by circumventing it. Some researchers have criticized the simplicity of these models and have suggested more complex ones to explain company behavior in a political context (Ring *et al.* 1990). Jacobson *et al.* (1993) extended the theory by including the diversity of the related actors and presenting a network view; a few others introduced the idea of the social dimension in interaction.

In summary, the critical issue is where the researchers put the boundary for researching the enterprises. Instead of studying the relationship between the firm and its environment, several other streams of research explain the behavior of the firm in the context of interorganizational relationships (Evan 1976; Hannan & Freeman 1977; Pfeffer & Salancik 1978). Contrary to the view in the first category of studies, the researchers in this track leave the inward focus for explaining strategic behavior and employ a more outwardly directed view. The primary focus of attention has been the resource control of the external components and their impact on the strategy and structure of the firms. The view is an extension of two major foundations. The first is the extension of the focal unit from "an enterprise" to "the interactions of enterprises." The second, in a number of studies, refers to the abundance of economic theory, its effect on behavior and other activities, and the use of social theory.

In the track of interorganizational relationships, some researchers have extended the boundaries and studied the firm's behavior by using institutional theory (e.g. DiMaggio & Powell 1983). Some marketing and management researchers have focused on the firm and its environment. Researchers adopting this approach lean on political science and the social sciences, and use institutional theory. They see factors in the environment as components of the firms. For the political environment, some recent studies, building on institutional theory, have explicitly rejected the hierarchical view and presented a wider perspective. The dyadic view, for the explanation of business behavior, considers two enterprises undertaken by a firm to be the focal concerns. Both actors are part of the exchange paradigm: how to maximize cooperation and minimize conflict. Among the most important variables to be considered in this regard were cooperation (often seen in terms of contractual obligations), conflict (defined in terms of disagreements), and opportunism (describing self-interested seeking with guile).

Some apply the dyadic view in studying the business relationship with political actors. Yarbough & Yarbough (1987) suggested a dyadic view in analyzing the roles of political and business actors. The main contribution of the relationship concept is that both sides are seen as active in influencing each other. The model further sees the interaction as constituting a market that functions in parallel to the business market (Boddewyn 1988). This view is contrary to that of Doz (1986) and Poynter (1985) in which governmental policies toward foreign investors must be responded to by absorbing the cost of governmental intervention, either by avoiding it or by circumventing it. For this, one needs to identify the legal power of policymakers as manifest in their ability to control the firms. The most widely held explanation for business behavior refers to governments' hierarchical view of, and unidirectional effect on, firms. Studies such as those by Jacobson *et al.* (1993) and Lenway & Murtha *et al.* (1994) criticized the main studies of linkages and questioned the use of hierarchical power by states. Boddewyn (1988), who studied the role of the government for foreign firms, contended that the political actions of firms do not fit with the predominant models of the behavior of enterprises. These researchers have criticized the simplicity of these relationship models and have suggested more complex ones to explain company behavior in a political context (Ring *et al.* 1990). Jacobson *et al.* (1993) extended the theory by including the diversity of the related actors and presented a network view.

The relationship view is essentially a dyadic one (Dwyer, Shurr & Oh 1987; Petterson 1995). In contrast to the exchange paradigm, the network paradigm focuses on the relational: how to develop mutually reinforcing long-term relationships. Network theory, therefore, is an extension of the dyadic relationship boundary from two to several identities. Further, it leaves the economic base in the dyadic exchange and incorporates behavior analysis. The view is

Table 1.2: Summary of views.

	Business to Non-Business	**Business to Business**
Unidirectional view	The focus is on political issues and the governance structure of the political system. Homogeneity in the influence on the types of industry (see, for example, Jacobson *et al.* 1993; Maddison 1991; Miller 1993).	The unit for the analysis is the firm. The assumption is based on the homogeneous impact of political rules, international marketing and business studies, adaptive strategies and risk evaluations (see, for example, Kotler *et al.* 1996; Porter 1986; Ting 1988).
Dyadic view	The explicit focus is on the interaction of the political and business actors. Some studies in institutional economics introduce a political market (see, for example, Boddewyn 1988; Yarbough & Yarbough 1993).	Studies such as those by Håkansson (1982) and Sheth & Parvatiyar (1993) use a relationship approach for the analysis of the business-to-business exchange. The political actors are treated vaguely and in a similar way to the traditional view on the political environment.
Network view	Studies in political and social science, such as those by Esping-Andersen (1985), Maddison (1991), and Nowtotny (1989), that strive for integration of business actors in the whole system. The principal literature includes the business aspect but still at a macro level (seeing it as categories of industry, etc.). Later business studies realized the need for studies at the level of the firm. They present a triadic model that concerns the interaction of two business actors and a political actor (see, for example, Hadjikhani & Ghauri 2000; Ring 1990).	In studies on business and industrial networks — such as those of Ford (1990), and Håkansson & Snehota (1995) — the dominating approach is to focus on the business actors in the network. The political actors are in the background, having only implicit impact. A few studies, such as that by Jacobson *et al.* (1993), look at political embeddedness in terms of buyer-seller interactions.

presented as a device to advance understanding of the market system. The social dimension in the network perspective enriches the concept of business behavior and introduces issues such as relatedness of the dyadic relationships, trust/mistrust, and commitment. Business network theory, which is borrowed from social network theory and is specifically developed for understanding business behavior, has several major differences with the earlier concepts, which have their roots mainly in economic theories. Business network theory, in contrast to those mentioned above, further expands the explanatory dimension of the firm. Due consideration is given to the importance of the environment. Firms' environments, which in other theories are analogous to a category of components with various constraining positions and abstract weights, are appraised in network theory as actors or components with a clear identity interacting with the focal enterprise. Furthermore, the theory shifts the economic base and founds the analytical perspective on social behavior. The economics of different activities are explained as a part of other constructions, and the social dimensions of business activities dominate the explanation of business behavior. Traditional thinking is focused on how to prevent disintegration of inherently apathetic or opportunistic partners, the implicit assumption being that the dominant forces in a relationship are destructive forces. Relationship cultures in a network, however, are based on the assumption that the exchange is inherently constructive and that the key variables are trust and socially accepted norms of behavior (Macneil 1980; Morgan & Hunt 1994 Table 1.2).

4. The Disposition

The introduction presented in this chapter was intended to introduce the aim and direction of this study, the purchasing behavior of the firms in Iran. The book has two fundamental bases. One is to depict a conceptual framework; the other is to examine it in relation to a specific case. The content of the next chapter follows this specific direction. Tracking the principles in network theory, the focal relationship is considered first, and subsequently the factor of embeddedness is introduced. In the first part of the next chapter, the focus is on different exchange dimensions. In the second part, the field of embeddedness is discussed, and an attempt is made to include business and political connections. This structure is used to bring in analytical tools for understanding: (1) how the relationships are organized; and (2) why the strength in the relationships contains a specific structure. In all of the following chapters, the effort has been to conduct a comparison between the market behavior of the Iranian firms and firms in the IMP2 study.

The book has three parts. The first part is devoted to the introduction and theoretical framework. The second part comprises the empirical study. The third part considers the analysis and findings. In the empirical part, the first three chapters are subjected to the core elements in the network. The first chapter in the empirical part (Chapter 3) focuses on the product and technological exchange relationships. In Chapter 4, attention is paid to the adaptation behavior of the firms, and Chapter 5 is devoted to the social interaction, although Chapters 3–5 are directed at different relationships and ties between the focal firms. In all these chapters, an effort has also been made to compare the results from the Iranian study with the findings from the IMP2 study. Chapter 6 considers business and political embeddedness. Part Three consists of three chapters: Chapter 7, in which the facts are analyzed; Chapter 8, which describes the theoretical analysis and its implications; and Chapter 9, in which some concluding remarks are presented.

Chapter 2

Business Networks and Non-Business Actors' Embeddedness

As briefly discussed in the preceding chapter, there are a number of disciplines and theories pertinent to business firms and their interaction with the environment. The market factors that are the focus of this study take into account both business and non-business components. In order to study these components, some researchers base their analytical framework on economic theories, whereas others borrow from behavioral theory. This study is attracted by behavioral theory and uses industrial network theory as its basis. The study extends the boundary of the network and incorporates non-business, specifically political, actors into the network. This chapter aims to construct a theoretical framework designed for studying a business network that is infused with the concept of the embeddedness of non-business actors. The chapter begins with a general discussion on industrial networks and continues with ideas about relationships and embeddedness. The study has distinguished two types of business and non-business exchange relationships, and introduces them in connection with the two fields of relationship and embeddedness.

1. Business Network Theory

Business network theories, which have been borrowed from social network theory, have several major differences from the other concepts. The aspect of environment, a critical aspect in traditional and relationship theories, gains another feature in relation to this theory. In this discipline, the firm's boundary is expanded, and environmental components are interwoven into the business arena with the assumption that no business activity is carried out in isolation. The network model of the firm-environment interface stems originally from the observation that business firms often operate and interact in environments that include only a limited number of identifiable groups of actors. The proposition of the network model considers situations in which the environments of the organizations that exert influence and interact with the firms are concentrated and structured (Håkansson & Snehota 1989). The model's basic classes of variables are *actors, activities,* and *resources.* Individuals, firms, and organizations can be actors. Actors are defined as those who perform activities and/or control resources with counterparts having identities. As a result, the relationships between these actors present as continuous and complex rather than discreet and simple transactions. Thus, a firm's perception of the external impact on its activities and resources refers to its network context, the total connected reality that is constituted by the entities that have a major effect on its condition and performance (Snehota 1990; Thilenius 1997).

In a business context, therefore, network is a social perception of organizations or a number of entities that are connected (Axelsson & Easton 1992). The investigation, thus, can limit the population in terms of numbers of organizations and concepts that are theoretically meaningful. The environment that really matters to the firms is the perceived environment, and its social meaning for a focal firm is constructed by groups of relationships affecting focal business. These entities are actors involved in the economic and political processes of relationships, which convert resources to finished products and services for consumption by customers and customers' customers, buyers and buyers' buyers, and end users.

If the entities have no important relationships, then the free-market models beloved by economists prevail. But, with the use of the network model, the basic approach is through the relationships, specifically that

(1) Relationships contain more than economic transactions.
(2) Every single relationship is to be regarded as a part of a broader context, a network of interdependent relationships.

Each relationship is embedded or connected to some other relationship. Its development and function cannot be properly understood if these connections are disregarded.

In the context of this study, the networks differ from social networks and networks in general by being coupled to business activities. Each business activity in a relationship is more or less dependent on the performance of a number of other activities, and each activity is linked to one or several other activities which are more or less extensive and closely linked. The actors, thus, are embedded in the wider web of business activities performed by other firms and organizations. The activity of one actor is always more or less dependent on a number of other actors. This raises the aspect of embeddedness and interdependency, which are the fundamentals in any business network. There is direct interdependency between supplier- and customer firms doing business with each other, and also indirect interdependence between two firms, as one or the other imports or exports products from or to a third firm. The following theoretical section is composed of two major components of relationship and embeddedness. The two components are introduced in the four areas of:

(1) Business Relationship.
(2) Business-Political Relationships.
(3) Embeddedness.
(4) Political Embeddedness.

The first area is to present the basic factors in a business relationship and the main features affecting the strength/weakness of a relationship. The second section purely discusses the types and contents of the relationship between business and political actors. The third section is devoted to the concept of embeddedness, specifically business embeddedness, and the last chapter discusses political embeddedness.

2. Business Relationships

The business relationship is the basic unit in business network theories. It is assumed that exchange involves several actors and that the relationships are characterized by mutuality and continuity. The notion has occupied researchers in different disciplines, and when explaining the types of exchange relationships, they propose a variety of tracks of thought. In these disciplines, some stress the social and others the economic dimensions in relationships. From a business network perspective, it is difficult to isolate one from the other. The exchange relationship does not solely involve economic or social aspects. Accordingly, exchange relationships have interwoven social and economic dimensions. These dimensions are also explored in a variety of ways, depending on the specific needs of the business research. Some explain the content of the exchange using only the two dimensions: social and economic. Others subdivide these dimensions and present the content in more detail. Following the latter track, the content of exchange relationships can be specified in terms of the following three dimensions (see also Johanson & Mattsson 1988): (1) Business Exchange; (2) Social Exchange; and (3) Information Exchange.

2.1. Business Exchange

This relationship refers to the flow of resources (such as products, service, technology, and finance) between actors. The flow of some resources, such as finance or products, is from one to another; the flow of others (such as technology and knowledge) can be either in one direction or bi-directional. Studying the flow from an interdependency point of view, however, shows that the actors, by whatever means, are functioning in a network. Aspects such as the distribution channel, in which the raw material flows from one firm to another and to a third until it is in the hands of the customer, is a way through which network relationships can be conferred for a business exchange. When each resource type flows just one way, and short-term flow is from one actor to another actor, the exchange has a weak economic nature. An exchange relationship is more developed when the resource flow is induced with long-term cooperation and adaptation. The strength of the relationships is an outcome of how extensive the exchange relationships are. The type, development, amount, and continuity in a business exchange are among the indicators specifying the strength of the exchange relationships.

A constant business interaction, which proceeds with a large flow of resources, cooperation, and adaptation, creates an interface among the actors and a structure of high interdependency and strong relationship. The interaction between buyers and sellers is constructed on the basis of the resource flow between actors that are somehow interconnected with, and interdependent on, each other. A large number of studies manifest the cooperation and adaptation needed for technological development. In such cases, the strength of relationships is reinforced through the processes of mutual adaptation and mutual orientation. Accordingly, parties exchange information and knowledge about each other's competence, experience, and limits (Demsetz 1992). The strength of the relationship is weak as parties aim at short-term benefit, and abandon cooperation and adaptation. The firm's knowledge and resources are used unilaterally, merely within the firm. The benefit of the complementarity that results from the combination of firms' resources is thus restricted. However, the process of mutual adaptation can strengthen the interdependence between the parties further. It can involve considerable investment that often cannot be transferred to other business relationships. As a consequence, the ties between parties are reinforced. Mutual orientation implies that the firms are prepared to interact with each other and expect the other party to behave accordingly.

2.2. Social Exchange

The discrepancies, conflict, and cooperate in the relationships relate to the next element, namely social exchange relationships or atmosphere. The social exchange relationship has an important function in reducing uncertainties between parties. One specific component in studying social exchange is the factor of trust. This factor of social exchange is particularly important when there are spatial or cultural differences between the actors, or experience is limited. The interaction between two actors with different value systems can develop uncertainties in business relationships.

The social aspect in the exchange is important in avoiding short-term difficulties. The higher the strength is in the social ties, the greater the probability that actors work for long-term relationships, and short-term difficulties can be resolved increasing mutuality and trust. Consequently, the social ties between actors are also measured by their strength. Weakness and strength are indicators of how the actors are interdependent on each other. The most important function of social exchange is the long-term process through which successive social exchanges gradually interlock the firms with each other. This functions as glue that binds actors to each other and, at the same time, facilitates the business relationship. It makes the actors realize the potential mutual benefit and reduces their mobility. The fundamental acquisition in social exchange is an atmosphere of mutual understanding, and the willingness of the actors to recognize each other's goal and conditions.

As a consequence, the element of trust in social interaction becomes important for social exchange, as it lays the groundwork for other elements, such as conflict, cooperation, and power in the business atmosphere. Trust is defined as willingness to rely on an exchange partner in whom one has confidence. In contrast, the legalization of relationships or a high dominance of formalized interaction confers a condition of lack of trust and confidence. The opposite condition results when relationships are based on trust and the mutual interest of partners, which minimizes legal and formalized procedures. Trust has its foundation in mutuality, whereas mistrust is based on uncertainty and opportunistic behavior or the exercise of power. The outcome of a coercive power in an exchange relationship, for example, exposes uncertainty and mistrust, which influences the actors to adapt their commitment or search for alternatives. Ultimately, trust functions as a regulator of the amount and type of the social exchange. The opportunistic behavior of an actor is decisive for the opportunistic behavior of another. The uncertainty which emerges is linked with a weak relationship. This behavior influences a condition of weak relationship in which price and short-term mechanisms bind enfeebled actors. Actors can switch from one to another on the basis of economic advantages.

Thus, we can presume that trust appears as a continuous scale. On one end, the exchange is based on trust and long-term relationships, and on the other, exchange has a short-term profit or economic basis. An easy switching of alternatives is an indicator of the economic nature in exchange relationships, which have a high degree of mobility. Lack of trust can elevate other mechanisms in the exchange, such as price, although actors can choose a position on the continuum from trust to price. In this scale, the element of high trust stands on one edge and economic exchange on the other edge. Business actors can choose one of the elements or to some degree combine the two elements.

Trust and mistrust, or uncertainty, contain the characteristics that are explained in the form of dyadic relationships. The explanation incorporates aspects such as the diffusion of trust/mistrust to other relationships. This means that, because of embeddedness, trust and mistrust in a dyadic relationship spreads or transfers to other exchange relationships. Furthermore, trust and mistrust in a relationship are outcomes of several partners' willingness in cooperation. As trust diffuses in the network, so also does opportunism.

Some define trust in terms of a willingness to rely on exchange partners in whom one has confidence (Dasgupta 1988), and therein willingness is related to dyadic interaction and capability through connected relationships (Larson 1992). Others extend this further and explain that trust and mistrust in a dyadic relationship are outcomes of the accumulation of expectations and events of different types and at different levels or parts of the network (Hadjikhani & Håkansson 1996; Macaulay 1963). Trust and mistrust exist on different levels (i.e. from the level of the personal and dyadic to those of the firm and political actors). Any change in the trust in one level or relationship affects the trust at other levels and in other relationships. The explanation assumes that trust in a dyadic relationship is an outcome of the accumulation of trust in dyadic and other connected relationships.

2.3. Information Exchange

Concerning information, the process of exchange relationships between actors entails access to and the use of information. The social and business exchange is processed by an exchange of information among actors. Thus, the customer-supplier relationship is considered as a vehicle through which each actor can gain access to and make use of a counterpart's knowledge. The information exchanged and combined involves a change in the knowledge base of partners. That implies processes of interactive learning. These processes involve technical, communicative, and social interactive learning and enhance the innovative capabilities of the producer-supplier and the competence of the user-customer (Lundvall 1988). This knowledge can then be transferred through formal and informal means with their bases in technical, commercial, and social areas. The content of the information can vary for different types of relationships. The range can contain complex technical or market information, which calls for high interdependency and strong relationships. In other cases, relationships can develop on the other end of this range, low interdependency and a weak relationship, and contain standard and formalized or only simple product information. One aspect in the exchange is the depth of the information. On the one hand, information can just contain simple and standardized technical/social knowledge, and have a low adaptation and interdependency. On the other hand, a relationship may be strong and have a complex nature requiring adaptation. Connecting this element to the social dimension and organizational nature, the aspect of formality in the information exchange becomes important. An interaction that places greater stress on the social relationship and on trust will elevate both formal and informal interactions to a higher degree.

In summary, the three elements mentioned above — business, social, and information elements in exchange relationships — themselves provide no grounds for the construction of networks. The two fundamental bases that glue the actors and relationships together are adaptation and interdependency. One specific characteristic, for example, that distinguishes between long- and short-term exchange is the aspect of adaptation. Coordination and cooperation, which link the actors and enable them to attain extra value in the relationships, have their foundation in the view that actors are interdependent and that this also requires adaptation. The process nature of network theory implies the development of exchange relationships, and that leads to change in interdependency and adaptation. On the whole, the relationship is reinforced through the mutual adaptation and mutual orientation processes. Without it, the exchange is in an isolated arena for a short space of time. This view of the attributes of adaptation and interdependency give life to the dimensions. A further development of the terms adaptation and interdependency in the relationships brings out the notion of relationship outcome. The outcome can be explained by the strength and weakness of relationships, illustrated in Table 2.1.

These characteristics encompass the basis of exchange relationships in the market in this study, namely, that the actors are functioning in a business market

Table 2.1: Some characteristics of weak and strong interdependency.

Weak Relationships	Strong Relationships
Simple exchange	Complex resource exchange
Few exchanges	Large numbers of exchange relationships
Low adaptation	High adaptation
Few actors engage	Few or large number of actors
Economic bases and low social exchange	Exchange combined with large social exchange
Small and simple information exchange	High and complex information exchange

constructed of both business and non-business actors. The buyer and seller have an exchange relationship not only with each other but also with other actors belonging to business and non-business structures. An actor may aim for, or pursue, different aspects with these actors. The relationship with one group may be exclusively based on technical concerns, whereas with other groups, the relationship may be politically based. These will be discussed in more detail later.

3. Political Exchange Relationships

This section presents a view on the political exchange relationship, which has an essential role for the business-exchange relationships. Following the discussion, the actors can be classified into two distinct groups of business actors and non-business actors. In the exchange between two actors belonging to two different systems, the reciprocity is not necessarily achieved through any direct benefit to one actor over another, but may be achieved through an indirect benefit (Bagozzi 1975; Ekeh 1974; Hadjikhani & Sharma 1999; Levi-Strauss 1969), although mutuality can have both a direct and indirect nature. The interaction between the two requires not only an adjunct of conflicting interest but also an arena for exploring options and sharing common values (Hult & Walcott 1990).

Some researchers observe the exchange between the business and political actors as the focal relationship. Following this, researchers such as Ring *et al.* (1990) argued that the view of the power of authority based on the unidirectional influence of political actors suffers from an economic bias and a passive perspective. Integration of the social dimension and a network perspective enrich the concept of the political behavior of business actors and introduce issues such as interdependency, influence and power, trust/mistrust. These elements together determine the strength/weakness of a political relationship. Within this area of thought, researchers have used different approaches to study how business actors behave to reach an outcome from their political relationships.

The perspective of this study presumes that political actors have institutional legitimacy based on values and norms from actors such as voters and the media, and subsequently are able to undertake coercive and supportive actions in their relationships with business actors. Business actors are driven by business legitimacy based on profit and growth (Hadjikhani & Sharma 1999; Jacobson *et al.* 1993). The purpose of business actors in this interaction is to convert the dependency on political actors to mutual interdependency (direct or indirect) and gain influence. Otherwise, the dependency to political actors leaves the business actor with weak relationships to the political actors, and the only option left in such a case is adaptation.

Political actors, with their legitimate power, use different tools for or against the business actors interacting with firms. They support business firms through procurement policies. Such support is distributed selectively, favoring certain sectors and firms. To regulate business activities and market forces, governments implement laws on the formation of cartels and pricing, which influence both local and international firms. In general, political actors employ a variety of tools that affect firms interacting with international firms, with the aim of encouraging economic growth and satisfying other non-business actors on whom the political actors are dependent. Business actors experience the supportive or coercive actions of political actors through the political rules governing tariff and non-tariff decisions. Political actors use these rules in different measures to regulate the behavior of business actors that interact with foreign MNCs. In a traditional theoretical scene, political actors have the legitimate power, and business actors are politically dependent on what decisions are made. Through this, the content of trade policy, and whether it is coercive or supportive, affects the confidence of business actors in their relationships with political actors. However, the political actors are also dependent on business actors.

Business actors control financial and technological resources, and produce products services, thus creating jobs. Political actors control financial and non-financial resources, and possess the power to make laws to regulate the business activities of firms (Booth 1993). These activities affect income distribution and employment, which are essential for economic growth and the GNP. For business actors, the economic outcome dominates the interactions, and political actors are driven by public needs, political ideology, or general economic values. Based on this reasoning, researchers discuss mutuality in the needs of both. Marketing researchers make claims for strategic actions to convert the dependency of political actors to interdependency and thereby gaining influence. Business actions are to manifest interdependency, and an exchange between the two benefits both. Thus, though with some modification, political exchange becomes similar to business exchange. In political exchange, financial transactions with politicians is prohibited as the public recognize it as corruption. Furthermore, product and technological interdependency is missing. In business relationships, the mutuality is more direct, and an actor seldom gains legitimate power. However, despite such differences in the other analytical tools in business relationships, such as social and information exchanges, strengths and weakness are as prevalent as in political exchange relationships.

Similar to a business relationship, one of the principle foundations that binds and forms the strength in the relationship between two actors is trust (Hadjikhani 1996). Political actors in gaining trust need to show a fairly stable value system. But the discrepancies between the proclaimed political values/slogans and political

Table 2.2: Political activities of the business actors.

Influence	Adaptation
Mutual interdependency	Dependence on political actors
Mutual interaction and benefit	Supremacy of the political actors
Cooperation	Conflict
Trust	Mistrust
Negotiation and convincing	One-sided decisions

decisions make some business actors lose their trust in political actors (Brunsson 1986). This, as Brunsson (1986) noted, is because governments are expected to satisfy different actors who have conflicting demands. In terms of network, political actors themselves are embedded in a network with non-business actors, including media, voters, and unions, all of which drive the behavior of political actors in different directions. Although, similar to the business-exchange relationships, trust/mistrust between these actors can be discussed in terms of weak and strong relationships, which correspond with the influential and adaptive positions of business actors (see Table 2.2).

In terms of influence, the political and business actors enjoy cooperation and the mutual benefit of the relationship, which is trustful. There is a complex exchange of market and technological information for each political issue (Boddewyn 1988; Boddewyn & Brewer 1994; Hadjikhani & Sharma 1999). Political decisions and consequences are negotiated with powerful business actors. Political actors, despite their legitimate political power, acknowledge the market power of the firms. The next setting is based on a weak relationship and mistrust. It derives from the coercive actions of political actors, which can be far from the needs of business actors. In this option, the exchange is unidirectional.

Ultimately, the exercise of influence by business actors is to gain subsidies and strengthen market positions. Although, contrary to passive support actions which are designed for unproblematic relationships (DiMaggio 1988), business actors can actively undertake actions to build interdependency and strong relationships with political actors. Influence embodies those activities intended to convince political actors to provide specific political support. The extent of influence varies. This is strictly connected to the political power of governments and their interdependency with the actors in the political system, the market power of firms, and the political issues. In the next setting, business actors have a very low influence and high adaptation, which requires adaptive strategies for production activities, organization structure, purchasing and marketing behavior, for example, and in severe cases, firms are forced to leave the market to the supremacy of political forces. This portrays weak or conflictual relationships. On the whole, such issues as continually changing political concerns and the repositioning of political actors make the political relationship complex and dynamic.

Generally, an interdependent relationship has its basis in the reciprocity of gains and losses. In political exchange, this interplay is always threatened since the interaction is based on dissimilar value bases and the temporary nature of the position of political actors. These two characteristics thus cause weakness in the political exchange. However, business actors make commitments with the intention of developing and maintaining such dyadic relationships (Hadjikhani & Sharma 1999). The interactive forms can be through co-option, absorption, and coalescence. The interplay has probably been the reason for the emergence of studies investigating the extent of cooperation under conditions ranging from bargaining to non-bargaining (Boddewyn 1988; Roth & Schoumaker 1983), bribery (Rose-Ackerman 1978), lobbying (Milbrath 1965; Potters 1992), and collective action (Olson 1975). Several studies can be mentioned, including one by Jansson *et al.* (1995), which concentrated on the influence of MNCs on political actors. Hadjikhani & Sharma (1999) and Ring *et al.* (1990) extended these dimensions of exchange and connected this cooperation to trust, giving the cooperation a social dimension. The bargaining and non-bargaining factors listed by Boddewyn & Brewer (1994) illustrate the varieties in cooperation and conflict, which are also related to trust in a political relationship, and which can result in outcomes of either influence or adaptation.

A reason for the weakness in the relationship is the resistance of political actors to engage in cooperation, and thereby mistrust and conflict fill the content of the relationship. Business actors, in such an urgent position, respond either by continuing to remain in the relationship and adapting (Hadjikhani 1996; Wells 1977) or by exiting (Hadjikhani & Johanson 1996; Hirschman 1970). Some of these conditions of cooperation can degrade trust in the connected relationship when, for example, the public learns of a case of bribery, which is recognized as illegitimate.

The political relationships are treated in this study as the main connected relationships. The extension lies in the presumption that non-business actors have a dominant position in the business network and affect/become affected by the business relationships. This view raises the most important aspect of the network — embeddedness. The aim of the following is to introduce and discuss the attributes of embeddedness of business actors, which in the later section will be connected to political embeddedness.

4. Firms and Government

Business firms interact with other firms and government to pursue their business goals. In these terms, a firm's relationships with other firms and government can be discussed in terms of embeddedness. Thus, a business firm is connected to other parties to make business and political exchanges. Connected relationships are considered to be an essential condition for the existence of a business network. Two exchange relationships are connected to the extent that exchange in one relationship is positively or negatively contingent upon exchange in other relationships (Cook & Emerson 1984). When a business entity is supposed to act in such a structure, there is reason to believe that the firm is embedded in a network of interdependent actors exerting both influence and making adaptations to achieve mutual gains. Embeddedness refers to the fact that economic activities and their outcomes affect and are affected by the focal actors' dyadic relationships (Andersson 1992; Grabher 1993). So, in order to understand a specific business relationship, it is not sufficient to view it as an isolated unit (Blankenburg Holm 1996); rather, it must be studied on the basis of a larger context, which consists of connections to other relationships. In this vein, the business networks are composed of the focal relationship and a number of connected relationships that somehow are interrelated with each other. This view interrelates a restricted focal actor and relationship with a number of other relationships. In some cases, the principle of direct mutuality is preserved and in others reciprocally is indirect. The environment of business firms, as illustrated in Figure 2.1, is constructed of connected relationships so that the strength of, and

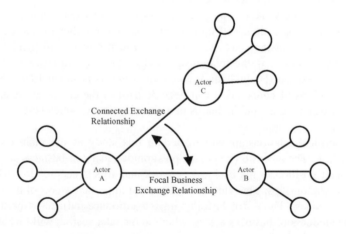

Figure 2.1: Business embeddedness.

changes in, the connected (for example between actors A and C) and focal relationships (between actors A and B) affect each other. The explanation implies that other actors connected to actors A, B, or C may affect the focal exchange relationships.

Embeddedness can be analyzed through aspects of strength. The degree of strength forms the type of structure in the network. High strength and a limited number of connected relationships constitute an extreme and bounded structure. Low strength in connected relationships and a large number of actors constitute a loosely coupled structure. The more a focal actor is dependent on the embedded actors, the weaker the relationship, the higher the adaptation, and the weaker the focal actors' position in the network. The closer these embedded actors are (in terms of direct and indirect exchange relationships) to the focal actor, the greater the strength in the network. In connection to the aspect of types of actors within the structure, the view explains that firms are embedded in a network in which the context incorporates actors of different natures. The view permits identifiable and known political actors to be enclosed within the boundary of the network. In this vein, the environment, contrary to a classical specification of the business network, is not completely given or seen as less important. The view implies that embeddedness in the political realm can be as important as, or even more important than, embeddedness in the business realm. Following the construction of interdependency of the embedded actors, business actors can exercise influence on actors which have different values.

4.1. Embeddedness in a Political Context

The complexity of embeddedness in this argumentation lies in the notion that the network expands its territorial observation and involves actors who do not have similar value systems (Hadjikhani & Sharma 1993). As presented in the earlier section, network theory constructs a view of political actors that is different from many studies where a laissez-faire market condition is assumed. In a laissez-faire market condition, business actors dominate the market. Such a presumption explored in terms of the network recalls the traditional industrial network that homogeneously constrains the business actors in the formation of their network context. Political actors are in, or even beyond, the horizon of the network context because they are very distant from the core activities.

In this study, a network is seen as a set of sociopolitically and economically interrelated actors. Some actors have a generalized exchange, while others have a specific exchange in which the reciprocity is not necessarily achieved through any direct benefit of one actor over another. Instead, it may be achieved through an indirect benefit provided for another actor, which is embedded in the network (Bagozzi 1975; Ekeh 1974; Levi-Strauss 1969). The view of interdependency is explored to indicate that the political embeddedness requires not only an addition of conflicting interest but also an arena for exploring options and sharing common values (Hult & Walcott 1990). Business actors' political behavior is seen as being governed by activities intended to adapt to the outcomes of the behavior of political actors, although the firm's aim is to exercise influence on political actors. Otherwise, firms become dependent on political actors, and the option remaining for the firm is adaptation, which causes structural change and increases costs. Such a view relies on a network explanation (Forsgren 1989; Johanson & Mattsson 1994), which is as follows: international firms are dependent on the government because political rules affect their business. At the same time, the government is dependent on foreign enterprises because firms make investments that, in turn, affect groups on which governments depend, such as the media and the public at large (Hadjkhani 1996; Jacobson *et al.* 1993). This calls forth the explanation that these two actors are interdependent, and their interplay is contingent upon a set of actors from both business and political systems. Such interdependency may be invisible or indirect, but it exists.

The focal actor's two types of exchange relationships and connections are depicted in Figure 2.1. In one relationship, the political exchange, the political actor undertakes coercive and supportive actions for, or against, the focal actor. Types and content of the political actions lie in the strength of embeddedness between the political and other business and non-business actors. Political actors undertake actions to convince those with whom they are highly interdependent. In this manner, business actors exercise influence to gain subsidies for their business activities.

The presumption in the idea of embeddedness is that the connected political and business relationships affect the focal relationship. Imagine a case where a government decides to make a drastic change in the customs duty. The new decision, first, will influence the focal firm's relationship with the political actor because of the influence of the decision on the cost structure. Because of the interdependency, the focal firm also has to change its business relationship with its counterpart. The purchasing or selling value between the two has to be altered. The decision will affect the cost structure of the production and distribution systems, which will further affect the other embedded business. Furthermore, it affects factors like employment, which are important for the political actors. As a result, the embedded actors also may have to change their organization and their marketing or purchasing activities. As a consequence of the decision and the rule of interdependency, such a political decision also influences social relationships. It has an impact on trust between the political and the focal firm, and subsequently on those businesses that are embedded. The degree of impact lies in the degree of strength in the connections or, in other words, the degree of embeddedness.

However, because of the role of interdependency, the impact from an embedded actor transfers to the focal and other embedded relationships. Thus, cooperation and conflict between a focal and political actor affects the trust in the focal business relationship, and that transfers to other interrelated businesses (Macaulay 1963). In cases where a powerful embedded actor discredits a firm's market activity, or when governments use the power of their authority, there is a conflict and consequent mistrust. A political actor, which discredits a firm because of its interdependency with a powerful interest group or political ideology, will affect the atmosphere in the focal relationship as well as those businesses that are embedded.

The higher the number of firms interdependent with political actions, the greater the density in the political zone of the context in the business network. The higher the level of impact from political actors on a focal actor, the higher the level of impact on embedded business actors. The complexity lies in where to set the boundary of the network. Incorporation of the political system also includes non-business actors, such as media, unions, and the public. Their numbers are large and vague, and the benefits of the actors are much more ambiguous. These complicate the measurement of density. But density is a significant issue as it represents a map of the business and non-business actors who have direct and indirect exchange relationships with the focal actor. No matter what the types of embedded actors are, the terms interdependency and adaptation the density assist in measuring the degree of embeddedness and the structure.

The atmosphere, expressed here in terms of power and trust, has its impact on the focal relationship, which transfers to others. The higher the degree of interdependency, the higher the degree of impact on the focal actor. A crucial issue, specifically important in political embeddedness, is the aspect of the political power of political actors, which can be used for the creation of interdependency. Such a condition is an outcome of a high degree of dependency of political actors towards non-business actors. A strong degree of dependency between business actors and political actors becomes equivalent to a weak political-business connection. An interesting issue for such a case is that there is a high degree of embeddedness, but the relationship has a weak nature. Under a condition of weak relationship with a high dependency, the only option left for the focal firm is adaptation, which subsequently affects others who are embedded in the network.

5. Summary

The attempt in this chapter has been to develop a model for studying the business network. The model has its basis in network theory, but it infuses non-business actors into the boundary of the network. The model integrates two problematic issues of business-to-business and business-to-non-business actors. The chapter continued with a discussion about the business relationship and its composition, introduced by: (1) business exchange; (2) social exchange; and (3) information exchange. The political exchange relationships were introduced to differentiate the contents of business and non-business relationships. The model then elaborated discussions about embeddedness. As far as the embeddedness considered business actors, the model is not unique and is similar to a large number of business network studies. The model's distinctiveness lies in the notions introduced, concerning the embeddedness with non-business actors. Since political actors control other types of resources than the business actors and have legitimate power, the study presented other notions to examine the content. When studying the content concerning non-business actors, the model introduced different types of actions varying from negotiation to cooperation. For the strength in these relationships, the model introduced the two concepts of influence and adaptation. The conceptual tool that integrates these two problematic issues is the strength in the negative and positive relationships. These concepts unify the two areas in such a way that a business network can be identified by its structure. This structure is discussed and is said to be composed of the accumulation of the strength in the focal and embedded actors.

The next section is devoted to a presentation of the facts. This model will be used to operationalize the empirical facts, and to present and analyze the conclusions reached by the Iranian and IMP2 studies. The analysis is to lead to additional findings that can enrich the conceptual framework.

Part 2

Decomposition of the Facts

In the preceding chapter, different perspectives on market and firms' behavior were presented. The aim was to introduce the benefits and shortcomings of different disciplines and to construct a theoretical framework. A distinct specificity in this construction was the requirement to include non-business actors in the industrial network. Yet, a business relationship is fundamentally embedded in connection with different types of actors. The specificity lies in the extension of the industrial network boundaries; the integration of non-business actors will shed new light on our understanding of the business firms' behavior. While the non-business actors have been referred to in other industrial network studies as assuming a non-active role in the network environment, this study integrates these actors into the network and gives them an identity.

No doubt, such a theoretical framework can be applied to different firms in different societies, since business firms both influence and are influenced by non-business actors. A presumption of linear, measurable impact — or indeed of no impact — from the side of the non-business actors produces doubtful results and conclusions. However, the inclusion of non-business actors will increase the complexity of the framework. This is because: (1) the number of the factors increases; and (2) the selection of the factors and a cross-sectional analysis become much more complicated. However, if the results, as these chapters will demonstrate, prove to be to some extent complementary and far-reaching, then the extension of the industrial network boundary is a necessity. The world of business is too complex to be explained away by any industrial network model that excludes non-business actors.

The survey is constructed to measure the content of focal relationships between Iranian firms and foreign MNCs, and also to study embeddedness in terms of the connections between the focal Iranian firms on the one hand and other local and foreign business and non-business actors on the other hand. Following this construction, the presentation of the empirical facts will first study the nature of the focal relationship, before proceeding to examine the connected actors. The main aims in this part of the book are:

(1) To study the strength/weakness of the focal relationships as this impacts on the content of the relationship. This is achieved by three chapters which cover different aspects of relationship development, adaptation and social interaction;
(2) To study the embedded actors' interaction with the focal relationship. The purpose is to understand the types and strength of these connections and, further, to illuminate the impacts of these connected relationships on the focal businesses between the Iranian and foreign firms. The impacts are discussed in terms of strength in the negative/positive connection with the focal relationship.

The subsequent four chapters present the empirical findings from the survey. While studying the focal relationship, the three aspects of relationship development and adaptation are presented in the three different chapters. In these chapters, the results of the Iranian cases are compared to those findings from the IMP2 (see Part 1, method section). For some of the questions, the results from both studies are compared. The comparison is designed to assist this study when drawing conclusions.

The fourth chapter is devoted to the topic of embeddedness. In each chapter, before the presentation of empirical results, a theoretical discussion is presented. The concepts can be considered as views that have their bases in the theoretical framework presented in the theoretical part of this study.

Chapter 3

The Focal Relationship

This chapter is devoted to the empirical facts about the relationship between the focal actors, namely, Iranian firms and their foreign partners. The relationship can be defined and analyzed in various ways, depending on the selected theoretical framework. In this chapter, the structuring of the survey results is based on the relationship content. Relationship content is defined in terms of: (1) a temporal continuum covering past, present and future transactions; and (2) the types of ties that constitute the relationship. The strength of the ties is dependent on these two dimensions of the content. Subsequently, the survey presents facts and findings about the history of the relationship and about present and future expectations. The next section sets out the results obtained for the exchange ties between Iranian and foreign firms. This covers aspects like product exchange and technological cooperation between the firms.

1. A View on Relationship Content

The exchange within the relationships exists on several different levels. The *content* is a dimension that encompasses several aspects. Content can be described as a factor which includes aspects that determine the strength of the relationships. Some researchers (e.g. Håkansson & Johanson 1987) signify the content by the nature of the flows between partners and view the technical and social flows as a decisive factor for the content. Others (e.g. Ford *et al.* 1998) focus on the exchange of products, services, money or social interaction. Still others (e.g. Hadjikhani 1997) extend this conceptual boundary and include different aspects like the residue left after the exchange. The latter study embodies the time dimension in the content along a continuum of past, present and future. The time dimension holds for duration of business relationship. A significant aspect of this dimension is durability, which maintains the network for a long period. This is important since the composition of the content at present has a connection to the past. Furthermore, the past and present affect expectations influencing commitment, which is essential for the future exchange.

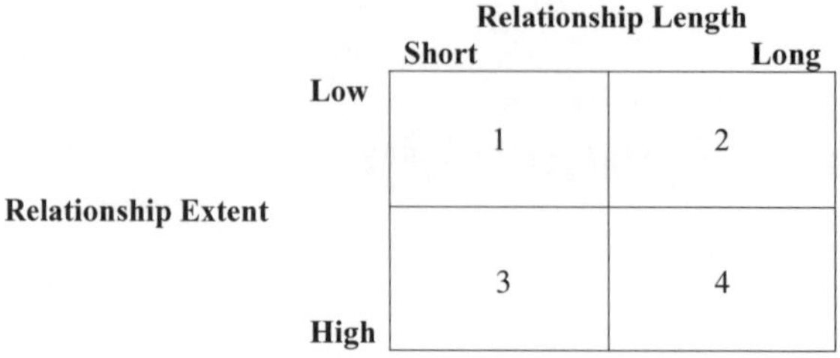

	Relationship Length	
	Short	Long
Low	1	2
High	3	4

Relationship Extent

Figure 3.1: Relationship length and extent.

The second dimension is the *relationship* extent. This dimension considers the technical and social contents of the exchange. It includes the number and extent of the business exchange. These two dimensions are exhibited in Figure 3.1. One considers the relationship development serving the dynamic aspect, i.e. the actors' present and past activities, and also their future expectations for the development of the business relationship.

The view of content is specifically important when studying linkages between the actors. A study on content provides no further knowledge if actors and relationships are identical. But, a network's relationships are diverse, and there is no standardized content; actors are linked to each other differently, and each relationship's content is specific. One specific aspect that distinguishes the content of each relationship is its strength. In Figure 3.1, the strength of both dimensions is expressed in terms of weak/strong and also positive/negative attributes. They simply indicate the duration and composition of the relationship. Cell 1 refers to a relationship of short-term interaction containing few and simple exchanges. A newly established relationship would belong to this cell. Cell 4 exhibits the opposite situation; here, the relationship is composed of intensive exchanges and is of a long-term nature. A long-term relationship between firms with an extensive technological cooperation for technical development (Håkansson & Johanson 1987) would fit the cell 4 categorization. In cell 2, the actors have had a long-term interaction, but the relationship contains few and simple exchanges. A long-term exchange of standardized products would indicate this situation. Finally, cell 3 refers to a relationship of intensive and diversified exchange which has existed for only a short period of time. Cases like market entry with project selling can denote a high level of exchange within the time limit of a project.

These cells are composed of different contents representing four different levels in the relationship strength. Cell 1 reflects a situation where the ties are weak and can easily be broken by alternative choices (e.g. choosing a different supplier).

Cell 4 reveals a diametrically opposed situation. Cell 2 shows a very low level of cooperational development. The relationship has a more formalized and narrow structure, and the number of the exchanges is limited. The experience gained in the long-term cooperation seems to indicate a lack of adaptation in technical capacities, and therefore a weak relationship. The potentiality to upgrade a weak relationship to a stronger one is depicted in cell 3; here, the extensive and large number of complex exchanges contains the seeds for further cooperation in the future (Hadjikhani 1996).

2. Historical Development

When studying the focal relationship, the aim of the questionnaire was to measure aspects like the development of the relationship and its content. Some of the questions consider the process, aspects like the history and initiation of the relationship, while other questions related to the composition of the relationship and the characteristics of the actors themselves. In studying the process, the respondents were asked questions on the commencement of the relationship; when the firms made their first purchase from their foreign partners; how these relationships developed; and their future expectations for their relationships.

The answer to the first question, "the year of initiation," is presented in Figure 3.2. As indicated, the initiation of the relationships does not follow a gradual development or specific trend. The number of relationships, along the vertical axis, and number of years, along the horizontal, show a rapid increase and decrease, respectively, in the years 1956–1997. However, the significant aspect of the figure

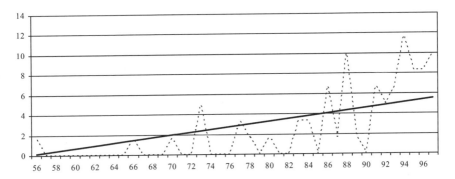

Figure 3.2: Relationship initiation.

lies in the values given to the initiation of the relationship. Whereas the relationship initiation seems stable until 1970, it rapidly increases in the years around 1973 and then declines until 1980. After 1980, it increases up to the year 1986 and then again decreases rapidly. The next positive development occurs around the year 1995 and then again rapidly decreases. In 1996, it starts to increase slowly. As shown, a steady incremental progression in the initiation development years is absent.

In the original IMP2, the decade that the relationships were started was the 1920s, and in each year, the number increased steadily. In the Iranian study, on the contrary, the first relationship started much later, and the successive development trend for the majority of the firms is by the year 1988. In this study, one firm starts purchasing in 1956 and the next one in 1966. Furthermore, the values are not of a progressive nature.

One explanation can be attributed to radical political and economical change in Iran. As depicted in Figure 3.2, the rate of value for the first purchase is intensified in the years around 1973, 1988, and 1995. This is related to the positive expectations of the Iranian firms because of the improvement in the general business environment.

As stated above, the intensity in the initiation of the relationships can be explained by economic and political changes. During the period 1970–1998, the Iranian political and economic milieus were faced with several dramatic changes. These periods can be divided into three substantial periods: pre-revolution (prior to 1977), revolution and war (between Iran and Iraq, 1978–1988), and post-war (1988). Expansion, revolution, and consolidation in the economic and political systems correspond to the changes in the development of the business relationships.

In 1973, the same year that the Shah's fifth plan was instigated, oil prices rose, and likewise Iran's oil revenue. The government started to make huge investments in different industrial sectors. The expenditures in 1974 increased 141% compared to the year before, and Iranian firms intensified their exchange relationships with the foreign MNCs. Local demand was increasing. For example, the consumption of electricity was increasing at a rate of 18–20% a year (Looney 1982). The result was a rapid demand for electricity and an increase in the interaction of local firms with foreign firms.

As the figure indicates, after the first expansion period, the number of relationships decreased. The explanation for this lies in the political developments after 1977, combined with increasing business uncertainty and hostility against foreign MNCs. In the autumn of 1978, the political and economic situation became more unstable (*Financial Times*, 29 July 1980). As Figure 3.2 portrays, there is a radical decrease in the number of new relationships at this time. Unfortunately, there is no

Table 3.1: Historical development.

Question	*t*-Value	df	Significance (Two-Tailed)	Mean Difference
1. What was the first purchase made from this supplier, years ago?	7.380	119	0.000	16.24

reliable information about the total imports by Iran during the period 1982–1992 (*Monthly Bulletin of Statistics* 1993, December, United Nations). According to the study by Rezayi (1986), the total value of imports dropped from 1000 billion Rials in 1977 to around 700 billion between 1978 and 1980, and increased to 1300 billion Rials in 1985 (see also Hadjikhani 1996). A similar development trend can be observed in the number of exchange relationships during the crises and consolidation periods illustrated in Figure 3.2. We can see that the number of relationships decreased in 1977 but thereafter increased and assumed a positive trend. However, it seems that the rate of increase is repressed. There is a further dramatic change at the time of the war between Iran and Iraq. In 1988, after the termination of the war, suddenly the number of relationships increased. The positive degree of intensity after 1988 is unmistakable; the only explanation for this development can be the termination of the war between Iran and Iraq. This can also be verified by the sudden and rapid increase in the import and export values to Iran. After 1988, it seems that the number of new relationships increases but at a much slower pace.

As depicted in Table 3.1, the first aspect of the focal exchange relationship under consideration concerned its historical development. Interesting enough when comparing the average age of the relationships, the relationships between the Iranian customers and their suppliers are significantly older than the relationships in the IMP2-study. An examination of the mean difference of the age of the relationships shows that those between the Iranian firms and their foreign counterparts are, on average, 16 years older. This might be attributed to the relatively long period (1970–1998) where the relationships which had already been established remained, although with a very limited interaction.

2.1. Relationship Development

Several sets of questions were constructed in the research to examine the relationship between the focal actors. Some questions measure the general content

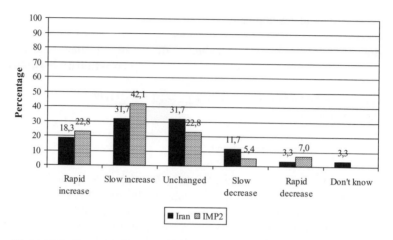

Figure 3.3: Pattern of purchase development over the previous 5 years.

of the relationships, in order to determine the parameters important to the survival of the relationships. Others refer to specific ties and measure the product exchange or technological cooperation.

Concerning the general aspect, in the set of questions relating to the *Development Patterns* in the focal exchange relationships, the trend in purchasing (over the past 5 years) was examined, i.e. the stability, regularity and quantity of the purchase. The first question examines the purchasing trend during the previous five years, and the response scale offered five options from "rapid increase" to "rapid decrease" (see Figure 3.3). The answers reveal a degree of increase in the last five years for this factor. The percentage of the rapid and slow increase taken together is 50.0%. The rest, 31.7%, selected the alternative "unchanged," and 15.0% chose "rapid decrease" and "slow decrease." The accumulated value given for the "slow decrease" and "unchanged" trend is 43.4%.

However, the combined value for the options "rapid increase" and "slow increase" is 50.0%, whereas for "rapid decrease" and "slow decrease," it is 15.0%. This shows that a large number of the Iranian firms have observed a positive trend in the relationship development. However, this trend is much lower than the trend in the industrialized societies. The corresponding alternatives in the IMP2 study are 64.9 and 12.4%. For the alternatives "rapid increase" and "slow increase," the IMP2 scores are more than 30% higher. Furthermore, the value of the "unchanged" is much less in the IMP2. In the question for the Iranian firms, the score is 31.7%, and for the previous study, it is 22.8%. This gives an indication of the development in the content of the relationship. A simple conclusion is that the growth in the

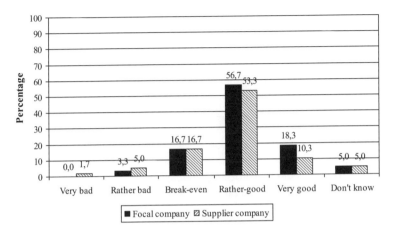

Figure 3.4: Profitability for the past 5 years.

content of the relationship in the Iranian case is much less than the previous study.

Two other questions that cover the development pattern reflect the importance of the economic relationship over the next five years. One question examines the profitability of the relationship for the supplier and another for the customer. The main question is "Considering all costs and revenue associated with this relationship, how would you assess its profitability over the coming five years: (a) for your company; and (b) for the supplier's company?"

Figure 3.4 illustrates the anticipated profitability for the coming five years via a response scale ranging from "very bad" to "very good." As shown, the combined values given to the first two options of "very bad" and "rather bad" in the customer question are 3.3%. The same options in the question for the supplier have the score value of 6.7%. The values for "break even" are higher, both at 16.7%, but are much less than the next two options. The combined scores for the alternatives "rather good" and "very good" are 75.0% for the customer and 71.6% for the supplier questions. These scores lead to several interesting conclusions.

These measures signify: (1) the anticipated high level of economic gains over the next five years; and (2) the mutual benefit in the interaction. The first has its basis in the high percentage scores for the options "rather good" and "very good." This implies that the Iranian customers predict a high economic benefit in their exchange with the foreign suppliers.

Further, the Iranian firms as reaping high economic gains in this interaction also predict the same for the foreign suppliers. Moreover, and this is crucial, the Iranian customers believe that this relationship is important not only because of the amount of the exchange but because of the mutuality in the economic gains. If the scores for the last two options had lower values, the relationship would be viewed as having only weak economic ties; or the relationship could have been considered unimportant. Also, if the values for the customer and suppliers revealed substantial differences, the relationship could have contained an imbalance in the exchange. Imbalance is an indicator of a weak relationship conducted by the exercise of power.

The positive view held by the Iranian managers vis-à-vis the importance of the relationships emphasizes the fact that whatever the relative strength of the other questions, both partners considered the exchange to be essential for their market activities in Iran. The results from these questions will later be used to support or reject other variables in the relationships. A crucial finding is that the Iranian customers believe in the absence of opportunism in the behavior of their foreign partners. This is important, since opportunism is a criterion for a weak and short-term relationship.

Another interesting set of questions in the context of relationship development is the expectation of the Iranian customers. The question was: "What are your expectations regarding purchases from this supplier for the next five years?" As shown in Figure 3.5, the degree of expectation for the option "rapid increase" is very low, viz. 8.3%. But for the option "slow increase," it is much higher, 25.0%. Unfortunately, the future expectation for the options "slow decrease" and "rapid decreases" are 28.3 and 5.0%. This means that the number of firms that expect a

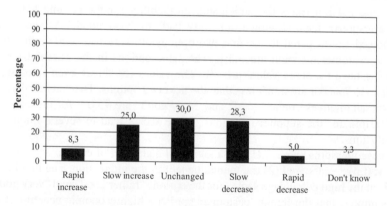

Figure 3.5: Expectations regarding purchases for the next 5 years.

reduction in the business exchange in the future is higher than those who anticipate a more positive development.

This is based on the accumulated values for the two first options (33.3%) and the two options "slow decrease" and "rapid decrease" (33.3%). However, the answers to other questions reflecting the past dimension, for example, "the total purchase during the last five years," as shown earlier, reveal a positive trend. For the question relating to the past five years, the values that the Iranian managers give to the options "rapid increase" and "slow increase" are 50.0%, while the combined value for the two options of "slow decrease" and "rapid decrease" is 15.0%.

The comparison of the results from the last five years with the future expectations reveals that the low degree of future expectation can be related to the higher degree of uncertainty for future development. This uncertainty can have its source in other parts of the network; for example, it may derive as a direct consequence of uncertainty in the political sphere. This explanation has its basis in the economic and political development, which corresponds to the volatility in the past dimension of the relationship development.

The comparison of the values for future expectations with another question (which is not set out in this chapter), considering regularity in purchasing behavior over the past five years, underscores the above conclusion. This is because the combined value given to the options "fairly regular" and "irregular" is about 65%. The answer for "very regular" is extremely low (5%), and for "very irregular" it is about 7%. The highest scores are given to the options "fairly regular" (45%) and "fairly irregular" (21.7%). However, the interaction contains a lower degree of uncertainty concerning the past five years than for the coming five years. However, future uncertainty is not manifested because of the problems in the focal relationship, since the focal relationship contains a high level of profitability for the both Iranian and foreign firms.

Despite the fact that the development trend in the past is better than that of future expectations, the values in the past, compared with the results from the industrialized countries (IMP2,) are not so high. Another question that examined the past dimension was: "How stable was the purchasing pattern?" in the last five years (see Figure 3.6).

The Iranian managers were presented with a response scale, ranging from "very "stable" to "very volatile." The scores presented, as depicted in Figure 3.6, are compared with the values from the earlier IMP2 study.

The response for the option "very stable" is 8.3%, and for "rather stable" 56.7%. The values for the "rather volatile" and "very volatile" options are 10.0 and 6.7%, respectively. The answers show an interesting prevalence of the "rather and slow" for these questions. The result can also be compared with the values from the

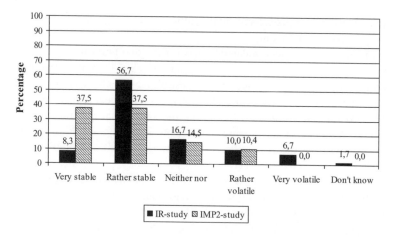

Figure 3.6: Stability in the purchasing pattern over the past 5 years.

IMP2 study. In the IMP2, the dominant values have a very positive nature. More than 37% chose the option "very stable," and for the same alternative, the score given by the Iranian firms is below 10%. However, in the industrialized countries, purchasing patterns enjoy a degree of stability that is three times greater than in Iran. In the Iranian case, the combined value for the options "rather volatile" and "very volatile" is 16.7%, and for the IMP2 study, the same combined value is 6.7%. This means that the degree of volatility is more than double for the Iranian firms. The comparison verifies the discussion above about the uncertainty. The purchasing pattern of the Iranian firms over the past five years has been less stable than IMP2. Instability has caused a degree of uncertainty higher than that perceived by the firms in the previous study. This also confirms the lower degree of dependency and a higher degree of uncertainty for the Iranian firms. But still, the scores in the Iranian firms' study indicate stability in the interactions.

Concerning relationship development (depicted in Table 3.2) the comparison between the IR-study and the IMP2-study shows that the Iranian customers overall have a more positive view on the development of their relationships. In the group of questions used to investigate this, we find that four out of seven test for significant differences between the answer from the IR-study when compared with the IMP2-study. It is clear that the relationship for both the customer and the supplier is viewed as more profitable in the IR-study, and that the stability and regularity in purchasing is higher (see Table 3.2). The trend in purchasing and the expectations for the future shows, however, no difference compared to the IMP2-study, indicating that the long-term nature of the relationship between the Iranian

Table 3.2: Relationship development.

Question	*t*-Value	df	Significance (Two-Tailed)	Mean Difference
1. What has the purchase trend been over the last five years?	1.527	115	0.130	0.38
2. Considering all costs and revenues associated with this relationship, how would you assess its profitability over the last five years for your company?	2.408	115	0.018	0.73
3. Considering all costs and revenues associated with this relationship, how would you assess its profitability over the last five years for the supplier?	3.051	112	0.003	0.80
4. What are your expectations regarding purchases from this supplier for the next five years?	1.897	114	0.060	0.45
5. How stable was the purchase pattern?	2.719	106	0.008	0.62
6. How regular was the purchase pattern, i.e. have purchases been made at regular intervals?	2.370	87	0.020	0.97

customer and their foreign suppliers is very similar to the relationships in the IMP2-study.

3. The Focal Exchange Relationships

This part of the study reflects several aspects in the exchange relationships. The first section considers the product and technological exchanges, and the second section considers the activities of the focal actors in product specification or technological cooperation. This section also integrates areas like market share and product delivery. The results from the Iranian study are compared with a selection of the evaluations reached in the IMP2 study.

3.1. The Product and Technological Exchange

In this context, the study seeks to measure two areas, viz.: (1) the type; and (2) the nature of the products flowing from the foreign suppliers to the Iranian customers. The survey includes six different questions covering aspects like product classification and the newness of the product. One question seeks to determine the type of products. The five options are: raw material; semi-finished product; component; light equipment; and heavy equipment. The type of product selected by 50% of the Iranian customers is raw materials, and 29% select industrial components. The rest constitute heavy and light equipment. The values given to these alternatives almost correspond with the results from the previous study, IMP2, with two major differences. The percentage in the heavy equipment option for the IMP2 study is 27%, whereas for this survey, it is 8%. Furthermore, in the Iranian study, the option "raw material" rates 50%, and in the IMP2 case, it rates 31%. However, the values for the other options are similar. However, the high rating for the "raw material" option prepares the ground for the assumption that half of the Iranian customers operate in the processing industry.

Another question (not depicted here) examines the knowledge of the Iranian firms about the specificity or the degree of standardization of the exchanged product. The results show that 60% of the firms classify the exchanged product as similar to the existing products. The rest (40%) responded that it was a "totally new" or "somewhat modified solution." These values are also similar to the results achieved in the IMP2 study, with one major difference. The percentage of the alternative "a totally new solution" and "new in several aspects" in the Iranian case rate both scores of 13.3%, but in the IMP2 study, the scores for the corresponding alternatives are 3.6 and 10.9%. However, the novelty in the exchanged products between the Iranian firms and their foreign partners is three times greater than in the IMP2 study. Reflecting on the product exchanged, the type of the product is one of the factors that determine the content of a relationship. The finding above, for example, requires a high technological competency for at least 40% of the Iranian firms to handle the product exchange. Further, it requires complex technological cooperation between different units of the Iranian and foreign firms. Consequently, the relationship content has to be consolidated, at least for this group of the firms, with a number of strong ties. One aspect in a business-exchange relationship is the engagement of both interacting parties. In terms of relationships, the partners need to have some degree of cooperation regarding issues like the specification of the product exchanged. One of the questions in this respect was: "Who specifies the product?"

As Figure 3.7 illustrates, the role of the supplier alone in specifying the product is very low. The response option "both supplier and customer are engaged" rated 22.8% (for the IMP2 study, it is 39.3%), and the option "mostly the customer" rated

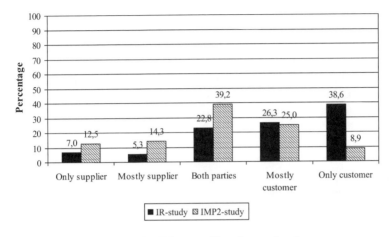

Figure 3.7: Who specifies the product?

26.3%. The interesting option that fixes the exchange relationship as being weak is "only customer," which rated a high score of 38.6%. For the same option, the value in the IMP2 is about 9%. These results can be analyzed in different ways. One is that in the Iranian study, cooperation between the supplier and customer regarding technological issues is weak. A further detailed question examining aspects like technological cooperation will approve/reject this hypothesis. The other possible reason is that the Iranian customers know what they want to buy. However, this possibility can be rejected by reference to the question above, which studied the requirement of the product in terms of the content of the relationship. This will be analyzed further in subsequent chapters.

Studying the possible differences and similarities (see Table 3.3) concerning the product and technological exchange reveals that there are no significant differences

Table 3.3: Product and technological exchange.

Question	t-Value	df	Significance (Two-Tailed)	Mean Difference
1. How much does the product depart from the products you have used previously?	1.072	113	0.286	0.28
2. Who specifies the product?	3.795	112	0.000	0.90

between how the companies in the IR and the IMP2 studies perceive the current product compared to previously used product. This implies a similarity between the characters of the relationships when it relates to the product technology. If a large portion of the relationships in either study had concerned product with very specific attributes, it is likely that this could have been observed as a significant difference. Contrary to this similarity, the Iranian firms state that the customer, to a higher extent, specifies the product compared to the firms in the IMP2-study.

3.2. Importance of the Customers

Another crucial area in the exchange relationship centers on the importance of the customer and supplier to each other. The scores measure this interdependency. Examining how this interdependence operates in practice will help to develop an understanding of the partners' needs vis-à-vis each other. In this respect, we focus on two sets of questions: (1) the importance of the customer for the supplier; and (2) the importance of the supplier for the customer. In each set, the questions measure the importance for a specific area in the relationship, like "the amount in the exchange." Each question offers the respondents a response scale of five options: "strongly disagree," "partly disagree," "uncertain," "partly agree," and "strongly agree." The first main question of the set is: "In what respect is your firm important to this supplier?" This topic contains 11 sub-questions, from which the study will present the results for only seven. The answers to these seven questions provide a good basis from which to extrapolate the importance of these partners to each other.

The first question is "What was the share of this supplier's total sale of this product in your country?" The alternative choices are scores from 10 to 100%. More than 28% of the firms had no knowledge about the activities of their foreign partners in Iran. For 100% of the market share, we have a response rate of more than 18%, which means that more than 18% of the foreign firms have only one customer, i.e. the foreign firms are completely dependent on their Iranian partners. About 55% of the firms select the values from between 30 and 100% of the market share. The percentage indicates again that the foreign firms have few customers in the Iranian market and that these customers are important. The rest (17% of the firms) judge the degree of importance to be in the range 1–30% for their foreign suppliers. Accordingly, the conclusion is that the majority of the foreign firms are heavily dependent on these customers in the Iranian market.

Another question sought to measure the relationship content in terms of market share. One question in this group was "How large a share of your need does this supplier meet?" The values are interesting since almost 27% of the firms buy 100%

of their needs from their foreign partners. About 70% of the firms declare that they purchase 50–100% of their needs from these foreign firms. This means that many of these Iranian firms are completely dependent on their foreign suppliers. As the Iranian firms are large firms spending over U.S.$200,000 every year, the amount or market share of the purchase is important.

The next question examines the importance of the amount spent by the Iranian firms with their foreign partners. More than 45% strongly agree that the amount they purchase has made them important to the foreign suppliers. This percentage response is double that given in the IMP2. The second highest value is 30%, and this is allocated to the option "uncertain." Apart from this option, the responses generally give the impression that the foreign firms are heavily dependent on their Iranian customers on the basis of the amount of the exchange relationship. However, such a conclusion requires further supporting evidence from responses to other types of questions.

The next question in the first set is about the "range of the product they buy as a reason for the importance of the supplier." More than 55% "strongly disagree" or "partly disagree" with the statement that the firm is important for this supplier because of the range of their products. However, 30% partly agree with the statement. This means that there are some Iranian customers that do purchase a variety of products from their suppliers. But the product variety is not a determinant for the interdependency, at least for the majority of the firms. In order to further our understanding of the interdependency between the Iranian customers and their foreign suppliers, we should focus our attention on the technological aspect in the content of the relationship. The study, as follows, refers to some questions in the survey that relate the degree of interdependency to the technology factor. The following two questions in the first group measure this factor. The results obtained for the question that studies the "importance of the partner for the range of technological development" is presented in Figure 3.8. One question in this group is phrased as a statement to which the respondents were asked their reactions. This was "Suppliers are of importance for technological development." The answers in Figure 3.8 reveal that 51.7% (in the IMP2, 28.6%) "strongly disagree" with this statement, and for the option "partly disagree," the score is 10.0%. The development trend in the values is digressive for the alternative options ("partly agree" and "strongly agree"). Comparing these scores with the IMP2's study discloses another picture. After the first option, "strongly disagree," the scores in the IMP2 reveal a positive trend.

For the option "strongly agree," the percentage is almost five times greater than in the Iranian case. This leads to the conclusion that the cooperation between the firms involved in the IMP2 that belong to developed countries is more common than between the suppliers and customers in this study. However, values like 15% for the

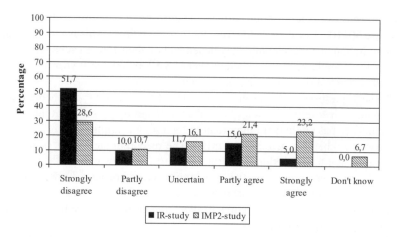

Figure 3.8: Partner's importance in the technical development.

"partly agree" option can be questioned, since the value for the same option in the IMP2 is 21%. Such a value (15%) is surprisingly high as the other questions arrive at different results. Connecting this question to the earlier question, for example, can help us to understand these measures. The comparison gives the impression that the fundamental basis of the cooperation relates to aspects connected to the quantity of the purchased products. Thus, the cooperation is revealed via other variables, such as quantity and price. This also means that for a relationship with only a low level of technological aspects, the role of price becomes paramount. Such a conclusion requires verification. One finding that supports this conclusion relates to the statement that "The firm is important for this supplier because it is a source of technological ideas." As indicated in Figure 3.9, about 51% of the firms select the option "strongly disagree," and the score for the option "partly disagree" is about 11%.

A comparison of the above values with the values from the IMP2 shows that combined scores for the "disagree" options are much higher for the Iranian firms and much less in the values for the options "partly agree" and "strongly agree." The results confirm an important aspect regarding the content of the relationship: namely that the relationships are simple and that cooperation mainly revolves around the aspect of quantity. In addition, the findings illustrate that technological cooperation is not at all extensive among the partners in the Iranian case.

The next group of questions analyzed the theme of "In what respect is the supplier important to your firm? The study examines the importance from the supplier's side." The survey contained eight questions to examine this issue. But,

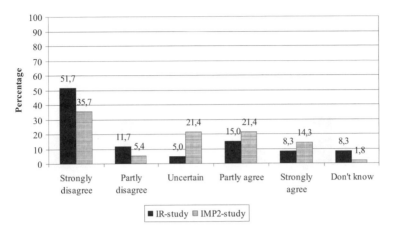

Figure 3.9: Supplier's importance as a source of technological ideas.

following the principle of relevance and similarities, the study will present only two of them.

The first question is (see Figure 3.10): "Is the supplier important because it is used as a safeguard?" For the options "partly agree" and "strongly agree," the total percentage is almost 70%. The answers display an interesting issue in the relationship that refers to another dimension of uncertainty in the relationship. The relationship content in this interaction can be measured by the values in the

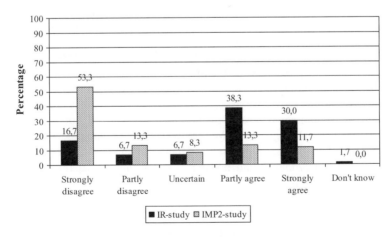

Figure 3.10: Concept of the supplier as a safeguard.

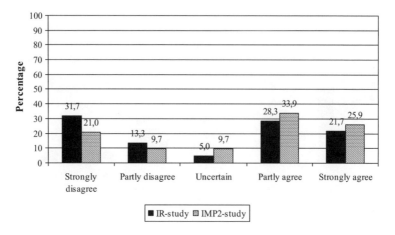

Figure 3.11: Important partner in technological cooperation.

options selected. The combined value of 68% for the two above options shows that Iranian firms' interaction with foreign firms is not founded on a strong business relationship. Figure 3.10 above shows explicitly that the suppliers can be measured as a safeguard for the majority of the Iranian firms. It can also be concluded that the Iranian customers, because of a low level of interdependency, can move to alternative suppliers. The level of certainty in the relationship is so high that the Iranian customers seriously evaluate business offers from the suppliers' competitors.

The results above can be verified by the answers to the next question, shown in Figure 3.11. This question is about "the importance of a partner in technological development." A total of 45% of the interviewees "strongly disagree" or "partly disagree" with the postulation that the foreign suppliers assist them in technological development, compared with around 30% in IMP2. During private interviews, we asked the interviewees how they understood the question of technological development. Their answers did not correspond to the usual definition as given in Western countries. Technological cooperation was perceived to be the suppliers' assistance in understanding the function of the purchased products, and not permanent technological relationships for innovation or the modification of products. It is therefore possible that the combined score for the "partly agree" and "strongly agree" is higher than it needs to be. Such complementary information affects the discussion presented above about technological cooperation. Consequently, before reaching any conclusion, we should try to incorporate several values from different questions.

Table 3.4: Importance of the customers.

Question	*t*-Value	df	Significance (Two-Tailed)	Mean Difference
1. What is your share of this supplier's total sales in your country of this product?	2.890	74	0.005	22.66
2. In what respect is your firm important to this supplier? For the amount we buy from them	2.028	116	0.045	0.70
3. In what respect is your firm important to this supplier? For the range of products we buy from them	0.965	117	0.336	0.36
4. In what respect is your firm important to this supplier? Important partner in technical development	−1.363	114	0.175	−0.48
5. In what respect is your firm important to this supplier? Source of production technology ideas for them	2.509	113	0.014	1.02
6. In what respect is the supplier important to your firm? Safeguard	5.419	118	0.000	1.52
7. In what respect is the supplier important to your firm? Important partner in technical development	−1.384	120	0.169	−0.39

Table 3.4, detailing the importance of the customers, shows some interesting notions when comparing the IR-study to the IMP2. First, the Iranian customers account for a significantly higher portion of the foreign suppliers sale in the customers' home country, compared to the customers in the IMP2-study. On average, the Iranian customer share of the suppliers' total sale is 20% higher than for the customers in the IMP2-study. This is enhanced in the difference between the studies when focusing on the importance of the Iranian customers

for the foreign suppliers. Here, we find that the Iranian firms also are comparably more important than the customers in the IMP2-study concerning the amount bought, but are also relatively more important than the IMP2 when it comes to being a source of production technology ideas for the foreign supplier. There are, though, no significant differences in the importance of the customers, relating to the range of products bought and the aspect of being an important partner in technical development. The fact that there are a great number of similarities between the Iranian relationships and the IMP2, with regard to technological development, is supported by the absence of a significant difference concerning the importance of the supplier to the customer in that area. On the contrary, when studying the importance of the supplier as a safeguard for the customer, there is a highly significant difference between the IR-study and the IMP2. The Iranian customers regard their foreign suppliers as much more important compared to the other group of customers. To conclude, the analysis proves that the two groups of relationships function very similarly, concerning the importance of the customer in some fundamental aspects of the relationship.

3.3. Product Performance

To examine the level of technological cooperation, we raised another question. Generally, technological cooperation between buyer and seller means that they discuss and specify their needs and together try to find technological solutions. The situation may also arise whereby the partners do not have a strong technological cooperation, and one needs to specify to the other its particular needs. Questions in this direction alone do not play a decisive role but, in combination with other questions, can promote a deeper understanding of the content of the technological ties between the two partners. On this subject, we raised two more questions, one of which was: "To what degree can performance requirements for the products be specified by you?" As shown in Figure 3.12, the following percentages were given for the various options: "very low" (0%), "low" (8.3%), "neither low nor high" (15%), "high" (41.7%), "very high" (35%). This means that the Iranian firms have a high degree of power to specify the products; more than 76% specify what their needs are. The firms can then determine the performance requirements in their relationships with the supplier. In the survey for the IMP2, the total value given to the combined options "high" and "very high" is almost the same (76.7%). But if we compare the results from this question with the results from, for example, an earlier question, the picture will shift. In the last question for the IMP2 study, the values consider the development of a new product. But for the Iranian study, the "high" and "very high" options for product specification relate just to the product itself and nothing else.

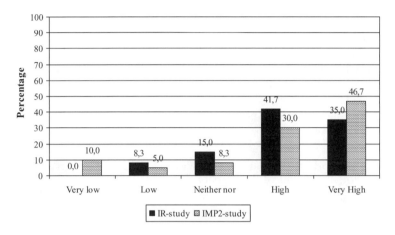

Figure 3.12: Specification of product.

Another question in studying the business relationship, specifically, the exchange of product in a deeper context, is the effect of delivery problems on the production system. In industrialized countries, in order to increase efficiency, the firms work in cooperation with the suppliers to regulate precisely when deliveries should take place. Methods like just-in-time and a well-organized buying-selling system are developed to reduce the production costs. The customers benefit from reduced production costs by not having the input products sitting in the warehouse for a long time. A delivery from the supplier enters the supplier's production system directly by its arrival time. The longer the products sit in the warehouse, the less efficient the production process is, and the higher the final production costs will be. Well-organized internal units and stability in the environment are required for such efficiency to be achieved.

Before we see the results of the impact of delays on the customer, we need to ascertain the number of deliveries in a year. The results from the question on the number of deliveries can support/reject the findings related to the delivery problems. For 18% of the firms, the number of deliveries is once a year, and 30% of the firms have deliveries twice a year. For deliveries three, four, and five times a year, the scores are 7, 13 and 12%, respectively. However, half of the customers receive deliveries from foreign suppliers only once or twice a year. About 32% of the firms receive deliveries three to five times a year. Even if we take into consideration the nature of the product, which may require a large quantity per delivery, the findings point to the conclusion that the firms are obliged to import large quantities because of uncertainty. This uncertainty is not related to

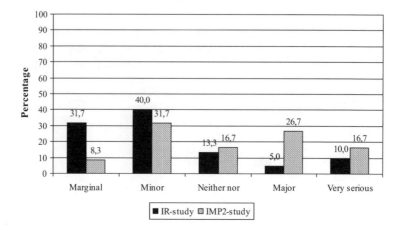

Figure 3.13: Effect of delivery delays.

the relationship with the foreign suppliers but rather has its basis in the surrounding actors. This conclusion can be verified by the following questions.

We raised two questions to examine the impact of the delivery on production. The topic question was "What are the consequences to your firm of a delay in delivery?" The first question asked what the consequences would be of a "one week delivery delay." As shown in Figure 3.13, the percentage for the "marginal and minor effect" is about 72%. For the "major and very serious effect," it is 15%.

In Figure 3.13, the question is compared with another question, which is about the delay for one month. For the option, "marginal effect" and "minor effect," the values are about 8 and 32%, respectively. However, the scores, contrary to the first question, increase. The options "major effect" and "very serious effect," are about 27 and 17%, respectively. It seems that the delay of a month has a much greater impact than the delay of a week. But still, the total value for the two alternatives of "major effect" and "very serious effect" is not more than 44%. This means that the strategy of Iranian firms is to reduce interdependency on their foreign suppliers by purchasing the product in bulk quantity. The values presented for the delivery and delay imply that the Iranian customer, because of uncertainty somewhere else in the network, uses the delivery to reduce the impact. They buy a large quantity and store it in the warehouse to minimize the uncertainty that derives from elsewhere in the production system.

The issues tackled in the last questions complement each other. They indicate at least two problems. The first refers to impacts within the organization of the Iranian firms. The second reflects on the relationships between Iranian customers

Table 3.5: Product performance.

Question	*t*-Value	df	Significance (Two-Tailed)	Mean Difference
1. To what degree can performance requirements for the product be specified in advance by you?	0.244	118	0.808	0.05
2. How frequently are deliveries made to your firm? Regarding more or less continuous sales	−2.422	71	0.018	−13.65
3. What are the consequences to your firm of delivery delay? One week's delay?	−5.656	117	0.000	−1.43
4. What are the consequences to your firm of delivery delay? One month's delay?	−6.382	115	0.000	−1.32

and the foreign suppliers. One conclusion is related to the matter of efficiency in production, and the next focuses on the strength of the relationship. The first concerns organizational aspects; as discussed above, the Iranian customers invest in the construction of large warehouses to reduce their dependence on the flow of input products. The reason for such an organizational system is not uncertainty in the capacity or willingness of the supplier to deliver the products in a smaller quantity. Management, rather, relies on other aspects of their environment. Firms make substantial investments in importing a large quantity of these products (which negates any possible savings or increased organizational efficiency which the just-in-time delivery method could have made). Firms have also invested massively in the construction of warehouses and maintenance of the buildings and products. When considering the second aspect, the minimal concrete transactions (in the form of few deliveries in a year) indicate a weak relationship between the two partners.

Table 3.5 manifests the final comparison between the IR-study and the IMP2-study related to the focal exchange relationship concerning product performance. The first question, measuring whether the customer can specify performance requirements for the product in advance, reveals very high similarities between the Iranian and the IMP2 customers. But this is the only similarity on this topic. The other three questions, all related to the delivery of products, indicate that the opinion of Iranian customers differs to a large extent compared to that for customers in the IMP2-study. Interestingly, the Iranian customers receive deliveries significantly less often than the customers in the IMP2-study. Also, the Iranian customers find the consequences of delays in delivery much less severe in comparison with the customers in the IMP2-study.

4. Summary

In the first section of this chapter, the concepts of extent and development were introduced as the determinant factors of the relationship content. The number and the depth of the relationships define one dimension of extent, while the dimension of development is explained by the history and future of the relationship. These conceptual tools were used to understand the relationship's strength and interdependency. When presenting the facts, these concepts were used to select, structure, and analyze the empirical results. Accordingly, the empirical study was initiated with a presentation of the historical development and preceded by the study of the product and technological ties. To increase the validity of the arguments, comparisons were made with the results obtained from the IMP2 study.

   An interesting finding in studying the development of the relationship was the apparent connection between the relationship intensity and socio-political development in Iran. The answers revealed that the increase and decrease in the number of relationships correspond with periods of political stability/instability. In the early period of the 1970s and the post-war period in Iran (1988), when greater political stability and economic prosperity prevailed, the level of intensity in the relationships increased. However, during periods of the revolution (at the end of 1970s) and the Iran-Iraq war (1980–1988), the number of relationships decreased. In the IMP2, on the contrary, the results show a more stable and incremental development. Furthermore, the relationships in that survey are more longstanding, dating back, on occasion, more than five decades. In the Iranian case, the oldest relationship originated in the 1970s.

   In further examining the relationship, the study focused on changes in relationships over the previous five years and anticipated changes for the next five years, so the survey looked both backwards and forwards. In the Iranian case, the rate of increase (50%) was far higher than the rate of decrease (15%) over the previous five years. However, this rate of increase in the Iranian case is much less than the rate in the case of IMP2. Another factor examining the future dimension was the anticipated rate of profitability over the next five years. Two results are obtained, one a high rate in the profitability and one the mutuality in the gains between the Iranian customers and foreign suppliers. Profitability and mutuality represent two important bonds greatly affecting the strength of the relationship. Apparently, the focal firms in the Iranian case consider their relationships to be essential, as they are keen to preserve the mutuality. Because of the mutuality in the benefits, the rate of opportunism is low. The expectation is that the high degree of mutuality in the future will positively affect the relationship development.

Connected to the development dimension, the future aspect examined the factor of expectation. Apart from a small group that believed in unchanged content, the values given by the other firms revealed an uncertainty about future development. The firms are skeptical regarding an increase in the strength of their relationships over the next five years. This uncertainty is not necessarily because of the problems in the relationship between the Iranian and foreign firms but rather is linked to their uncertainty regarding other actors in the environment.

A number of questions measured the content of the product and technological exchanges. Some questions measured the factor of product specification, and the others evaluated the importance accorded by the Iranian firms to technological cooperation. For the first criterion, the data disclosed that the Iranian firms alone are very active in specifying the products they require to their foreign suppliers. Only 23% of the customer and supplier firms interact equally in the technological areas of the product. This shows that there is a low degree of interdependency between the Iranian customers and foreign suppliers. Further, when measuring the foreign suppliers as a source of technological development, the score given to the factor of "unimportance" is more than 60%, which is very high. These scores are much higher than in the study of the firms in the IMP2. However, in another question that measured the supplier's role as a partner for technological development, the value is a little higher. This is mainly because some of the Iranian firms are engaged in project activities, and therefore they recognize the foreign supplier's importance for technological development. However, the Iranian firms purchase large quantities, and that makes them important customers for the foreign suppliers. From the results, it can be concluded that price is an important factor binding the actors in the Iranian study. Both firms, as will be discussed in the social interaction, have an understanding about the role of the price.

In a further analysis of the strength of the ties, the study examined product delivery. It seems that the Iranian firms purchase their products in large quantities and very few times per year. About 50% of the Iranian firms make their purchases only once or twice a year. Thus, they are necessarily obliged to buy their products and store them in warehouses. A late delivery of several weeks does not greatly affect production for the Iranian firms. This shows the absence of "just-in-time" methods to increase the efficiency in the production system. The purchase of a large quantity in each delivery can be explained by the uncertainty in the business environment. The analysis in the chapters that follow will help us to establish whether the hypothesis of low interdependency between the Iranian customers and foreign suppliers is in fact true. The principle of just-in-time has an inbuilt interdependency.

Chapter 4

Adaptation

In the previous chapter, the aim was to understand the content of the business exchange between Iranian customers and foreign suppliers. We also compared the results from the IR-study with the results from original IM2. The measures considered the general and specific bonds in the exchange of products and technology. This chapter follows the same track and focuses specifically on the adaptation behavior. Adaptation is perceived in this study as an activity that enforces the willingness of the partners to invest in a relationship. High levels of adaptation require a large investment and generate a strong relationship. In contrast, in a situation with a low level of adaptation, a weak relationship is produced, and the mobility of the parties is increased. In considering the content of the relationships, this section is devoted to the presentation of results for two specific aspects of adaptation. The first considers the adaptation for technological cooperation, and the second implies changes in the routines to ensure a smooth cooperation. The aim is to measure the extent to which parties are willing to invest in the relationship. The chapter ends with a study on how the organizations are adapted to handle the relationships.

1. Views on Adaptation

The concept of adaptation refers to the ways in which a fit is achieved between interacting units. International marketing strategies generally consider standardization versus local adaptation as a way of fitting the firm (and product) to its environment (Cateora 1996; Keegan 1969). Standardization is seen as a tool to minimize the cost of specific adaptation. Local adaptation is phrased in terms of the needs of the customers (Ansoff 1979). From a network perspective, the business market is seen as consisting of interactions dominated by few partners with long-lasting relationships, in which adaptation is one of the major components for long-term relationships (Hallén, Johanson & Seyed-Mohammed 1991). Adaptations are based on the needs of the partners. They take place between individuals, units, and organizations that are dependent on each other.

According to Johanson & Mattsson (1987), adaptations are important for several reasons. First, they are an indicator of the strength of the bonds between interacting firms. Adaptation makes the parties increasingly dependent on each other. Partners, who have made extensive technological and organizational changes and are flexible to their counterpart's needs, construct strong relationships. A high level of interdependency results from modifications and changes in the rules and structures for fitness. In contrast, exchange partners structuring standardized rules and fixed procedures construct weak interdependency, although adaptation may be expressed in terms of high and low degrees. This naturally correlates with the level of interdependency and mutuality. A high symmetric adaptation is an indicator of mutual interdependency. An asymmetrical adaptation refers to a case of dependency of one to another and imbalance in the power relationship.

The second dimension considers the durability of the relationship. Mutual and unique adaptation consists of a balance in interdependency and long-term interactions. This in turn means that an understanding in the relationship contributes solutions besides those of the formal rules. The partners' "voice," as Johanson & Mattsson (1987) explain, is better as a conflict-resolution mechanism than strategies such as reference to a much-detailed contract or exit. This dimension amplifies the learning and social interaction processes that enable the actors to understand each other. This, in turn, affects the mobility of the actors and their degree of freedom to switch to competitors. In the long term, a large investment in unique adaptation will delimit the degree of mobility.

The third dimension is related to the second above. A situation with high adaptation and low mobility requires flexibility from the actors. This is important as it indicates that there is some space for changes in the relationship. The cooperation and adjustments in the activity process mean that rules are not given. The relationship content is unfixed, and partners always need to make new investments to deal with adaptations. In the context of change, adaptation investment aimed at maintenance and progress is necessary.

Finally, adaptation also brings changes in the attitudes and knowledge of the parties, which, in turn, enrich the relationship through a mutual orientation. The mutuality is manifested through common language regarding products, technology, and administrative rules and processes. This also implies adaptation in strategies and resource contribution. Partners modify their strategies to enrich mutuality in goals and investments. In the process of cooperation, conditions of misfit may arise in a number of activities. The parties act to influence and adapt to reach common purposes in the interaction.

These dimensions amplify the degree of adaptation in relation to the strength of the relationship. Corresponding to these dimensions, adaptation reflects a range of operationalization aspects varying from administrative to technological areas.

These aspects indicate how two partners are willing to change and adapt their production and organization. This can vary from simple routine administrative or technological changes — a low degree of strength — to a more extensive change in the technology or to some aspect of organizational structure — a high degree of strength. An extensive administrative adaptation affects criteria such as the delivery of product and timing. This subsequently affects the internal costs, as firms change their boundary-spanning units, such as stockholding. By contrast, a low administrative adaptation makes the relationships similar to economic exchange. The supplier delivers just the requested products, and the customer pays the fee according to the agreements. The partners have the flexibility to change their partners. Buyers or sellers have alternatives, and the cost of changing a partner is low. This mobility, however, has another cost. The cost is connected to the nature of the relationship that appears to have a weak character. A relationship with low interdependency is accommodated with an absence of high adaptation in the resource exchange.

In the opposite condition, partners have made an extensive technological adaptation and become strongly interrelated when they change their marketing, purchasing, production, or management and administrative units. The routine in production or other units of one firm become interrelated with the internal structure of the other. Any change in the units or the structure of a partner will directly affect the other. Alternatives become limited and costly. The high level of interdependency reduces the mobility and forces the firms to live together even if other market opportunities exist. On the one hand, partners obtain mutual benefit but, on the other hand, they lose their mobility. The cost aspect becomes more serious when adaptation is unidimensional. One actor completely adapts itself to another, enjoys its powerful position in the relationship but loses its mobility. This condition arises when an actor has control over a resource that is needed by another. Large MNCs purchasing a large quantity of exchange from small firms can force small firms to follow their application, as they are the major buyers. These factors are among those that measure the strength of relationships.

2. Adaptations

In this chapter, the two aspects, technological and administrative adaptations, are presented. In the technological part, the aim has been to measure: (1) the effort of partners to make unique changes adapted to the counterpart's request; (2) the modifications that partners have made in the products to fulfill the needs of their partners; and finally (3) the suppliers' effort to provide technological advice to the customer. Following the discussion of technological adaptation, the next part of this chapter considers administrative adaptation and adaptation in service, specifically in the training of personnel. The final section is devoted to a discussion on relationship investment and management.

2.1. Specificity in Adaptation

Following the track of adaptation, the degree of originality in adaptation to the partners is examined with two questions. The first question was directed at an evaluation of the supplier's adaptation, and the second was with respect to the customer. The purpose of these questions was to understand the specific adaptation that the firms had made towards each other. The more particular and original the adaptation was towards the partner, the more specific and privileged was the partner in the relationship. The uniqueness of the technological adaptation has a direct relation to the degree of product complexity delivered by supplier to customer. Thus, the more specific the adaptation, the more sophisticated will be the technological adaptation. Thence, when a product is customer-specific, collaboration and adaptations make the partners interdependent. Consequently, the high strength in the relationship decreases the rate of mobility.

However, studying the two questions in this case provides contrary evidence. A large group of the firms in these questions selected the alternative that indicated non-specific or general adaptations. In measuring the degree of specificity in adaptation, one of the questions considered the suppliers and another the purchasers. The results are depicted in Figure 4.1. The accumulated value for the

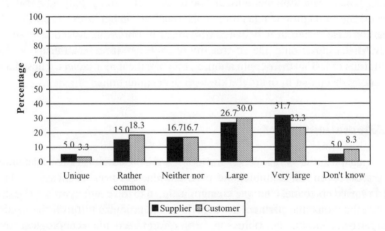

Figure 4.1: Extent of adaptation.

measurement of "large" and "very large" in the question "unique to this supplier" was 58.4%. The accumulation for the same alternatives in the question related to supplier adaptation was 53.3%. This value becomes much higher if the value from the alternative "neither" is included, although the managers explained that adaptations made by the two focal actors were of a general nature. The discussion becomes more interesting if the values in the alternative "unique" are also studied. In almost none of the answers was the adaptation described as "unique." As illustrated, in the questions the values for a unique adaptation were 5.0 and 3.3%, respectively. Even these values do not necessarily mean that this group of firms had made a sophisticated technological adaptation. It could be that these so-called "unique activities" were actually standardized but considered by the firm to be specific (although regular) activities. They may refer to administrative areas, such as a specific agreement connected to the product delivery.

As illustrated in Figure 4.1, both partners have changed their routines and technology. But the dominating values reflect the change with a general or standardized response. The generality in the adaptation leads to a conclusion. As far as these firms have not made large specific changes, they have a high mobility in their relationships and the ability to change their partners and interrupt relationships. Interruption of relationship is an outcome of a weak relationship. This can be a result of two major factors: (1) there exist large numbers of alternative choices; and (2) it is a result of constraints from other dependent actors. In this case, the weakness can only be depicted in terms of the specificity of the change. The study needs to elevate other facts in order to have a deeper understanding of the content and implying forces in the adaptation.

Table 4.1 compares the results from IM2 and IR studies. The first area investigated in relation to adaptation concerns the specificity in adaptation. Here, there are clear differences between customers in the IR-study and in the IMP2-study. The comparison of the answers for the both questions manifests that, in the Iranian customers' opinion, both themselves and their suppliers have made changes that are more unique in their relationships than the customers in the IMP2-study.

2.2. Product Modification

Following the questions above, several others were raised to evaluate the adaptation in the areas of product modification and new product development. These questions had a twofold objective. One was to examine the validity of the answers in the above two questions, and the other was to find clues to understanding the specificity in the adaptation. The result can approve or reject the conclusion above on the weakness of the relationship. In Figure 4.2, two of these questions are presented: one is

Table 4.1: Specificity in adaptation.

Question	*t*-Value	df	Significance (Two-Tailed)	Mean Difference
(1) To what extent are the changes you have made unique to this supplier or similar to those you have made with regard to other suppliers?	2.732	107	0.007	1.24
(2) To what extent are the changes this supplier has made unique to you or similar to those he has made with regard to other customers?	2.026	107	0.045	0.81

about product modification, and the other considered new product development. The topic question was "what changes have been made by your supplier to adapt to you, your products, or procedures?"

As shown in Figure 4.2, the dominating value (more than 48%) in relation to product modification was given to the alternative "none." For the alternative

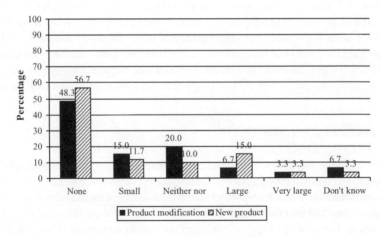

Figure 4.2: Suppliers' adaptation.

"small," it was 15%, and "neither small nor large" was a little higher at 20%. The most important alternative is "very large." Unfortunately, no more than 3.3% was given to this value, meaning that the foreign suppliers had not made large product modifications. In a general sense, it is possible that the interviewees saw product modification as technological adaptation, and therefore there was a low rate for the alternative "very high." The critical issue is that the score given to new technological development is even lower than that given to product modification. The percentage of the value given to the alternative "very large" was 3.3%, with 15% given to "large." The accumulated value for the alternatives of "none" and "very small" was more than 68%. Such a high value can only lead to one conclusion: that the majority of the firms do not have an established technological relationship. Cooperation between the two, other than in a few cases, did not have a deep technological context. The interaction did not contain new product development designed for the Iranian customers. The questions above provide enough evidence to draw the conclusion that the very low technological cooperation among these firms has elaborated weak technological ties.

Concerning changes made by the suppliers in order to adapt to the customers' products or procedures (illustrated in Table 4.2), there are similarities between the groups when it involves product modification. However, when it involves suppliers' adaptation regarding new product development for the customers' sake, there is a statistically significant difference between the opinion of the Iranian firms and

Table 4.2: Product modification.

Question	t-Value	df	Significance (Two-Tailed)	Mean Difference
(1) What changes have been made by your supplier to adapt to yourselves or your products or procedures, regarding product modification?	1.625	119	0.107	0.60
(2) What changes have been made by your supplier to adapt to yourselves or your products or procedures, regarding new product development for your sake?	2.081	119	0.040	0.77

the firms in the IMP2-study. The Iranian firms consider the changes made by the supplier to be higher compared to how the customers in the IMP2-study see it.

2.3. *Technological Advice*

The questionnaire contained 10 questions directed at the further study of technological bonds. The aim was to penetrate deeper into technological cooperation at the level of service and advice. The questions measured the strength of ties among individuals and organizations for areas like technological assistance. All the answers from these 10 questions indicated one specific direction, and the study will, therefore, only present three of the questions that demonstrate the trend of the answers. The topic question, covering several of the questions, was formulated as follows: "Do the suppliers provide any of the following services to you, and if so to what extent, compared with what you consider normal practice?"

In this group, one of the questions considered the technological advice and cooperation between Iranian customers and foreign suppliers. As illustrated in Figure 4.3, surprisingly, the rates for the values "average" and "above average" were 44 and 20%, respectively. The percentage given to the accumulated alternatives of "no" and "less than necessary" was 30.6%. Despite the fact that the value of 30.6% is not that low, the accumulated value for the alternatives of "average" and "above average" is very high, more than 64%. This means that the supplier provides a high degree of technological services to the Iranian customers.

A preliminary snapshot analysis of the measures above indicates that the majority of the firms have a high degree of technological cooperation at the service

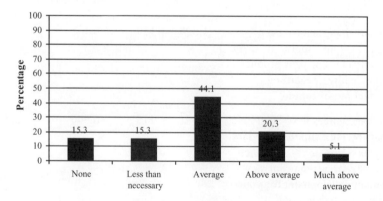

Figure 4.3: Technological advice.

Table 4.3: Technological advice.

Question	*t*-Value	df	Significance (Two-Tailed)	Mean Difference
(1) Does the supplier directly provide any of the following services to you, and if so to what extent as compared to what you consider normal practice? Technical advice, cooperation & development	1.997	100	0.049	0.46

and assistance levels. The first review gives an idea that, despite all the facts discussed before, there is a technological relationship between the partners (i.e. the majority of the foreign firms provide technological assistance). This question compared with the earlier question (Figure 4.2) shows the different degrees of strength in the technological bonds. Technological advice, for example, which refers to the simple transfer of technological information, contains a higher degree of interdependency and stronger bonds than the technological bonds created in developing new products. The results from IR and IMP2 are compared in Table 4.3.

One specific aspect of the suppliers' adaptation concerns the provision of certain services and whether any extra effort has been made. In the present study, technical advice, cooperation and development was examined in this respect. The analysis revealed a significant difference between how the Iranian firms and the firms in the other group looked upon these aspects of technological advice. The Iranian firms noticed that the suppliers provided a higher degree of technological advice in their relationship, in comparison with the relationships the firms in the IMP2-study had with their suppliers.

2.4. Service and Delivery Adaptation

The results from the above questions provide a deeper understanding of technological bonds. In one area, that of new product development, the degree of interdependence and strength was very low. This section refers to technological ties in a rather less complex area. It considers areas such as service and delivery.

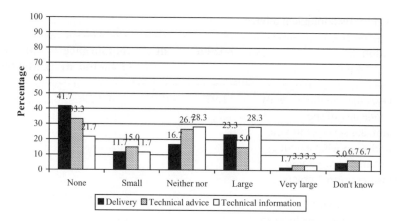

Figure 4.4: Suppliers' adaptation behavior.

The question is how the relationship is organized in those areas that require a lower level of intensity in interaction. A group of questions was used to measure these factors. In the following section, three will be presented, which measure the suppliers' adaptation behavior in relation to: (1) the delivery procedure; (2) the technical advisory service; and (3) technological information. These questions aim to provide knowledge about the strength in the other bonds. The findings are illustrated in Figure 4.4.

Questions (2) and (3) are related to the technical aspects. Both examine the suppliers' adaptation to Iranian customers. Question (2) is about change in the field of technical advice, and question (3) concerns the change in the flow of technical information. However, these two questions examine two factors with different levels of cooperation intensity. Question (2) studies a factor that requires deeper or more intensity in the interaction than the factor studied in question (3). Technical advisory services are accommodated through personal interaction beyond the standardized information flow. Such services are concerned with more specific technical problems and solutions. In contrast, question (3) measures adaptation of a more standardized nature. Such an adaptation is specific only when considering a particular product, but it is far from an adaptation that requires specific and comprehensive technological adaptation. The technical information (question (3)) is transferred in forms such as simple standardized brochures and catalogues. Question (2), however, reflects a more personal interaction.

The comparison of the answers to these two questions shows that the percentage of technical information adaptation is higher than that of the technical advisory service. The accumulated values for the alternatives of "none" and "small" for the question on the advisory service was 48%, compared with 33% on the technical information question. Further, the accumulated value for the alternatives of "large" and "very large" for the question on the advisory service was 18%, compared with 31% on the technical information question. These measures indicate that the technical bond in relation to technical information is stronger than that which is in relation to technical advisory services. However, the degree of the values given to standardized relationships was higher than that which required a stronger bond for a long-term interaction (although ties with a low intensity of personal interaction were stronger than ties with high intensity when just information exchange was included).

In question (1), which was concerned with delivery procedure, the alternatives of "none" and "small" adaptation change have a value higher than 53%. However, the percentage for the category "large" is more than 23%, which is more than the percentage for the questions requiring higher technological cooperation. The score given to "very large" was only 1.7%. A possible explanation for this low value could be that delivery change does not necessitate a very large adaptation commitment. In a condition with high mutual technological interdependency in terms of technological cooperation, a high value for delivery would have been necessary. As the mutual technological cooperation in this study is low, as shown earlier, so the need for delivery adaptation is low. In the question of the delivery, the values given to delivery adaptation were lower than the values given to the information service question. The value in the delivery question was 40%, in the question on advisory assistance 31.7%, and on the information service 56.6%. But, the values for the first two alternatives "none" and "small" in relation to delivery were high. This explains that in delivery adaptation, the majority of the Iranian customers were not highly dependent on the foreign suppliers. In general, the answers show that the rate of adaptation for the delivery procedure was higher in relation to the other bonds. This finding confirms the earlier conclusion about the purchasing behavior of the Iranian firms. As discussed, Iranian firms, because of the high uncertainty generated by the connected actors, are obliged: (1) to buy large quantities; and (2) to make only a few purchases per year.

Comparing the result from question (3) with the result on questions (1) and (2), a regression trend for the adaptations is shown. Ranking these three questions, adaptation for the technical advisory service requires more interactions than the delivery procedure, and delivery requires more interactions than the pure exchange of information. This means that the degree of adaptation of the foreign suppliers has been greater for alternatives containing standardized changes. The suppliers did not specifically adapt their activities toward Iranian customers. Adaptation in the Iranian case was of a more general nature, but there were specific adaptations in areas such as information needs, which require a more standardized and lower commitment.

The degree of generality or specificity of the adaptation had its impact on the strength of the business bonds. Adaptation demanding a general change generates lower interdependencies and weaker bonds. In contrast, in cases where business partners have made specific adaptations towards each other, there will be stronger bonds. Thus, the degree of strength depends on two areas, namely: (1) the type of selected adaptation alternative; and (2) the degree of commitment to the selected alternative. For the first area, some alternatives, such as the three discussed above, represent adaptations containing a low degree of interdependency. But others, such as extensive technological cooperation, represent interdependency that contains a higher degree of strength, although the degree of interdependency for the cause of adaptation varies from standardized to more complex depending on the types or areas of the adaptation. For the second area, each adaptation alternative contains a degree of strength. Generally, adaptation can have a low or high degree. The low degree of technological adaptation in the Iranian case manifests a low degree of strength in the technological bonds.

Another area of adaptation studied involves changes made by the supplier to service and deliveries. In this context, three questions were analyzed for similarities and differences between the IR-study and the IMP2-study (see Table 4.4). The results indicate that there are clear differences in the opinion of the Iranian customers and the customers in the IMP2-study relating to delivery procedures, technical advisory as well as technological information. In all three cases, the Iranian firms find the changes made by their foreign suppliers to be more considerable than those observed by the customers in the IMP2-study.

2.5. Adaptation in Administration

The survey contained a group of questions that specifically examined aspects such as administrative adaptation. For this group, the top question was "What changes has your firm made in order to adapt to the supplier or his products or procedures?" There were 38 questions related to this topic. They examined administrative, product, and production routines. As follows, only two questions represent the general trend in the answers. Of these, one considered adaptations in the administrative routines. The question was "To what extent have Iranian firms changed their administrative routines for this specific supplier?" In this question, the value for the alternative "large change" was only 1.7%. For the alternatives of "large" and "very large" adaptations, the value was 11.7% (see Figure 4.5). This means that the rest, more than 78%, had selected the alternatives "none," "small,"

Table 4.4: Service and delivery adaptation.

Question	*t*-Value	df	Significance (Two-Tailed)	Mean Difference
(1) What changes have been made by your supplier to adapt to yourselves or your products or procedures, regarding the delivery procedure	2.301	117	0.023	1.11
(2) What changes have been made by your supplier to adapt to yourselves or your products or procedures, regarding the technical advisory	3.322	116	0.002	1.66
(3) What changes have been made by your supplier to adapt to yourselves or your products or procedures, regarding technological information	4.936	118	0.000	2.37

and "neither small nor large" changes. For the first two alternatives, the value was more than 68%. This further reveals some facts about how the Iranian firms have only weakly adapted their administrations to their counterparts. A similar answer was obtained in relation to the suppliers' administration. The values in the alternatives for the question concerning "his administrative routines" were lower, with more than 16% selecting the alternative "don't know," although both firms conducted a low degree of administrative adaptation. This result is natural, as there is a low degree of interdependency in technological cooperation.

In business interactions with strong relationships, partners adapt their administrative routines to increase efficiency in the information and product flow between the focal partners. The adaptation is also a means of reducing the conflicts. Otherwise, an administrative routine not adapted to the range of interdependency fabricates a mismatch in the management function. The conclusion is that in this

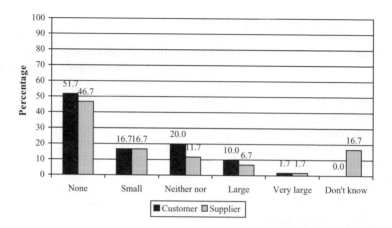

Figure 4.5: Administrative adaptation of the focal actors.

study, the very low administrative adaptation is not an outcome of a mismatch. Rather, it is because of the strength of the ties, which do not require a high degree of administrative adaptation.

As depicted in Table 4.5, in the area of adaptation in administration, the comparison between the IR-study and the IMP2-study reveals some interesting results. It can be concluded that the Iranian firms' foreign suppliers make significantly more changes to adapt themselves to the Iranian firms' administrative routines than the suppliers in the IMP2-study. At the same time, the changes made by the Iranian firms to adapt to the foreign suppliers are highly similar to the situation for the customers in the IMP2-study.

2.6. Personnel Training

The discussion above raises some uncertainty concerning the rates of the technological bonds given by the interviewees. What had really been rated by the respondents? In this connection, we introduce three other questions. The presentation of these questions had two objectives: first, to gain more knowledge about the interviewees' perception of the questions, and second, to gain a deeper knowledge about adaptation in the personal interactions. One of these questions referred to the personal training and instruction of the Iranian firms by the suppliers. As depicted in Figure 4.6, the rating given by the Iranian firms is somewhat different from the rating given in response to the earlier question.

Table 4.5: Adaptation in administration.

Question	*t*-Value	df	Significance (Two-Tailed)	Mean Difference
(1) What changes has your firm made in order to adapt to the supplier or his products or procedures, regarding administrative routines	0.474	117	0.637	0.10
(2) What changes have been made by your supplier to adapt to yourselves or your products or procedures, regarding the administrative routines	4.145	115	0.000	2.65

The results show that about 60% received no personal training. This is quite a high percentage for partners who claim to have a strong technical advice and information service (see Figure 4.4). Furthermore, the accumulated percentage for the category of "above average" and "much above average" was less than 14%. This reveals two facts: (1) the product exchange technological advice referred to

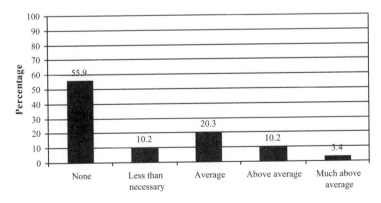

Figure 4.6: Personnel training.

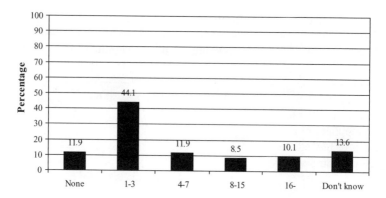

Figure 4.7: Frequency of meetings per year.

in question (3) displayed in Figure 4.4 is of a standardized and general nature; and further (2) the exchange of technological information is below the acceptance level of the customers. For the majority of firms, the technological knowledge exchange was composed of advice provided by simple instructions rather than through personal involvement.

For a validation of the discussions above, the following three questions, which consider the personal meetings and number of personnel involved in the meetings, are presented. Two of these questions provide information about the structure of the technical bonds. They can give further knowledge about the strength of the technical bonds as well as the degree of interdependence of the partners. The presumption is that a higher degree of interdependency is also related to the frequency of meetings and the number of people involved. The results from the answers are depicted in Figure 4.7.

Regarding the question "How frequently do personal meetings take place?" as Figure 4.7 above illustrates, there was a low frequency of meetings. The percentage for "no meetings" was about 12%, with 44% reporting one to three meetings per year. For four to seven meetings, the value was 11.9%. An important aspect is the high percentage for the low frequency of the meetings. A strong technological bond requires an intensive relationship and a number of meetings to modify and develop new products. Only through a high frequency of personal meetings can partners develop new products and solve technological problems. The more complex the technology, the higher the requirement is for personal meetings. This is contrary to the facts given in the case of Iranian firms.

Figure 4.8 connects the former question to the number of people engaged in the relationships. The question was "How many people are directly involved in the relationship?" One question concerned the Iranian customer firm, and the next was

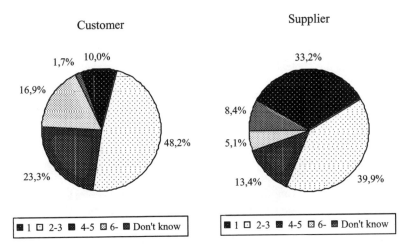

Figure 4.8: Number of people involved.

about the foreign supplier firm. The result shows the same trend as the previous question. For the category one to three people, the value was 58.3%, and for the alternative of four to seven people, the value was 26.7%. Thereafter, the values decreased rapidly. The value for the category of four to seven people is high (26.7%), but this is mainly because 15% of the respondents were involved with four people, at the lower end of the category. This simple illustration shows that even in those few meetings, the Iranian customers were involved with few people. The combination of the questions above reinforces the fact that these meetings have a more standardized nature. Nevertheless, it has to be mentioned that four to seven people were engaged in more than 26% of the cases. This means that the meetings in this group of firms engaged several engineers and managers. As there were few meetings, as depicted above, the main conclusion is that in the meetings of this group, the discussions were about the quality and quantity of the products, and not about product development. This conclusion can be confirmed in the last section of this chapter, which is about the units engaged in the relationships.

In this connection, another question was raised about the number of people in the relationships from the supplier firms. The answer is interesting, as the frequency shows that there were even fewer people from the suppliers than there were Iranian customers. Thus, in the meetings, the Iranians out-numbered their foreign partners. As shown in the figure above, the percentage for the accumulated number of 1–3 people was more than 73.3%. This number drops very fast by the increasing number of people engaged in the meetings. The results obtained in this question confirm the conclusion that the meetings are about product specification and not about complex technological changes.

The comparison of the above questions leads to some fundamental conclusions. One considers the content of the exchange. The facts reveal that the technological bonds have a simple nature for three reasons. First, the specificity in adaptation refers to information exchange, which mainly touches on the functional aspects of the products. Second, the products exchanged were not complex, and the Iranian firms had enough technological knowledge and did not need assistance from the foreign suppliers. Finally, and a more conclusive result, as the relationships have a general nature and are not specific, the level of interdependency between the partners is low, and the relationships are weak.

Personnel training is another aspect discussed in the connection to adaptation. In this area, the comparison (see Table 4.6) shows large similarities when comparing the opinions of the Iranian firms with those of the firms in IMP2. The frequency of personal meetings, and the number of people involved in the relationship from the customers and the suppliers, are almost the same for the two groups of firms. This is also the case for the suppliers' provision of personnel training and instructions where no significant differences between the groups can be found.

2.7. Investment for Adaptation

An important area in the interdependency between two firms is the commitment of the focal firms. The more investment the partners have made in a relationship, the more interdependent they are. Investment is another key that measures interdependency and the strength of the relationship between partners. When only one firm invests in the relationship a condition of dependency arises, as the firm investing in the relationship becomes dependent on the other. Following this discussion, the study presents another question that examines the investment of the Iranian firms in the relationships which they have introduced as the most important in their business network.

The question asked was: "In all, how large is the investment made by your firm in your relationship with this supplier?" (see Figure 4.9). There were five alternative responses: "none," "small," "neither small nor large," "large," and "very large." The accumulated percentage for the alternatives "none," "small," and "neither small nor large," was 80%. In general, the answers illustrate the fact that a large majority of the firms have not made a financial investment in their partners. For the first two choices, the percentage was 50%, and for the last two ("large and very large"), the value was 16.6%. Financial investment in a relationship is one of the indicators of the importance of the partnership. The higher the importance of a partner, in

Table 4.6: Personnel training.

Question	*t*-Value	df	Significance (Two-Tailed)	Mean Difference
(1) Does the supplier directly provide any of the following services to you, and if so to what extent as compared to what you consider normal practice? Personnel training and instructions	−0.763	114	0.447	−0.17
(2) How frequently do personal meetings take place?	0.179	94	0.858	1.99
(3) How many people are directly involved in the relationship from the customer?	1.759	90	0.082	1.26
(4) How many people are directly involved in the relationship from the supplier?	−1.865	96	−0.065	−4.72

terms of technological or other relationships, the higher the need is to invest in and change the technology and organization. In the case of Iran, the situation is the opposite. As discussed above, the majority of the firms do not see any reason to make an investment in this foreign supplier.

Figure 4.9 compares two questions of relationship investment. One concerns the customer, and the other is about the suppliers. As shown, the trend in the answers is almost the same as for the first question. The total value for the two alternatives "none" and "small" in the question concerning customer investment was 50%, with 31.6% responding in this way to the question of the suppliers' investment. If the alternative "neither small nor large" is added to these values, 80% is obtained for the customer and 66.6% for the supplier. These values show that the Iranian firms believe the foreign suppliers to be more dependent on

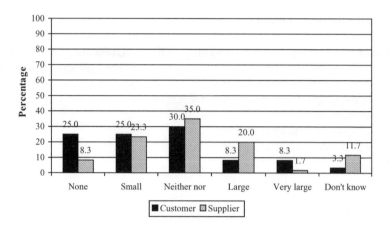

Figure 4.9: Relationship investments.

the Iranian customers, as the suppliers have made a greater investment in the relationship.

In contrast, the values for the alternatives "large" and "very large" are low. A great number of Iranian customers believe that the suppliers have not made a large investment (1.7%) in the relationships. The values also show that the suppliers act similarly to the customers. The comparison of these results also gives the impression that the Iranian customers believe that foreign suppliers have made a larger investment in the relationships than the foreign suppliers do, as the value for the category "large" in the first question was 8.3%, and in the second question, 20%. Despite the fact that the accumulated values for the categories of "large" and "very large" in the first question was 16.6%, and in the next question 21.7%, it can be concluded that the majority of the firms have not made any investment in the relationships. The conclusion is that the low degree of investment has generated a high degree of mobility. This naturally is embedded with a high level of uncertainty. But, despite a high degree of mobility, as the questions in Chapter 3 have shown, the focal relationships are not so short-lived. There must be a reason why the partners continue the exchanges with some suppliers. With reference to this finding, it can be concluded that Iranian customers have become more dependent on their foreign suppliers because of their connections with other actors (i.e. the dependency has gained strength from the connected relationships).

As mentioned in the previous discussion, investments made in the relationship between the focal firms are central. A comparison of the answers given on the two questions used to analyze investment reveals that the investments made by Iranian firms in the relationship with their foreign suppliers are at a similar level

Table 4.7: Investment for adaptation.

Question	*t*-Value	df	Significance (Two-Tailed)	Mean Difference
(1) In all, how large is the investment made by your firm in your relationship with this supplier?	−1.122	115	0.264	−0.38
(2) In all, how large is the investment made by this supplier in the relationship with your firm?	2.489	116	0.014	1.29

to those made by customers in the IMP2-study (see Table 4.7). The investments made by the foreign suppliers in their relationships with the Iranian customers are, however, at a significantly higher level in comparison with the investment made by the suppliers in the relationships in the IMP2-study.

2.8. Organization Adaptation

An important aspect is how an enterprise manages its exchange relationship with an important partner. The term "management" considers the units or individuals that are responsible for handling the relationship with a focal partner. The main question is: "How important were the following different units within your own company, for this relationship?" One question measures the role of the headquarters, and the other examines the engagement of other groups within the firm.

The first question was to measure the degree of importance of the headquarters. An interesting result can be observed in the answers on the importance of the different units. The five alternatives ranged from "very highly important" to "not at all important." More than 60% of the firms interviewed selected the "high importance" of headquarters. This explains the high dependency of the purchasing units on the strategic apex for the final decisions. Generally, headquarters delegate responsibility for decisions to the purchasing units, because they do not have specific knowledge about the purchasing market, product technology, or the content of each specific relationship. The involvement of headquarters in a specific relationship can only occur for reasons such as production technology. However,

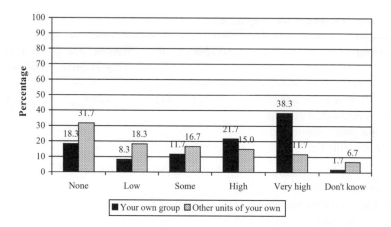

Figure 4.10: Adaptation of the organization units.

the results in the questions generate another factor, management style. The factor of management style can be verified when we compare the values from the questions in the Iranian survey with the values obtained from the corresponding alternatives in the IMP2. In the IMP2 study, the value in the alternative "high importance" of headquarters was less than 30%, indicating that headquarters in the industrialized countries devote 30% less time to managing the relationship with their foreign partners (see Figure 4.10).

This does not mean that the management in the IMP2 was less complicated than in the Iranian cases. Rather, it shows that the management among Iranian firms is structured by a hierarchical system (i.e. the purchasing units' activity is vertically controlled by the headquarters). A speculative conclusion would be the degree of importance of the exchange. The Iranian firms' headquarters have a large degree of engagement because of reasons such as the recognition of this specific exchange as an important part of their business activities.

The conclusion of a centralized management system is also confirmed by the values given to the next question. This question measures the importance of other groups in the relationship. The accumulated value in the two alternatives "rather strong" and "very important" is less than 27%, but the value for the alternative "no importance" reached 31.7%. The accumulated value for the alternatives "no importance" and "minor importance" was 50% and, together with the alternative "some importance," totals 66.7%, although the influence of the other units, such as marketing or production units, is minor. It seems that the purchasing units have a low power position, and their major tasks are centralized and handled mostly by

Table 4.8: Organization adaptation.

Question	*t*-Value	df	Significance (Two-Tailed)	Mean Difference
(1) How important were the following different units within your own company, for initiating the relationship? Your own group HQ	4.487	105	0.000	2.31
(2) How important were the following different units within your own company, for initiating the relationship? Other units	4.486	106	0.000	2.43

headquarters. The answers also lead to the conclusion that, despite the importance of these relationships with foreign companies, the exchange is weakly related to other units within the Iranian firms. The headquarters vertically controls purchasing units. Functionally, headquarters delegate the essential part of the exchange to purchasing units because of the units' competence. These units have knowledge about the production system and have specific information about the local needs.

The last aspect of adaptation investigated concerns changes in the organization. In this respect, the comparison between the IR-study and IMP2-study in Table 4.8 displays clear differences. It is obvious from the previous discussion that the Iranian firms consider other units, including the group headquarters, to be of great importance for managing the relationship with the foreign supplier. This conclusion is supported by the highly significant difference between the opinions of the Iranian firms and the firms in the IMP2-study.

3. Summary

The factor of adaptation between the Iranian and foreign firms has been examined in this chapter with respect to several areas. The first attempt was to understand the degree of the partners' adaptation in general, and the effort thereafter was to gain a deeper knowledge by examining the adaptation in different exchange areas. In general, when examining their particular adaptation, the research arrived at the conclusion that none of these actors have made a specific unique change to adapt their activities to their counterparts. Adaptation is largely general and not specific to the partnership. The study further presented the evaluation of the Iranian firms on adaptations of the products. Areas such as product modification and new product development are studied to measure the foreign suppliers' investments in these criteria. The results again show the absence of the suppliers' commitment in both areas.

For a deeper study of the adaptive behavior, the study examined the administrative areas. The aim was to understand the extent to which the partners changed their administration, service, information exchange, and personal training. Considering the administrative routines, the majority of the Iranian and foreign firms (about 70%) have made no or very small changes. A large number (16%) stated that they did not know of changes. This again discloses the absence of administrative adaptation.

In further examining the degree of adaptation, the study contained questions about the bonds that surround the core product and technological bonds. Service, delivery, and information adaptations are examples of these. Similar to the results above, there has been a low degree of adaptation in all these three areas. The results show a reverse connection between the administrative commitment and the types of administration. For the adaptation type "information exchange," the values given are higher than for other types of adaptations, such as delivery procedures. The degree of the commitment in information exchange was low and also contains a weak bond. The degree of adaptation was a little higher in the area of personal training, but still, about 65% of the Iranian firms received no or very little personal training. Besides the personal training, the study also examined the frequency of meetings and the number of people engaged in them. The small number of meetings over a year, and the few people engaged implicitly disclose a low degree of cooperation.

In one question, the study aimed to discover the level of investment for adaptation by each of the firms. The response indicated a very low degree of investment from both sides. Almost 80% of the firms made no or very little investment to keep the relationships alive. Another area that was examined was connected to organizational adaptations. The answers were clear. The main adaptation is that the headquarters undertake tasks. This means that the role of the other units is not considered as important in the Iranian firms. This excludes consideration of the technological aspects as the most important part of the interaction.

Chapter 5

Social Interaction

The questions in this chapter evaluate the strength of the bonds reflecting the social construction of the relationship. Some questions measure the social interaction in general; others measure specific social bonds. The survey comprised more than 60 questions measuring different aspects of the social interactions between the Iranian customers and their foreign partners. The comparison of the results from this survey with original IMP2 can enhance our understanding. The aim of this chapter is to generate an understanding of the atmosphere in which these actors are linked to each other, for not only Iranian firms but also firms studied in the IMP2. Depending upon the nature of the bonds, these questions can be grouped into two interrelated categories. The first category deals with questions that measure the general views of the Iranian firms on social interdependency. These refer to the strength in the relationship and incorporate aspects such as mobility and mutuality. The second category measures the outcome of the social and business ties, namely, trust. Trust is measured as the fundamental factor that binds the actors and facilitates the relationship. In this category, questions examine the view of the Iranian firms about, for example, cooperation, personal relationships, and attachment. Social interaction is presented in three sections of this chapter. The first two sections are related to interdependency and measure general aspects of mutuality and mobility. The third section is devoted to the dimension of trust in the relationship.

1. Short Notes on the Views

As mentioned in Chapter 2, every business enterprise is deeply rooted in its specific social context. It is the specific conditions and circumstances, in the form of economic and social interdependencies, that make a business enterprise possible and, at the same time, constrain its opportunities. Every enterprise connects various people and activities with a varying degree of mutual fit. In the earlier chapters, interdependency was discussed in terms of functional bonds, which contain the technological/product-related information, and administrative bonds. The concept of adaptation has also been examined in terms of how partners make offers in an attempt to get closer to each other. In a further study of the relationship, an important aspect is to understand how these interdependencies are conceived and conceptualized by the partners. In this chapter, the focus is on the atmosphere that is created. This is examined through the aspects of (1) mutual fitness, (2) mobility, and (3) the trust relationship.

The concept of social interaction — the atmosphere — is defined as the emotional setting between the partners. This differs in different networks with regard to the impact that can be expected from the properties of the network structure (Blankenburg *et al.* 1997). The social atmosphere is a variable linking the supplier and customer exchange (Ford *et al.* 1988). The elements in the atmosphere are stressed in many conceptualizations. They are presented in terms of factors such as power/dependence, perceived feelings, understanding, and trust, with power/dependence and trust being identified by researchers, such as Anderson and Narus (1990), as representing mutuality. However, all the studies agree on two fundamental aspects in the social interaction that are interconnected: interdependency and trust.

The relationship between two parties can be characterized as balanced or imbalanced with regard to interdependency (Hallén & Sandström 1991). Imbalance, which elevates the fact of power in the relationship, is indicated by an unmatched dependence. A business relationship with such an imbalance is characterized by mobility. Potential mobility is a resource that strengthens the position of an actor as it can change the partnership. An actor with high mobility can venture the existing relationship in favor of competitors. This element does not necessarily imply a condition of conflict, but it can provide evidence for the strength of the relationships. The exercise of power by one partner increases vulnerability, as a weak partner can move to a competitor when there is an opportunity.

The relationship of interdependence can also be perceived as balanced as partners can, to some extent, control resources, and mutual interdependency is preserved. The degree of balance can be discussed by the level of mutuality. In a condition where partners feel equal to each other, at least two different situations exist. One considers non-committed actors and is thus a situation of complete freedom in which parties are independent. Another implies a situation in which partners have made a high investment for adaptation and have become mutually interdependent. This exposes a continuum on which the balance of mutuality and adaptation can have different degrees of interdependency. Strength and weakness in the interdependency reflect the degree of mobility. The success of competitors in penetrating a relationship is a consequence of the degree of interdependence. Low mobility relies on a high level of interdependence and vice versa. This dimension has a correlation with adaptation, which may be low or high, followed by the role of mutuality.

The other dimension in the social atmosphere that is explored in this study is trust. Trust is an important factor in any relationship, as its absence has a strong bearing on the strategy an actor chooses. There are two dominant conceptualizations of trust in the literature. Rousseau *et al.* (1998) interpret trust as cognitive expectation, whereas Johnson-George and Swap (1982) define trust by "the willingness to take risks" (e.g. McAllister 1995). Some, like Moorman, Desphande & Zaltman (1993), combine the two definitions in a higher-order construct. Following the principle of reciprocity in exchange theory (e.g. Blau 1964), trusting behavior is defined in this study as being grounded in mutuality and stability (Anderson & Weitz 1992; Rousseau *et al.* 1998). Trust can also be built on expectations and can lead to a willingness to rely on a relationship partner in whom one has confidence (Dasgupta 1988). Trust is the concurrence of promise with real action. In the absence of uncertainty, the foreign affairs of firms can proceed because business actors can easily plan their future courses of action. There would be no problem of trust if people always did what they said they would and were expected to do. The vulnerability of an investigated actor comes from the increasing uncertainty associated with the inability to control the behavior of a counterpart. When actors use their power to influence other actors, mistrust may appear (Pagden 1988). The studies in trust are well documented.

Some studies treat trust as a commodity and regard its maintenance as a necessity (Hawthorn 1988); otherwise, uncertainty increases, and mistrust becomes a source of problems. Thus, trust can be seen on a continuum from high to low. At one end of the continuum, actions correspond with promises and reciprocity prevails. At the other end, there is a high disparity between promises and actions, and mistrust emerges. Changes can occur in either direction of this continuum. Reduction in trust or an increase in mistrust requires repeated deviations in actions from promises. Such deviations can arise for unforeseen reasons beyond the control of the counterpart (Hadjikhani & Sharma 1993). Another reason for deviating is a change in the credibility of trust (Dasgupta 1988). This refers to a situation in which actors do not follow the rule of reciprocity and do not consider themselves obliged to fulfill their promises.

Some studies, such as those by Hadjikhani (1996) and Hadjikhani & Håkansson (1996), also disclose another interesting dimension besides the continuum of trust, namely, levels (individual to institutional) in the trust. Cases like the positive relationship between governments (Hadjikhani 1996) or the belief of buyers in products made in different countries (i.e. country of origin and/or trust among individuals in the organization) are examples of trust relationships between actors standing at different levels. Conceptually, these aspects — levels of trust and the trust/mistrust continuum — constitute the multidimensionality of trust. Business trust should be seen as an outcome of the combination of trust among business and non-business actors at different levels (Håkansson & Östberg 1975). Trust can be classified at different interrelated levels. A change in business or political actions does not necessarily have similar effects on different levels of trust. A business actor can use trust at one level to obtain trust at another level where trust is low or absent. The mistrust at one level could also influence another level. Trust can be on an individual level (Macaulay 1963); it can also be on a corporate level based on organizational structure, rules, or process (Håkansson & Östberg 1975). Business trust may gain assistance from the relationship between governments. According to this view, the outcome in business trust is produced by the trust/mistrust relationships between the actors at these different levels. The multidimensionality of trust implies that each individual relationship concerns not only trust/mistrust between the two individual actors but also trust/mistrust at other levels. According to this explanation, trustworthiness contains not only the sediment left from relationships at the individual level, but also relationships among groups and firms with groups, units, and even perceptions towards the firm. This follows the rule of connection in the network: that trust in one relationship affects another.

2. Social Interdependency and Mutuality

Another dimension in social interaction is the customers' feelings about the mutuality in their relationships with their suppliers. The extent of high or low values in feelings constitutes a continuum for mutuality that extends from high dependent in one extreme to high power in another extreme. In examining mutuality, the questions in the survey were concerned with the aspects of dependency and power in the interaction. Mutuality in the resource exchange involves a feeling of interdependency in the relationship. The more dependent actors are on their partners, the more power the partner has in a relationship. The exercise of power is an instrument that affects the partner's behavior *towards the wishes of an actor* in the exchange. The case of equality indicates only one condition on the mutuality continuum when partners have a feeling and position of equal power in the relationship.

An important characteristic of this mutuality is the level of interdependency, which is directly connected to the content of the exchange. Equality in a highly developed business exchange includes technological cooperation and a high level of mutuality in the relationship. In contrast, an exchange containing a simple interaction has a low level of interdependency but also mutuality. According to the network approach, mutuality is a cumulative process that takes into account gains and contributions. In the long term, the content of an exchange develops successively, and the partners aim for a balance in what they offer and what they gain (i.e. equality in the exchange is preserved). Mutuality also has other characteristics. A developed multilateral activity strengthens mutuality and interdependency, as few exchange bonds, and a low volume of exchange will develop a weak interdependent relationship. The latter can arise despite a long-term interaction, as the content of the exchange is being kept at a low level. Thus, every exchange affects the behavior of actors, as it elevates a feeling of the potential and actual gains from a relationship.

To examine the aspect of mutuality in the survey, five questions were raised. Results from only three of the questions are discussed, as similar results were obtained from the other questions. The questions examine how Iranian firms realize the mutuality in their relationships with their foreign partners.

The first question (see Figure 5.1) considered the feelings of dependence of the Iranian firms. They were asked to respond to the statement: "We feel dependent on this supplier." Thirty-five percent of the firms either partly or strongly agreed with the postulation. This rate is somewhat higher than in the survey for the IMP2 study, where it was about 30%.

In general, however, the percentages for these alternatives were much lower than the rates for the disagreement alternatives. The accumulated percentage for the first two disagreement alternatives is 56.6%, that is less than the 50.0% value for similar alternatives in the IMP2 study. This implies that the firms in the IMP2 study

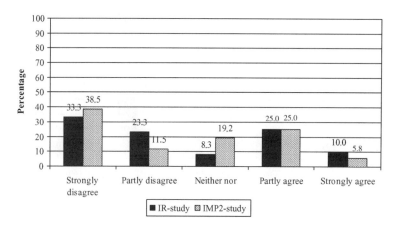

Figure 5.1: Feeling of dependency.

perceived themselves to be much less dependent on the suppliers than the Iranian firms did. Surprisingly, the difference is much less than expected. At the same time, a third of the Iranian firms felt that they were not dependent on the foreign firms. One reason for such a low difference is that, as will be discussed later, Iranian managers have the feeling that foreign firms are greatly dependent on Iranian firms because foreign firms have shortcomings in the Iranian market and lack social knowledge.

The next statement was: "We have a feeling of mutual dependence in our relationship with this supplier" (see Figure 5.2). The topic relates to a similar area in mutuality, with a clearer expression. In their responses, the majority of the Iranian firms selected the alternatives "partly agree" (41.7%) and "strongly agree" (13.3%). It seems that the firms' managers recognized mutuality as the basis for the interaction. Combining these categories, it can be seen that 55% of the managers (an even higher percentage than in the IMP2 study) were positive about the interaction. In the question, the accumulated score for the alternatives "partly disagree" and "strongly disagree" was not more than 30%. This value corresponds with the accumulated percentage in the next question, which examined the degree of frequency in the adaptation. Adaptation refers to the appropriateness of the partners' input into the technological and organizational bonds of the relationship.

As can be seen in Figure 5.2, the accumulated value for the "partly agree" and "strongly agree" categories in relation to adaptation was also 30.0%. As the result for the adaptation question shows, the accumulated rate for the "disagree" alternatives was more than 53%, which is much higher than the 30% accumulated

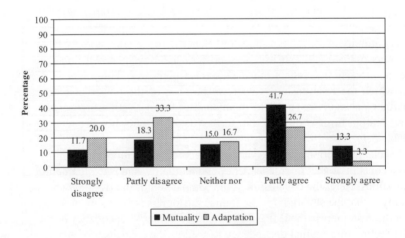

Figure 5.2: Mutuality and adaptation.

rate for the alternatives of partly and strongly agree. It is true that the majority of the firms in all of the three questions had a feeling of equilibrium in the interaction, but the values indicate that the rate of the imbalance in the relationships is not low (e.g. Figures 4.5 and 4.9 in Chapter 4).

Two speculative conclusions can be presented. One considers the power exchange, and the other is the balance in the mutuality in the relationship. The questions presented in the earlier chapters demonstrate the scores in the specific bonds, such as those of product or organization. The power in the relationship concerns the functional interdependency. The evidence shows the functional power of foreign firms, specifically, the technological dependency of the Iranian firms on the foreign firms. However, in the questions concerning the general feelings and perceptions of the Iranian personnel, the answers, as shown above, indicate a more balanced interaction. The questions in the earlier chapter generate a picture that is not completely the same. The earlier questions, displayed in Figure 4.9, were related to the functional aspects, and the answers reported the more objective facts. The differences between the results could be a function of the type of questions. The later questions examined perceptions and feelings, which can be directly associated with powerlessness in the sense that managers select those alternatives that do not disclose, for example, their powerless position. The explicit declaration of low power is sensitive, particularly for people who come from cultures like Iran: They perceive it as a personal shortcoming.

The next conclusion refers to the factor of mutuality. The answers show that, in spite of a weak relationship, the actors to some degree have a balance in their relationships, although mutuality has no direct connection with the strength of the relationship. In cases where actors have weak relationships, they may perceive the relationship as balanced. The aspect of balance is important, as it has an impact on continuity in the relationships. Imbalance in the relationship can be recognized as opportunism and can lead to short-term relationships. An imbalanced long-term interaction results from the exercise of power. This reflects a condition in which the relationship is coercive because of the power of one interacting partner on another. The field of mutuality in the relationship between Iranian and foreign firms is discussed in further detail in the following section (see also Table 5.1).

Social interaction relates to various aspects of the relationship's atmosphere. The first concerns social interdependency and mutuality, and is explored through three questions. Here, the conclusion of the comparison of the IR-study and the IMP2-study is that the situation for the Iranian customers is very similar to the situation for the customers in the IMP2-study. In the customer's dependency on the supplier, the feeling of a mutual dependency as well as the frequency of adaptation made by the customer, there are no differences between the two groups.

Table 5.1: Social interdependency and mutuality.

Question	*t*-Value	df	Significance (Two-Tailed)	Mean Difference
1. We feel dependent on this supplier	0.260	110	0.796	0.07
2. We have a feeling of mutual dependence in our relationship with this supplier	−0.233	110	0.816	−0.06
3. Adaptations are more frequently made by us than by the supplier	1.281	110	0.203	0.29

2.1. Interdependence and Mobility

The questions related to the factor of mutuality examine the perception of mobility and interdependency of the Iranian firms. The firms were asked to explain their willingness to change a partnership. In a way, the questions had a general character and aimed at measuring how Iranian firms recognize their own and their partners' position in the network. (That is, their position in terms of the strength of their partners compared with other alternative partners in the market). These aspects may enlarge our understanding in two areas. One is the positioning of the Iranian and foreign firms beyond the dyadic interaction. This is related to the aspect of connection and the power of suppliers' competitors in the Iranian market. The other area considers the strength of the dyadic relationship between the Iranian and foreign firms. In a case of high mobility, a condition of low interdependency follows. When firms note a low degree of choice, the condition is one of low mobility with high interdependency and a high degree of strength in the relationships.

Considering the factor of mobility, three questions are presented in the following discussion. They examine the mobility of the Iranian customers and foreign suppliers. The alternatives consider the degree of probability in changing partners. Two of the questions are related to the behavior of the Iranian buyers, and one is about the Iranian buyers' perceptions of the behavior of their foreign partners. In the first question, the study examined the Iranian firms' alternatives if they wanted to change or replace their foreign partners.

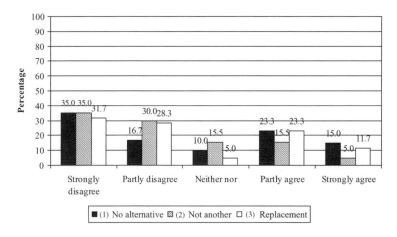

Figure 5.3: Mutuality and understanding.

Figure 5.3 illustrates the respondents' reactions to three statements: (1) "Considering everything, we actually have no alternatives to this relationship"; (2) "We would not buy from another supplier at the expense of our current supplier"; and (3) "It would be very difficult for us to find a replacement for this supplier." In statement (1), almost 52% of the firms indicated a high level of potential mobility. In other words, these firms explained that they would change their suppliers if another one appeared. However, the values given to the last two alternatives of "partly agree" and "strongly agree" were not so high (23.3% and 15.0%, respectively). The accumulated percentage of 38% is rather high if the value is compared with the results obtained from the questions previously presented concerning the business exchange. The earlier questions showed that for a large number of Iranian firms, the technological bonds contained a low level of interdependency. A comparison can be made with statements concerning the foreign partner as a source of technological development (see Chapter 3, Table 3.7). The answer shows that only one out of five of the Iranian firms perceived their foreign firms as technological partners. It is clear, therefore, that these partners have a weak technological bond. The difference between 38% in question (1) above and the measures for technological interdependency may have another explanation. This difference, as well as the conclusion of weak relationships, can appear because of the firms' connection. It may be that the selected alternatives in question (1) have their foundations in financial bonds. The terms of payment, cash, a form of installments, and the exchange rate, can all generate a dependency among the partners. Generally, firms acting in developing countries are obliged to find sources for financing their purchases. Financing is a significant tie in the interaction with firms from developing countries, as foreign MNCs recognize these countries as high-risk markets and are not willing to venture their capital. Suppliers that have a strong positive connection to sources for financing industrial activities are given priority by the customers. Conceptually, this impact enlarges the dyadic relationship view and gives greater importance to the aspect of connection. Thus, one can conclude that the stronger the connection of a supplier to supporting the actors' activities financially, the stronger the position of the supplier will be in the relationship. In the Iranian case, a number of foreign firms, by gaining financial support from others, have strengthened their own position and weakened that of their competitors'.

The results and explanation above can be verified by the next question that considers the view of customers in finding a replacement for their partners. As question (3) indicates, it seems that only 5% of the Iranian customers are uncertain of their position in the market, although this group does not have a clear view of their own and their partners' positions in the Iranian market as a whole. However, this small uncertain group also shows that a large group of the Iranian managers have good knowledge of their competitors. Among the Iranian firms, a large group (60%) selected the first two alternatives, indicating a high ability to change partners. These firms explained that it would not be difficult to find another alternative with which to substitute their foreign suppliers. The high potential mobility of these firms reveals the weakness in the strength of the relationships.

Statement (2) was: "We would not use another supplier at the expense of our current supplier." The accumulated score for the alternatives "partly agree" and "strongly agree" was just above 20%. The score of 35.0% for the alternatives of "partly" and "strongly agree" in question (3) is higher than the 20.5% in question (2). The reason for such a difference could have its foundations in the types of interdependencies. As mentioned above, a relationship is composed of several bonds, and each bond has a specific connection structure. The strength of a relationship is an accumulation of the strength in all of the focal and connected bonds. Firms can face a condition in which a supplier's competitors offer similar problems and opportunities, except in a few areas. Consider a case where the focal supplier and all of the supplier's competitors can contribute equal exchange to the customer except for one, which can offer, for example, different terms of payment. Generally, the strength of the connected bond that may result from an exchange is related to the strength of the connection between the supplier and its financial sources. Thus, the difference between the values 20.5% in question (2) and 35.0% in question (3) is because of the high dependency of the Iranian firms on foreign suppliers. This can be confirmed by the value of 38.3% given to the alternatives "partly agree" and "strongly agree" in question (1).

Question (2) measured the extent of customers' activity in changing partnerships. The question, ultimately, measures the reaction of Iranian customers if several suppliers offered a similar exchange. A comparison of the results between question (2) and the two questions (1) and (3) (see Figure 5.3) shows that the accumulated values for "partly agree" and "strongly agree" in question (2) were lower than for the other two questions. The value in question (1) was 38.3%, in question (3) 35.0%, and in question (2) 20.5%. This means that almost 38.3% (question (1)) of the firms had no other alternatives to that particular supplier. Even if a new alternative supplier appeared 20.5% (question (2)) were not willing to change suppliers. The rest of the firms are forced to retain their relationships.

The accumulated results for the first two alternatives, "strongly disagree" and "partly disagree," in question (1) was about 52%, and for question (2) 65%. These values also support the answers for the alternatives "partly agree" and "strongly agree," although, questions (1) and (2) are complementary in showing a high level of potential mobility among a large group of the Iranian firms. The degree of potential mobility, as the comparison of the cases shows, varies. The basis for variation was the degree of dependency of the customer, apart from the technological bonds. In a condition where a supplier's competitor can offer similar opportunities, customers can very easily change their supplier. This is a consequence of weak relationships.

In examining the aspect of mobility, the survey included another question (not depicted in this chapter) that asked the Iranian customers to explain their perceptions of the future behavior of the suppliers. About 30% of the firms believed that their suppliers could easily find other customers. This means that for this group, the exchange does not contain such a degree of benefit that the partners could expect a high level of development in the relationship. They perceived that these suppliers could switch to another in the near future. However, the majority of the firms, 55%, believed that the suppliers would continue their relationships in the future. Comparing this value with the values in the earlier questions is interesting. There is a 10% difference between the values given to these two alternatives, 55% in this question, and 65% in the answers to question (2). The difference can be explained by the Iranian customers' beliefs that the foreign suppliers are highly dependent on them. In question (2), the customers explained that they could easily change the supplier, but they did not realize that the suppliers also had such a freedom. Compared with the values for the freedom of the foreign suppliers, the Iranian customers believed that they had a higher degree of potential mobility to change partners than the suppliers, although, the foreign suppliers have a higher dependency on the customer than Iranian customers have on the foreign suppliers. This aspect, interdependency between these two partners, will be discussed further in the following section (see also Table 5.2).

Table 5.2: Interdependency and mobility.

Question	*t*-Value	df	Significance (Two-Tailed)	Mean Difference
1. Considering everything, we actually have no alternatives to this relationship	0.290	108	0.773	0.09
2. We would not buy from another supplier at the expense of this current supplier	−0.467	110	0.642	−0.12
3. It would be very difficult for us to find a replacement for this supplier	1.133	109	0.260	0.31

The second aspect of the atmosphere and social interaction of the relationship to be compared involves interdependency and mobility. The first question about the existence of alternatives for the customer in the relationship with the supplier indicates high resemblance in opinions between the Iranian firms and the firms in the IMP2-study. This is also the case for the other two questions relating to whether the customer would buy from other suppliers at the expense of the current one, and would have difficulty in finding a replacement for the current supplier. Like the result concerning social interdependency and mutuality, the relationships between Iranian firms and their foreign suppliers are very similar to the relationships between the customers and suppliers in the IMP2-study when it concerns interdependency and mobility in the relationship.

3. Trust

In this study, more than 30 questions in the survey specifically examined the factor of trust and its multidimensionality. In terms of trust, questions were connected to the fields of functional and personal trust. In relation to personal trust, the questions covered such areas as cooperation and personal relationship. In terms of functionality, questions were related to aspects such as the exchange of technical information.

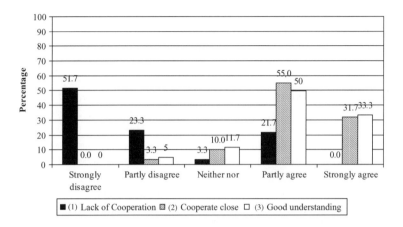

Figure 5.4: Cooperation with foreign firm.

The first four questions considered cooperation in general. The emphasis was not on relationship at an individual level, but rather was concerned with the perception of cooperation in the context of the organization. The first three statements were: (1) a lack of cooperation has caused problems in the relationship; (2) we cooperate closely with this supplier; and (3) the supplier has a good understanding of our problems as a customer.

The scores in Figure 5.4 indicate that Iranian firms have a very positive perception of cooperation with their foreign partners. For the first question, lack of cooperation causing problems, three out of four chose the alternatives "strongly disagree" and "very strongly disagree." The value for the first alternative, "strongly disagree," accounted for more than half of the answers. None of the respondents strongly agreed with the statement, and only 21.7% partly agreed. Thus, one in five of the firms realizes that lack of cooperation is a source of relationship problems. For this group, the cooperation problem will naturally elevate mistrust in the foreign firms. In comparing this with the values in the following two questions, this was the highest score given to mistrust.

When examining closeness in cooperation and good understanding in the partnership, the accumulated value for the equivalent alternatives of partial and strong disagreement in statement (2) was 3%, and in statement (3) was 5%. That is to say, the degree of mistrust for the two statements (1) and (2) was similar, and stood at a very low level. The reason for the degree of mistrust being higher in the first question is difficult to understand. One explanation could be that the last two statements examined the cooperation and understanding of the foreign sellers but not the content of the relationship. The first statement examined the achievement of cooperation in terms of whether there had been moments of mistrust. The statement was more specific than (2) and (3) (see Figure 5.4), which aimed to measure the cooperation more concretely.

Statement (2), which examined the closeness in cooperation, had a score of about 88% for the combined alternatives "partly agree" and "strongly agree." The alternatives "strongly disagree" and "partly disagree" had a total of only 3%. Similar values can be found for statement (3), which measured the understanding of the foreign partner. For the alternatives of strongly and partly agree, 83.3% of the Iranian firms believed that the foreign firms understood the local firms' problems. This means that a very large number of Iranian firms experienced a trustful relationship, as they stated that their foreign partners cooperated closely and had an understanding of their problems. However, the number of uncertain firms in relation to both statements (2) and (3) was quite large (more than 10%). The score for the uncertain group was lower in the first question, about 3%. The difference could be because of the nature of the statements. As mentioned earlier, the first statement was more specific than statements (2) and (3) below.

These three questions examined the perception of the Iranian firms regarding cooperation with their foreign partners. Questions measured general aspects in the relationship. Results from these three questions show that Iranian firms generally trust their foreign partners. They believe that their foreign partners understand the Iranian firms and act to satisfy them.

The earlier questions on the business relationship, which measured specific issues such as technological cooperation, have provided different results. They show a much lower percentage for the willingness of partners to cooperate. In contrast with the results from the above questions, it can be concluded that Iranian firms seem to have a strong belief in their partners' willingness to cooperate.

A contradictory result was obtained from the questions designed to measure the functional aspects of the relationship. In the following question, the focus was on measuring two specific areas in the content of trust. One was the short-term profit preference in cooperation, and the other was activity satisfaction. The statement put to respondents was: "The supplier puts cooperation with us before his short-term profit." The statement was a response to a crucial area in trust building, namely the actors' mutual benefit in a long-term relationship. Mutuality requires an equal gain and understanding of each other's needs and ability. Figure 5.5 illustrates how the foreign suppliers classified cooperation and satisfaction before short-term profit. There were five choices on a scale of cooperation to short-term profit. The question narrowly examined the perception of the Iranian firms concerning foreign firms' aim in cooperation. The values for the alternatives "strongly disagree" and "partly agree" were 5.0% and 11.7%, respectively, although, very few Iranian firms,

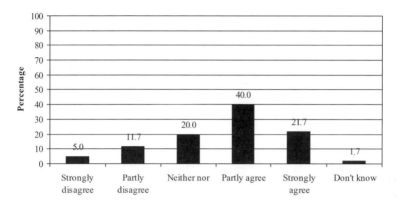

Figure 5.5: Cooperation and short-term profit orientation.

16.7%, saw the foreign firms' behavior as opportunistic. Rather, the majority of the Iranian firms, 61.7%, believed that foreign firms preferred to cooperate. These measures show that a large group of the Iranian firms "partly agree" (40.0%), and the rest (21.7%) "strongly agree" that the foreign firms prefer cooperation over short-term profit. The belief may be grounded in the presumption that these foreign firms aim to stay in the relationship. However, those firms that selected the alternative "strongly agree" were confident of a long-term relationship. The aim of a long-term relationship was verified by the 21.7% who answered in the alternative "strongly agree" category. This value was not quite as high when only one of the five firms interviewed had a strong belief that foreign firms prefer mutuality in the cooperation.

This result may depend on the uncertainty of the Iranian firms about the strategic purpose of the foreign firms in Iran. The interesting result that confirmed this conclusion was the percentage of Iranian firms that were uncertain about the preference of the foreign partners. The number of firms in this group was quite high 20.0%. A drastic analysis of the answer could be that the uncertainty was a signal for the profit orientation of the foreign suppliers, meaning that a group of Iranian firms declared their uncertainty as they had not observed any evidence showing the willingness of the foreign firms to cooperate. However, the majority of the Iranian firms, to some degree, still trusted their foreign suppliers.

One of the most interesting aspects of social interaction relates to the factor of trust. In the first set of questions, the focus is on cooperation in the relationship. Three of the four questions point towards high similarities in the relationships between the Iranian customers and their suppliers and the customers in the IMP2-study and their suppliers (see Table 5.3). The possible lack of cooperation causing

Table 5.3: Trust.

Question	*t*-Value	df	Significance (Two-Tailed)	Mean Difference
1. Lack of cooperation has caused problems in our relationship	−1.716	99	0.089	−0.46
2. We cooperate closely with this supplier	1.789	98	0.077	0.35
3. The supplier has a good understanding of our problems as a customer	2.071	98	0.041	0.39
4. The supplier puts cooperation with us before their short-term profit	0.052	96	0.958	0.01

problems, the closeness of cooperation, and whether the suppliers put cooperation before short-term profit are perceived similarly by the Iranian customers and the customers in IMP2. One difference in opinions can be observed when it comes to the supplier having a good understanding of the customer's problem. Here, the Iranian customers have a more positive attitude than the customers in the IMP2-study.

3.1. Personal Relationship — Individual Level

Arrow (1974) explained that trust is an important lubricant of a social system that saves time and trouble. In this social system, individuals representing different organizations interact and bring their own perceptions about the promises made. These link the individuals, even though they may have other perceptions about the interacting organizations. Some researchers go further and only predict trust at an individual level. Their effort is to explain the success of economic transaction by including trust at this level. In one case, Dore (1983) and Sabel & Zeitlin (1985), for example, present goodwill and sentiments of friendship among individuals as the basis for success in recurring economic exchange. According to this explanation, trust is engendered by the social norms that insist that business relations are personal relations. Trust at an individual level is not the same as general trust. The latter is an accumulation of trusts at different levels.

The survey included more than 10 questions aimed at evaluating trust at an individual level. But in this study, only a few questions that are representative and illustrate the general trend in the answers are included. These questions measure different aspects of trust at an individual level. Some examine personal contacts, and others are related to cultural differences.

The first two questions are related to the personal interactions between the two partners. The general outcome from the answers to these two questions is that the partners have a very good personal relationship, and this did not emerge because of the efforts made by the Iranian managers. The aim in the first question was to understand the level of social interaction; in the next, it was to gain an understanding of the partners' commitment in the relationship. In response to the statement "We have excellent personal relationships on a social level with people in the supplier's company," the total value given for the categories "strongly disagree" and "partly disagree" was 25.0%, with 16.7% being uncertain (see Figure 5.6). But the majority of the Iranian managers, just below 60%, stated that they have an excellent personal relationship with the supplier's personnel. In this group, 46.7% selected the alternative "partly agree," and 11.7% "strongly agree." Despite the fact that the percentage for "strongly agree" was not more than 11.7%, this should not be seen as a low value because the description "excellent relationship" (one of the choices) is a strong expression. The total value given to all the "agree" alternatives was 58.4%, compared with 25% choosing "disagree" alternatives. This indicates that the majority of the Iranian firms believe that they have a good personal relationship with the foreign suppliers' personnel. A dilemma in the answers is

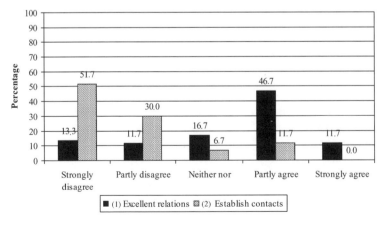

Figure 5.6: Personal relationship.

the score of 16.7% for the alternative of uncertainty. This could be the result of using the term "excellent." Perhaps if the question had been phrased using the word "good," rather than "excellent," the uncertain group might have selected the alternatives "partly agree" or "strongly agree."

Given such a result, the next question measured the commitment of the partners in social relationships. This question had two functions. The first was to provide information about the partners' investment in the social relationship. The second was to try to confirm the conclusion of a high level of mutuality in the personal relationship presented in the first question. The presumption was that a strong social relationship at the individual level indicates mutuality and that the partners are actively involved in establishing and maintaining the relationship.

In this question, 11.7% of the Iranian managers partly agreed with the postulation that they were more active in establishing relationships; none of them strongly agreed. Thus, very few Iranians made a bilateral investment in social interaction. As shown in Figure 5.6, the majority of the Iranian managers supported mutual investment in the social interaction. More than 80% of the Iranian managers disagreed with the postulation that they had initiated the social interactions. That value includes the 51.7% who strongly disagreed and the 30% who partly agreed. These results also confirm the values in the first question.

In the first question, the majority of the Iranian managers (58.4%) stated that the relationship was excellent. These two questions showed that personal relationships between Iranian and foreign managers are based on understanding. One clear conclusion is that mutuality and trust exist among these managers, but this conclusion can only be reached by comparing the results from the two questions (see Figure 5.6).

Table 5.4: Personal relationship – individual level.

Question	*t*-Value	df	Significance (Two-Tailed)	Mean Difference
1. We have excellent personal relations on a social level with people in the supplier's company	2.659	96	0.009	0.76
2. We usually make an effort to establish personal contacts with people in the supplier's company	−4.783	98	0.000	−1.22

Trust is not only related to aspects of cooperation. The personal relationship on an individual level is also decisive in the forming of trustful relationships between customers and suppliers. When comparing the IR-study with the IMP2-study in this area (see Table 5.4), some interesting differences between the groups are revealed. First, the Iranian customers have a significantly more positive view of the personal relations on a social level with the people in the suppliers companies, indicating trustful relationship. Second, the Iranian customers have a much less positive attitude toward making personal contacts with people in the supplier companies. These results confirm the conclusions drawn in the earlier discussion on this topic.

3.2. Formal and Informal Social Relationship

One aspect of personal interaction is cultural differences. There are a number of studies in international marketing which put the emphasis on how the cultural aspect influences the interaction (Hofstede 1991; Peters & Waterman 1982; Pettigrew 1979). While researchers such as Levitt (1983), Nordström (1990), and Porter (1986) point to the world of business as being made up of homogeneous cultural interactions, others stress heterogeneity and differences in cultural behavior. In this view, cultural differences present as a major factor causing friction, conflict, and a communication gap. Hofstede's (1983) study stressed cultural differences as a source of individual conflicts. The author, among several other researchers, stressed that the differences in deeply rooted values of managers from countries like Iran and those from developed countries are a source of problems in interaction. In the following questions, the purpose was to measure such concerns.

The four statements listed below were directed at examining the social impacts. The first two measured the cultural influence in terms of friendship and communication problems. These were concerned with the social interaction at an individual level (see Figure 5.7). The next two statements (3) examined the general impact of cultural differences and (4) considered the impact of cultural differences on business interaction (see Figure 5.8).

Statement (1): "It is difficult to make friends with the sellers and technicians."
Statement (2): "Language differences create problems in discussions with this supplier."
Statement (3): "Cultural differences have caused crises in the relationship."
Statement (4): "When we visit the supplier, we interact on a formal level."

In response to (1), the Iranian managers disagreed with the postulation. Forty-five percent of the managers selected the alternative "strongly disagree,"

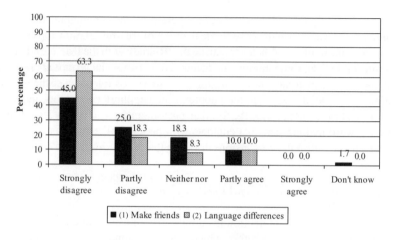

Figure 5.7: Cultural differences.

and 25.0% partly disagreed. This means that 65% of the Iranian managers observed no problem in social interaction with foreign buyers. Only 10.0% of the Iranian managers partly agreed, and none strongly agreed with the statement. The remaining 18.3% of the Iranian managers were uncertain. This is a high score, and it is difficult to explain why such a large number of the managers selected this alternative. However, a comparison of these results with the results from (b) laid the groundwork for the conclusion that there

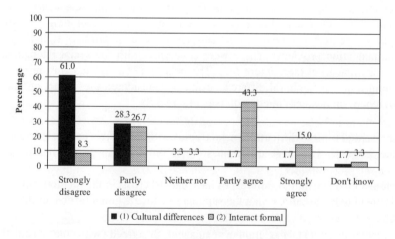

Figure 5.8: Formal and informal interaction.

are strong ties in the personal relationships between the Iranian and foreign firms.

Statement (2) measured another aspect of cultural differences, namely, communication. The statement was about language differences as a source of problems. As illustrated in Figure 5.7, 63.3% strongly disagreed 18.3% partly disagreed, and only 10.0% partly agreed, although about 81.6% of the Iranian managers stated that language was not a problem for their social interaction. Language was seen by very few of the managers as a hindrance in their social interaction. Statements (1) and (2) were complementary. Both signified a low level of social distance and strong social bonds. The results are interesting, as they illustrate the fact that social interaction contains different types of bonds. As illustrated in this section, some bonds are weak, and others are strong. In categorizing these bonds, one can observe that some of the bonds with a more sociofunctional nature are weak, and those that are related to purely cultural aspects are stronger. Another conclusion considers the cultural differences that have engendered a very low level of impact. This result is completely contrary to the findings in earlier research (Hofstede 1991). Previous results (see Figure 5.5) show a lack of cooperation for a group of the firms.

In adding knowledge about the social interaction at an individual level, two more statements were introduced. Statement (3) considered the cultural impacts, and (4) measured the formality in the relationship. The results for (3) verified the measures presented in (1) and (2) above, namely that mutuality and trust are not limited by cultural differences. Ninety percent of the Iranian managers did not observe the cultural differences as a source of problems. Only 3.3% of the managers realized that this factor affected their relationships. Among these managers, only 1.7% saw cultural differences as a source of crises. The aim of statement (3) was to understand the Iranian managers' general view about social interaction and its influence. As (1) and (3) measured the specific aspects in the relationships, this statement referred to the culture as a whole. The aim was also to detect if there was a significant difference between general and specific findings.

Statement (4) reflects the formality in the relationship. The question is interesting as it measures the personal relationship aside from the informal interaction, and can reveal facts about differences between the social-business and informal interactions. The answers were surprising. Almost 60% selected the alternatives "partly agree" and "strongly agree" with the postulation of formalities in the relationships (43.3% partly agreed, and 15.0% strongly agreed). However, 8.3% reported that they strongly disagreed, and 26.7% partly disagreed. The results indicate that the majority of Iranian managers clearly differentiate friendship from formal interaction. As the results from (1), (2), and (3) showed, there is no doubt about a strong informal relationship. It seems that the Iranian firms, because of uncertainty about unforeseen changes, have to rely on formal contracts. This could be because of the Iranian firms' connections to other actors that have a major influence on the focal relationship. The interaction with the foreign suppliers is based on trust of an informal nature, with Iranian managers showing little uncertainty, as discussed above, about the social behavior of the foreign suppliers.

The responses revealed that Iranian managers divide the social relationships into two bonds, one purely social and the other involving social-business interactions. When it is purely social, as depicted in the earlier questions, the relationship is strong. But when the interaction is functional (i.e. it has a social-business context), the relationship is more formal.

In further examining the formality of the business interaction, two questions concerning the arrangement of agreements between Iranian firms and their foreign partners must be considered. The first question, as exhibited in Figure 5.9, is about formalization of the agreements.

The question is interesting from two perspectives. One is the comparison of the values from the two studies. As illustrated in Figure 5.9, as many as 95% selected the alternatives "a great deal" and "entirely." For the same question, IMP2 showed the same trend but with some differences. In the IMP2, the percentage for the first two alternatives "very little" and "to some extent" was 21.4%, compared with only 5.0% in the Iranian study. Furthermore, the values for the alternatives "a great deal" and "entirely" were clearly lower in the IMP2.

The answers above become more interesting if they are linked with the next question, which aimed to measure a specific area in the personal interaction. The question was: "What effects do the written agreements have on the actual dealings between you and your two companies?" The Iranian firms, as illustrated

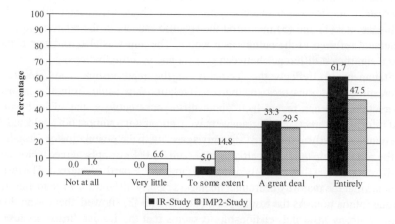

Figure 5.9: Formalization of the agreements.

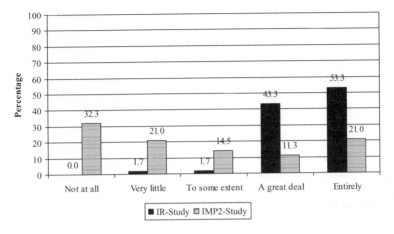

Figure 5.10: Impact of the written agreements.

in Figure 5.10, saw the written agreements as the main factor in the relationships. A massive 96.6% confirmed a high reliance on the written contract. For the same alternatives, the result for the IMP2 was only 32.3%. One can therefore suggest that the formal social relationship did not have as decisive a role as it did in the Iranian case (in the Iranian case, the value was 95%). This finding confirms the results obtained for the reliance on the written contract, with an accumulated value of 53.2% for the same alternatives. This means that, in reality, there is a much lower rate of formalization of the contract in industrialized countries than in countries like Iran.

In this survey, the Iranian firms recognized the written agreement and its impact as a means to challenge uncertainty in the relationships. Such an attitude reveals another fact in the relationship. This is connected to the issue of written contracts. Generally, a written contract is a management tool used to secure relationships under uncertain conditions. In cases where the firms have elaborated a strong relationship, the role of formal agreements becomes insignificant. Under such conditions, where the partners have a long-term relationship, the rules of the game are clearer for both. There is less of a need for written details in the agreements, although in the Iranian case, despite a strong informal social relationship (friendship), the relationship contains a weak social-business bond. This is not because of uncertainty in the social bonds but rather has emerged because of the impacts from other parts and levels of the network. The uncertainty in the relationships with business actors transfers to, and weakens, the social-business relationship.

Table 5.5: Formal and informal social relationship.

Question	*t*-Value	df	Significance (Two-Tailed)	Mean Difference
1. It is difficult to make friends with sellers and technicians in this firm	−3.779	93	0.000	−0.96
2. Language differences create problems in discussions with this supplier	−2.915	93	0.004	−0.75
3. Cultural differences have caused crises in the relationship	−2.841	91	0.006	−0.69
4. When we visit the supplier, we interact on a formal level	2.303	95	0.023	0.64
5. To what extent are the arrangements with the supplier formalized in written agreement?	2.770	119	0.007	0.42
6. What effect do these written agreements have on the actual dealings between your two companies?	8.415	120	0.000	1.81

The last aspect of social interaction relating to trust concerns the formality and informality of the social relationship. In all, six questions are used to investigate this area. When comparing the Iranian firms with the firms in IMP2 (see Table 5.5), all six questions disclose significant differences leaving no room for similarities between the relationships of the two groups. First, the Iranian firms find it clearly less difficult to make friends with sellers and technicians in the supplying firm than the customers in the IMP2-study. This is also the case with language difficulties and cultural differences, where the Iranian customers see these as much less of a problem than the customers in the IMP2-study. However, the Iranian customers give much more to attention to interacting on a formal level with the supplier, both on a social level and when it comes to writing and using formal agreements with the supplier, compared to the customers in the IMP2-study.

4. Summary

This chapter examined the strength of the social bonds. The results from the earlier chapters provide some answers about the degree of dependency and strength in the business exchange relationships. The chapter was concerned with the "soft" part of the interaction between the Iranian customers and foreign suppliers. The crucial question was how the social atmosphere influenced the business exchange. The social bonds reflect the following dimensions: (1) social interdependency/power and mutuality; (2) potential mobility; (3) trust and a personal relationship; and finally, (4) social-business interactions. The concepts presented in the introduction are used to operationalize the answers and assist in the analysis and review of the values obtained. Factors such as mutuality, power/interdependency, mobility, and trust have been followed in the presentation of the answers. When drawing conclusions, the values in each question have been connected to the values in other questions to gain support or sanction.

The first two questions reflect the factors of dependency and mutuality. Surprisingly, about 35% of the Iranian firms declared that they have feelings of dependency on the foreign suppliers. However, more than 56% of the Iranian customers declared that they are not dependent on foreign suppliers, and the values showed a higher dependency of foreign firms on Iranian firms. In connection with the mutuality in the dependency and in the rate of input for the adaptations, two other questions were raised. In contrast to the above results, the answers showed that the majority had a feeling of equilibrium and that they reported mutuality in the input for the adaptations. More measures are needed to confirm the above results.

In further examining the issue of interdependency, several other questions were raised to evaluate the mobility of the partners. The outcomes showed that more than 60% had a high degree of potential mobility because they did not observe their foreign partners as a partner with whom they could develop, for example, new technologies. Only 22% were unwilling to replace their partners with another. Strangely, more than 55% of the Iranian firms believed that their foreign partners were very satisfied and would continue to be in the future. However, the values in these questions disclose a high degree of potential mobility. This result could be because, even with a high degree of mutuality, the strength of the bonds for this group was insufficient to keep them together for a long period.

Considering the factor of trust, the questions measured the cooperation between the partners. More than 75% explained that the partnerships did not have any cooperation problem. When further examining trust, the question of "closeness" showed a very low level of mistrust among the managers. Similar values were obtained when measuring the level of understanding. More than 83% declared that they did not have any problem in understanding each other, despite the fact that they came from completely different societies. One evident conclusion was that the questions measuring the informal relationships resulted in higher values than those that examined the formal business interactions.

The factor of trust was also measured in relation to specific areas such as the preference for cooperation over short-term profit. Iranian firms perceived that more than 67% of the foreign suppliers preferred cooperation to a relationship built on short-term profit. This value is rather high. Thus, the value for the opportunistic behavior of the foreign suppliers is ranked very low (16%). However, the percentage of the Iranian firms who were completely sure that the aim of the foreign suppliers was a long-term relationship was also not that high, at only 21.7%.

While the above questions mainly considered the study of trust at an organizational level, the study also examined trust at the individual level. The majority of the Iranian firms, 60%, reported a very good personal relationship. Strangely, and in contrast to the studies on cultural behavior, the Iranian managers perceived that the foreign people mainly initiated social interaction. A deeper study of trust was conducted with questions about the formal and informal relationships. An interesting conclusion was reached from one question examining the problems related to the cultural differences. It was surprising to realize that the cultural and language differences have had a very low impact on the relationships. More than 93% of the managers, for example, did not see cultural differences as a problem in the interaction.

The above five questions mainly reflected the informal relationships. One interesting question was directed at whether there was any difference between these measures and formal interactions. One question was about formality in the agreements, and another reflected the impact of the written contract. Contrary to what was expected, the Iranian firms relied on formal agreements to a considerable extent. The scores given to formality in the business relationships were even higher than in the IMP2 study. Similar results were obtained for the question on the written contract. It seems that the Iranian firms, because of their uncertainty about their environment, prefer to resort to formal business exchange.

Chapter 6

Embeddedness

In the earlier chapters, the aim was to study the focal dyadic business relationship. The facts included information about the product and technology, adaptation, and social bonds. Clearly, this was a step towards understanding the strength and weakness of the focal relationships. It was necessary to limit the analysis to a study of the business-to-business relationships, but that is insufficient for a comprehensive understanding of the firms' behavior. Inasmuch as these firms have exchanges with other actors, this chapter attempts to study the embeddedness of the firms. The following questions are addressed: What is the nature of the Iranian firms' relationships with their embedded business and non-business actors in Iran? How do the embedded relationships affect the focal relationship between the Iranian and foreign firms, and how are these managed?

As discussed in Chapter 2, embeddedness pertains to both business and non-business actors. This chapter, after the presentation of the Iranian managers' general views, comprises two sections. The first section considers the business connection, and the second is devoted to the connections with non-business actors. The attempt in the first section is to understand the extent to which the focal relationship is interrelated with the local and foreign firms and organizations. In the second section, negative/positive connections and the strength of the connections are discussed in the context of political embeddedness (for government decisions over trade policy). The negative/positive nature of the bonds is indicated by the coercive or supportive actions of the government and the bureaucratic organization covering trade policy decisions. The chapter begins with the views on the interactions and activities between political and business actors, and finishes with a discussion on the management behavior of the Iranian firms.

More than 60 questions in the survey were concerned with business and political embeddedness, and interviewees gave complete answers to 53 of them. A selection of representative questions is presented in this chapter.

1. Some Conceptual Details

The complexity of the interface between business and non-business actors is treated differently in different marketing models, and the interaction problems between these two groups of actors are usually treated ambiguously. Traditional marketing research studies non-business actors as components of the environment and sees their impact as homogenous. In these analytical models, adaptation is proposed to deal with the uncertainty which derives from the coercive actions of non-business actors (Kotler 1999). In economic theories, the firms are viewed, primarily, as production units operating in a faceless market environment. Similarly, the literature based on organization theory does not have a pertinent view of the market environment.

However, studies that are more recent have taken two directions. One specifies the dyadic view for studying the interaction between business and non-business actors. Another extends that view further and insists on the application of network theory. These two views also introduce the concept of influence, instead of adaptation, on the marketing behavior of firms.

According to the network view, the most important implication of the existence of relationships is that firms cannot be regarded as independent units that choose their counterpart at any time but rather as interlocked units constituting a complex structure (Håkansson & Johanson 1987). One suggestion that has been made is to employ a dyadic view for the analysis of political and business actors (Boddewyn 1988; Yarbough & Yarbough 1987), but this approach still creates an analytical boundary as it delimits other relationships. In further developing the dyadic view, other studies have presented views on network theory for a more comprehensive understanding of connections between actors of different origins (Hadjikhani 1996; Hadjikhani & Sharma 1999; Ring 1990). These theories have been tested in studies carried out in industrialized markets, but the implication of such views needs to be tested in countries with a lower degree of industrialization.

This study expands the territorial boundary of explanation and integrates the non-business actors. The view implies that a network approach can preferably be used to analyze a structure built on interaction between business and non-business actors. Against this background, it can be postulated that any single actor is embedded in two different types of interactions. With reference to the discussion on various types of exchange (Bagozzi 1975), there are no theoretical obstacles preventing the use of this wider application of business relationships. Particular to this study, two types of actors in the business network, business and non-business, are distinguished. Political actors control financial and non-financial resources and exercise power to make laws and regulate business activities (Hadjikhani & Sharma 1999). Business actors, however, are involved in economic activities.

Nature of Actor I

	Business	Political
Business	1	2
Political	3	4

Nature of Actor II

Figure 6.1: Political and business interactions.

The political actors act for political ideas and values, and the business actors function on the economic outcomes. Following that explanation, the combination of types of actors leads to a matrix (see Figure 6.1) with four combinations. In the first cell, the situation for both parties is grounded on business rules, and their fundamental interest in the long-term is growth and profit. The power exchange is through business resources, and conflicts are resolved on business grounds. At the other extreme, combination four involves two political actors with non-business grounds for legitimacy. Political mechanisms govern the exchange, and the actors act to gain political legitimacy. These are the two least complicated situations. Situations two and three are more complicated as the interacting parties functionally rely on different principles. One acts on the basis of political values and the other on business gains. Management of the interaction thus becomes complicated.

Political embeddedness results in a business network structure, which links actors in all of these four conditions. A business actor, besides connecting with a number of business actors in business interactions, also has to deal with actors of a political nature. Critical to these latter interactions is the matter of the dependence of business actors on the political actors. The influential activities of business actors are introduced as a management tool to affect that interdependency (Boddewyn 1988; Lenway & Murtha 1994). Management activities are acts to strengthen the position towards non-business actors and to bring mutuality. In cases where political power and coercive actions are used, the position of business actors is weak. The types and contents of political and business action can be combined into a matrix (see Figure 6.2) with four situations.

A high degree of coercive action, for example, in situations one and two, leads to very weak relationships (Hadjikhani & Sharma 1999). A contrary situation can be seen in cell 3, where the political actions are specific and supportive. In conditions two and four, the contents of the political actions are general (i.e. they reflect on

Contents

	Specific	General
Coercive	1	2
Supportive	3	4

Types

Figure 6.2: Political and business actions.

several firms or industries). An aspect in this construction is the dynamism of the political action. An action that is coercive at one time may become supportive at another time. A business actor's strategy is to gain a position in cell three as it is accommodated with mutuality and a specific strong relationship. The later business studies elevate a variety of views on influential activities of business firms designed to overcome changes and bring strength to the relationships.

Embeddedness implies a principle of transfer of these supportive/coercive actions to other business relationships. Thus, business relationships are affected by the political exchange relationships between political and business actors. The degree of impact depends on the strength of the positive or negative political exchange. A highly negative connection with political actors naturally increases uncertainty in the focal relationship. Stability in political rules, for example, is proclaimed by business actors as an exigency to build a strong and positive business relationship. No matter which political society it concerns, stability is accommodated with trust that transfers from the exchange with political actors to the focal business relationships.

2. Embeddedness

In the empirical study, one important aspect in understanding connections was to measure embeddedness in general. The first three questions examined the general opinion of the managers on how the political and business connections affect the focal relationship. Respondents were asked: "In your relationship with this supplier, give a value to the role of the following actors." In this group, one of the questions was related to the connections of the political actors. The next two questions referred to the connections of the business actors. Question 1 examined the managers' opinions on "foreign trade" and referred to its impact on the focal

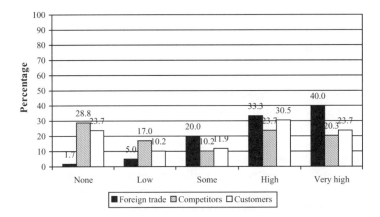

Figure 6.3: General opinions on the importance connections.

relationship. The second question related to "your competitors," and the third to "your customers." Figure 6.3 illustrates the values given to these questions.

Based on these three questions, the managers appeared to be knowledgeable about the environment in which they operated. This conclusion is drawn from the fact that none of the managers selected the alternative "don't know" in response to these questions. All the managers selected one of the alternatives ranging from "no importance" to "very high importance." None of the firms mentioned having difficulty in evaluating the actors and their actions.

As depicted in Figure 6.3, very few (about 5.7%) of the respondents saw the impact of foreign trade as having no or minor importance. Only one firm (representing 1.7% of the total) selected the alternative "no importance." For the question relating to competitors, 45.8% selected no or minor importance, and 33.9% selected these categories in relation to customers. These answers indicate that the managers assigned a lower importance to the market actors (i.e. customers and competitors).

A closer observation of the answers in the last three alternatives strengthens the arguments above. In the question of foreign trade, the answers in the last three alternatives "very high importance," "high importance," and "some importance" are interesting. They disclose two important aspects: one is the distinction of the degree of importance assigned to each bond, namely with foreign trade, competitors, and customers; and the other applies to the role of the political actors in the business market.

In contrast to the question concerning "your competitor," the scores in the questions on the importance of "foreign trade" and "your customers" are much higher.

The comparison of the values in the first two and the last two alternatives (each question taken separately) is interesting. It seems that the managers assigned a very high score to the importance of the trade policy (73.3%) and to customers (54.2%). The value is slightly lower in the question about competitors (44%). The comparison between the first and last alternatives in the question concerning competitors (45.8% for the first two alternatives and 44% for the last two alternatives) shows that the managers did not give a high value to the importance of the competitive market. By using network theory, one may speculate that the competitors are not important because of a high interdependency between the focal actors. In this study, such speculation can easily be rejected by reference to the earlier chapters on relationships. The results in the earlier chapters contain enough information manifesting a weak relationship between the Iranians and their foreign partners. However, in the question concerning the customers, the first two alternatives had a cumulative value of 33.9%, and the last two alternatives 54.4%. This simply implies that the managers had a higher dependency on their customers than on their competitors, although the negative connection to the competitors was weak.

The answers concerning the impact of the political actors (via foreign trade) are much more interesting. As mentioned above, the cumulative value of the first two alternatives "no importance" and "low importance" in the question on trade policy was only 6.7%. However, the cumulative value of the last three alternatives ("some importance," "high importance," and "very high importance") was 93.3%, meaning that the managers see the actions of political actors as a very important element in their market activities. Political actors play a crucial role in the Iranian market, and this was borne out by the fact that only 1.7% of the managers chose the alternative "no importance."

The comparison shows which actor in the market was considered to have the highest degree of importance for the focal relationship. While the cumulative value for the last three alternatives in the question concerning the political actors was 93.3%, the values for the similar alternatives in the next two questions were 54.2% (for the competitors) and 66.1% (for the customers). The differences between the values above have such a degree of significance that it is not difficult to draw the conclusion as to which connected actor has the strongest influence on the focal relationship. The survey contained several other questions that could confirm the strong influence of the political connection. Two of these questions are presented here. The first aimed at measuring the influence that each connected actor has on the Iranian firms, and the second at allocating a value to the selected actor. The first question was: "Which group most influences the focal relationship?" As illustrated in Figure 6.4, the actors can be classified into two groups: business and non-business actors. When ranking these two groups, 81% of the Iranian firms viewed the political actor as the one that most influenced their business with the

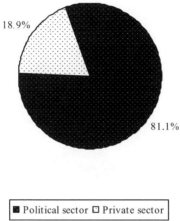

18.9%

81.1%

| ■ Political sector □ Private sector |

Figure 6.4: Connection with business and non-business actors.

foreign partners. This indicates that the Iranian managers are more dependent on the connected political actors than on the connected business actors. In another question (not illustrated here), the managers were asked to evaluate and select the alternatives that had the most influence on their business. The question measured the influence of non-business actors on the focal relationship. Here, 80% of the respondents selected the alternatives "very and high" influence, and the rest, 20%, selected the alternative "to some extent." These values confirm the conclusion that the focal relationship is highly influenced by the non-business actors. The values can explain the weakness in the focal relationship.

In further developing the question above, another question arose. Iranian firms were asked to evaluate relationships with business and non-business actors in different sectors. As shown in Figure 6.5, non-business actors also include intermediary actors such as the unions. The score verifies the results introduced in Figure 6.1. The score for government was 39%. This can be compared with the focal relationship (between Iranian firms and foreign suppliers) that had only 18.9%. The value given to competitors was only 2.7%. For the connection with business actors, the difference between customers (5.4%) and competitors (2.7%) can clearly be seen.

As discussed earlier, it seems that the firms consider the impact of local customers to be double that of competitors. The comparison of the actors in the intermediary group with business actors shows that even these groups have a higher influence on the focal relationships than the business actors do. The cumulative

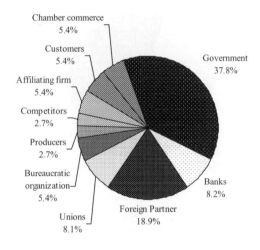

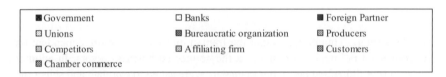

Figure 6.5: Evaluation of focal and connected relationships.

value for an intermediary group, such as a branch organization, was higher than the scores for customers or competitors. The score for connected intermediaries (chamber of commerce and unions combined) was 13.5%, which was more than for competitors (at 2.7%) or customers (at 5.4%).

The review of the questions above provides a general picture about the influence of the connected actors on the Iranian firms. The explanation reveals the high degree of influence of the political actors. It also provides general and even specific information about the role of the different political and business actors in the sphere of the connection. The purpose of the following sections is to understand the strength of these connections in relation to each separate type of connection. The concentration, however, is mainly on the connection with non-business actors.

3. Business Connection

In this respect, the survey included several questions. Only a few have been selected, as they contribute enough facts to draw some essential conclusions.

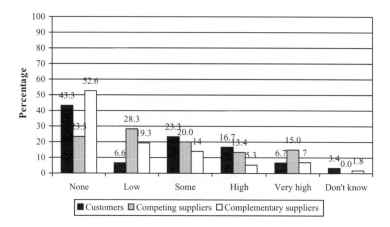

Figure 6.6: Business connection.

Two of the questions studied the connections to other suppliers, and to suppliers competing with the foreign firms. The topic question was: "To what extent is your business with this specific supplier affected by your own relationships with some of the following?" In Figure 6.6, the questions examine the impact of three business connections: (1) the Iranian firm's customers; (2) competitors to the foreign firms; and (3) complementary products to the foreign suppliers' products.

In the first question (1), which referred to the firm's own customers, about 50% selected the alternatives "none" and "low." The same alternatives in questions (2) and (3) scored 51.6 and 71.9%, respectively. It is interesting to compare these scores with the scores in the last two alternatives ("very high" and "high"). Here, the cumulative scores were 23.4 and 28.4%, and in question (3) 12.3%. In question (3), more than 52% selected the alternative "none." Seven percent selected "very high" in response to this question. This can be confirmed by the values for question (1) above. In that question, the alternative "very high" was selected by 6.7% of the respondents and the alternative "none" by 43.3%. The fundamental difference between questions (1) and (3) lies in the answer to the alternative "to some extent," which, on question (1), was 23.3%. This was a high score and made the scores for the other alternatives low. On question (3) the score was 14%, indicating that the suppliers of complementary products have a very low influence on the focal exchange relationship. This means that, similar to the focal relationship that contains simple product exchange, the complementary products are also of a simple nature. This character of the exchanged products affects the interdependencies between the focal and the connected actors. As the values for the alternatives "very high" and "high" are low, there is a low interdependency between the focal and connected complementary suppliers.

The picture is slightly different in question (2), which measures the extent of interaction with the competitors. In this question, the cumulative values for the first two alternatives "not at all" and "low," and the last two alternatives "high" and "very high," were 51.6 and 28.4%, respectively. There is a large difference between these values and the values in the similar alternatives in questions (1) and (3). The answers to question (2) also disclose that there is a weak connection between the Iranian firms and the suppliers' competitors. Some may interpret this result as evidence of a strong focal relationship, but the facts in the earlier chapters interposed a weak focal relationship. The exchanged products between the focal actors, for example, as discussed in Chapter 3, did not have a complex nature. Further, the values in question (2) do not indicate a well-functioning market. If one assumes that a product is not too complex, then the competitive market has to function in a traditional way (i.e. the price mechanism has to regulate the transaction). A high domination of the price competition will naturally lead to a low interdependence among actors. The study, however, produced results that show a weak price competition and a weak focal relationship.

3.1. Business Connection with Financial Actors

The survey also contained questions examining the dependency on the financial actors. One of the questions referred to the extent of the impact of the banks or financial organizations on the focal relationship. As depicted in Figure 6.7,

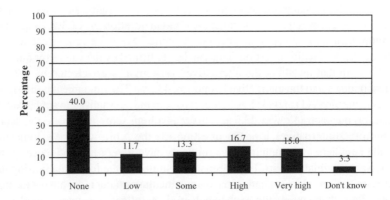

Figure 6.7: Financial connection.

the cumulative values for the alternatives "high" and "very high" were 31.7%. Compared with the values given in the other three questions above for the same alternative, this was the highest response. In question (2) above, which examined the aspect of competition, the alternatives "high" and "very high" had a value of 28.4%, which is slightly lower than the connection to sources contributing financial resources to the business activities. Otherwise, the financial connection compared with questions (1) and (3), in Figure 6.6, seems to contain a higher degree of strength than in question (3), which referred to complementary products.

For example, the value given to the alternatives "high" and "very high" in question (3) was only 12.3%. In question (3), in Figure 6.6, only 23.3% of the managers selected the first alternative "none." This is quite a low value compared with the question above, where it was 40%. A closer review of the answers indicates that the difference may lie in the two alternatives offered: "low" and "to some extent." For these two alternatives, the cumulative value in question (2), Figure 6.6, was 48.3% compared with 25% in the question above. This means that within the limits of "low" to "very high," the majority of the Iranian managers observed the competition to have low impact. One group of Iranian managers considered the financial connection to have an even lower degree of impact. This group, 40%, believed that the financial actors had little or no influence. However, 31.7% of the firms indicated the high influence of these actors. This value is much higher than the values in the similar alternatives in questions (1), (2), and (3) above. Thus, the financial connection was viewed as creating a stronger bond than these connected actors did. But, compared with industrialized countries, the connection is very weak.

Despite some differences between the values in these questions, one general conclusion is that these bonds have a weak connection with the focal relationships. Two connections displayed several major differences compared to the others. One was the connection to the suppliers' competitors, and the other was the connection to the financial actors.

4. Political Connection

Political actors use their legitimate powers to affect the business actors in different ways. In relation to foreign business, political actors direct their major actions towards two areas of policy: tariff and non-tariff trade policies. Business firms, however, create internal political capability and use external organizations, such as industrial branches and unions, to manage the political actors. When studying the political influence, some researchers (see for example, Brunson 1986; Sharma & Jansson 1993) subdivide the political actors into government and bureaucrats.

In accordance with this approach, the influence of the Iranian government and bureaucrats is discussed separately here. In the section on the government, the discussion considers the exchange on tariff and non-tariff policies. After the section on bureaucrats, an attempt is made to explain how Iranian managers have "managed" the political actors.

4.1. Political Actions — Tariff Decisions

One exchange bond considers the area of tariff in foreign trade. The political actors aim to decide the tariffs, and business actors aim to influence the content and adapt it to their conditions in the market. In examining this bond, the survey included more than seven questions. Two of the questions reflected the export and import tariffs. As depicted in Figure 6.8, when managers were asked to assess the influence of the two tariffs, there was a major difference between the two factors. The import tariff was considered to have a much higher impact on Iranian firms. In the first alternative "not at all," the value for the import tariff was 18.3%, and for the export tariff 36.7%. In the alternative "very high," the value for the export tariff was 16.7%, and for the import tariff 46.7%; thus, the degree of impact of the import tariff was twice that of the export tariff. This indicates that the Iranian managers believed that the import tariff has nearly three times more influence on the focal businesses. The degree of influence of the import tariff becomes higher when the two alternatives of "high" and "very high" are added together. The value for the influence of the import tariff then becomes 70%, and the export tariff 20%.

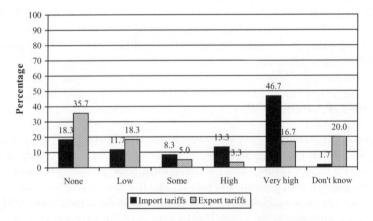

Figure 6.8: Tariff and non-tariff decisions.

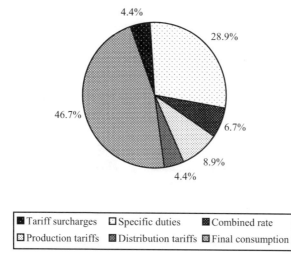

Figure 6.9: Important political actions.

These two questions reveal two facts: (1) the behavior of political actors towards product export constructs a weak negative connection; and (2) the dependency of the firms on the local customers.

The research also studied the influence of different types of tariff policies. In this line, in one of the questions, the Iranian managers were asked to choose one of the six important types of political actions. As Figure 6.9 illustrates, the factor selected by the managers as most important was "consumption of final products," with a value of 46.7%. The second-highest value (about 29%) was given to the factor "specific duties." The other factors were supported by 5–9% of the respondents.

The results in this question confirm the second conclusion above. The score of 46.7% for the factor "consumption of the products" indicates that the Iranian firms have a higher dependency on their final customers. The high dependency on local customers clarifies the low degree of dependency on political actions in relation to the export tariff.

In further studying the different types of tariff decisions, one question concerned government subsidies. As Figure 6.10 shows, more than 46.7% selected the alternatives "high" and "very high." If the value given to the alternative "to some extent" is included with the above two alternatives, 60% rated this value as having an influence, although a large number of firms believe in the influence of government subsidies. Eventually, government subsidies have a positive impact on the business interactions. However, a high degree of subsidies leads to financial

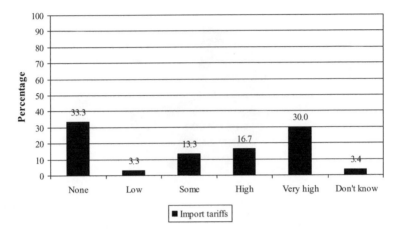

Figure 6.10: Government as financial actor.

dependency. In cases of weak industrial relationships, the removal of subsidies can damage the firms.

The answers to this question are in line with those of financial interdependency presented earlier. In those questions, the strength of the relationships with the financial sources was examined. As discussed, the financial dependency of the firms on external sources was very high. In relation to the subsidies, as shown in Figure 6.10, the core business is positively connected to the political actors. The high scores in the alternatives "very high" and "high" are to some extent related to the nature of the firms. The cross-analysis of the statistics showed that these firms are mostly state-owned and, without subsidies, could not continue in the market. However, for the other firms, the degree of dependency on the political actors was low as the subsidies they received were low. This does not mean that their financial needs are limited. They have a high dependency on private financial sources but receive low support. As a result, the core business is suffering because of a weak business relationship with the Iranian government and with banks.

4.2. Non-Tariff Political Actions

The study contained more than nine questions aimed at understanding the political action by using non-tariff regulations. All these questions examined the connection between the Iranian government and the relationship between the focal Iranian and foreign firms. They considered relationship areas such as product specification,

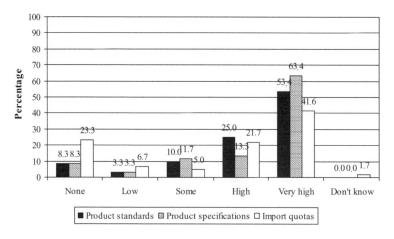

Figure 6.11: Product regulations.

standards, packaging, labeling, and exchange and credit control. In the following section, some of the questions that concern product import and their characteristics will be discussed. The basis for selection is not only to present those questions that confirm the earlier conclusions, but also to gain an understanding about other types of political actions.

The topic question for a group of the questions was: "To what extent is your business with this specific supplier affected by non-tariff actions?" Two of the questions referred to product standards and specifications, and the third to import quotas. In the questions on product standards and specifications, as illustrated in Figure 6.11, the values increase successively in moving from alternative one to alternative five. But it seems that the government decision regarding product specification has a higher influence than product standards. In question (1), on product standards, 53.4% selected the alternative "very high," and in question (2), on product specification, this was selected by 63.4%.

However, the cumulative value for the alternatives "high" and "very high" for questions (1) and (2) are rather similar (78.4% for the first and 76.7% for the second). The values for the other three alternatives are also similar. These questions also included the alternative "do not know." As none of the respondents selected this alternative, it seems that all the firms had a clear opinion about the impact on the product level. In another question, which is not depicted above, the aim was to measure the political impact on packaging, labeling, and marketing. In almost all of the questions, the values for the two categories of "very high" and "high" taken together were more than 53%. When the alternative "to some extent" was included, this reached more than 73.3%. These values are again similar to the values presented for questions (1) and (2) above.

However, the major finding was in relation to the high influence of both product standards and product specification on the focal relationship. Almost 80% of the Iranian firms considered the high regulation of the product standard as coercive actions influencing the focal relationship. In both questions, the managers gave a low value (8.3%) to the alternative of "not at all."

Question (3), in Figure 6.11, measured the import quotas. In this question, the Iranian managers considered political decisions concerning imports to be a hindrance in their business with their foreign partners. More than 41% saw the interference as having a major influence on the focal relationship. The cumulative value for the two alternatives of "high" and "very high" is 63.3%. This value is lower than the value for the same alternatives in the other two questions. Nevertheless, 63.3% represents quite a high score. An alternative that is substantially different from the other two questions is the alternative "not at all." This alternative, which had a score of 8.3% in the other two questions, was selected by 23.3% in answer to question (3). These facts show that the coercive actions of the government have a higher degree of influence concerning product standards and specification than concerning import quotas.

4.3. Non-Tariff and Flow of Financial Resources

As mentioned earlier, one connection that had a high negative impact on the focal relationship was the financial tie. The flow of financial resources considers two substantial areas. One is the connection to actors such as banks; the other is to rules imposed by the political actors to regulate financial transactions. As was shown in the review of business connections, the Iranian firms saw actors such as banks as a source of uncertainty.

The following review considers questions about political actions in relation to foreign exchange. Results from four questions are presented in this section. They evaluate the connection with the political actors with respect to foreign financial transactions that affect the focal partners. The attempt is to understand the content of the relationship and whether the government agencies exercise power over the Iranian firms. The topic question for all four questions was: "To what extent is your business with this specific supplier affected by non-tariff actions?" The actions considered were: (1) exchange control; (2) the exchange rate; (3) prior import deposits; and finally (4) credit restrictions.

Figure 6.12 measures the first two areas of Iranian government intervention in financial transactions between Iranian firms and their foreign partners. One

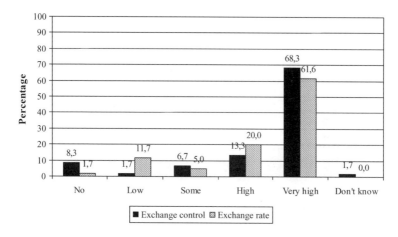

Figure 6.12: Political exchange regulations.

interesting result is the number of managers who selected the alternative "I do not know." In question (1), on exchange control, it was selected by only one firm (1.7%), and in question (2), on the exchange rate, none of the firms selected this alternative. This shows a high level of knowledge among the Iranian managers about the content of the foreign exchange relationship. The results in both questions indicated a high level of coercive action by the government, exposing strong negative connections. These contribute to the conclusion of a high dependency of the Iranian firms on the political rules regulating financial transactions between focal actors.

The values given to the two alternatives of "high" and "very high" are interesting. In question (1), on exchange control, the value for the alternative "very high" is about 8% higher than for that alternative in question (2), on the exchange rate. But the cumulative values on those two alternatives for questions (1) and (2), at 81.6%, are similar. However, the value for the alternative "not at all" in question (1), 8.3%, is much higher than the 2% in question (2). The cumulative values for the first two alternatives in question (1) are 10%, and in question (2) 12.4%. Thus, the cumulative values for the first and last two alternatives for these two questions are similar, with a low score in the first two choices and a very high score in the last two. The scores also show a high dependency of the focal firms on government decisions concerning foreign exchange regulations. The Iranian government uses its hierarchical power to control the flow of financial resources to foreign countries.

The following two questions examine two other financial bonds, namely prior import deposits and credit restrictions, in order to gain a more specific

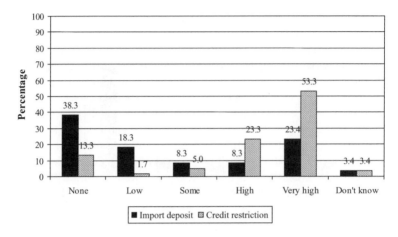

Figure 6.13: Import deposit and credit restriction influence.

understanding of the foreign exchange rules. As Figure 6.13 illustrates, it seems that the political actors wish to control all types of foreign financial transactions. To achieve this, they use different means in various degrees of strength to affect foreign trade.

As depicted in Figure 6.13, the value given to the alternative "not at all" was much higher in these two questions than in the earlier ones. On the question of import deposit, the value was more than 38%. The alternative of "not at all" (in relation to coercive action) is, thus, 22 times less in relation to "import deposit" than it was to the question on the exchange rate, as illustrated in Figure 6.12. The comparison of the scores in the category "not at all" in the question on import deposits (Figure 6.13) and on exchange control (Figure 6.12) shows the value on the deposits to be about five times more than that on exchange control. This also means that in the other alternatives, the values on import deposits are much lower than the values in relation to the credit exchange rate and exchange control.

In the question on credit restriction, the values given to the different alternatives are similar to the values in the questions on the exchange rate and exchange control. These three questions show that firms have similar opinions about the coercive action of the government. The cumulative value for the alternatives "high" and "very high" in the question on credit restriction is more than 76%. For the same alternatives, the value for both of the earlier questions was 82%. In the question on the exchange rate, if the value given to the alternative "to some extent" is also included, the cumulative value is 87%. In all three questions, the majority of the

Iranian managers realized that these coercive decisions had a negative influence on the focal business relationship.

One explanation for the lower values in the question on import deposits is that the firms themselves may have an opportunity to reduce the negative influence. It seems that Iranian firms have a high cash flow and capital that can be used as a deposit. This conclusion is also verified in Figure 6.6. This management tool is employed by the firms to reduce the strength of the negative political connection. While the firms cannot challenge the high degree of coercive actions, they have adapted their behavior, but the effect is to restrict their capital resources. This resource is thus withdrawn from the production process, which, naturally, has increased the production cost. Thus, the coercive actions of the Iranian government have increased the product price in the market.

The use of the power of government authority to control the flow of financial resources to foreign countries may have its foundation in economic conditions in the country, yet it has created a negative connection not only towards the focal business firms, but also against the final customers. The higher this negative connection, the weaker the Iranian firms' relationships with the foreign firms and local customers will be, and the stronger the need for organizational adaptation, surplus capital to deposit, or other management tools.

5. Supportive and Coercive Political Actions

The discussion to this stage considered the recognition and measurement of the content of the various bonds connected to the political actors. Each bond is measured separately, and some comparative discussions have been presented. The following section aims at two specific areas. One is to understand the positive or negative natures of the bonds; the other is to understand how Iranian firms realize the strength of these bonds. For each question, the managers were asked to recognize and evaluate the most and least influential of the political actions on the focal relationship.

Two questions are presented in the following discussion. One considers coercive, and the other supportive, actions. The questions were simple. Iranian managers were to select one among 12 alternatives. As Figure 6.14 illustrates, the least coercive actions recognized by the firms were actions such as export quotas and state trading. The most coercive were the actions related to the financial transactions.

The alternatives in the question concerning the positively connected bonds received values that are almost in direct opposition to those of the negatively connected bonds. Government subsidies were considered the most supportive.

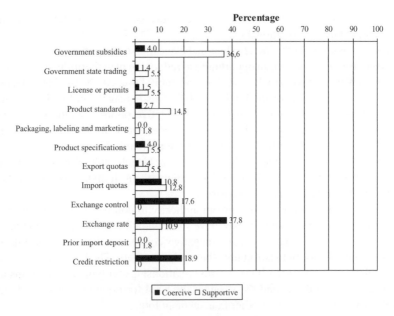

Figure 6.14: Coercive and supportive actions.

One critical issue is clear: there is a high negative connection to the government for its control of the financial flow to foreign firms. The score here was 74.1%. It seems that Iranian firms do not demand state control of the business exchange. The highly coercive political action has created a negative relationship with the political actors. The comparison of the cumulative values in all the supportive and coercive alternatives shows that the managers measure the degree of negative connection more highly than they do the positive connection.

The influence of financial control behavior by the political actors was also presented in the earlier sections. As mentioned, in some criteria the impact was as high as 81%. This is in line with the results obtained in the above questions.

Considering the supportive actions, the values have an almost regressive trend (i.e. the higher values are in the supportive actions, the lower they are in the coercive actions). Government subsidies scored 36.6% (the highest rate). Scores reduced with the questions referring to standardized products (14.5%), import quotas (12.8%), and finally credit restriction (0%). Although government subsidies had the highest value, it was still only 36.6%, which confirms the value for government subsidies presented in Figure 6.10. On that question, the positive impact of the government subsidies was valued at 46.7% (this was the support for the combined alternatives "high" and "very high"). The results indicated that the firms preferred tariff-trade supportive actions directed at specific areas. In the question of the exchange rate (Figure 6.13), only 10.9% of the firms interpreted non-tariff political actions as supportive. Figure 6.13 also shows that few firms (3%) selected the alternative of "not at all." In this figure, for the question on credit restriction, the value for the alternative "not at all" was 13.3%. However, the values for the same alternative referring to exchange control and the exchange rate were much less, 8.3 and 2%, respectively. The presumption is that those who selected this alternative received financial support from the state. The difference between these values, 13.3% compared with 8.3 and 2%, could be because of needs and the expectation of gaining support rather than because of what they actually received.

The comparison of the supportive and coercive actions showed that the most negative factor influencing the focal relationship was the influence of the Iranian government in financial transactions. These bonds, namely credit restrictions, the exchange rate, and exchange control, gained the highest score (74%) for coercive actions and the least value for being supportive (15.4%). The reverse pertained to government subsidies, which scored 44.2% as supportive and 8.2% as coercive. These values uphold the statement that the Iranian government uses coercive means more strongly than supportive actions. Such a conclusion is based on the explanation that the highest values in supportive actions are not as high as in coercive actions.

6. Connection to Bureaucrats

No matter what political decisions are made, it is the bureaucratic organizations that exercise and implement the political rules. These organizations can strengthen or weaken the political connection as they translate and regulate the firms' behavior. They can exercise power in relation to foreign trade rules for testing products, custom documentation, product classification, and financial transactions. The survey contained seven questions directed at these issues. Five of these questions are presented below. Three questions are related to product exchange, and two measured financial and product exchange control. For this category, the leading question was: "To what extent do trade administrative procedures affect your business relationship with this supplier?"

The measures depicted in Figure 6.15 show that the bureaucrats, at least, are not positively connected to the focal relationship. The questions were concerned with: (1) customs for product classification; (2) customs for product valuation; and (3) product testing. It is true that in all three questions, the alternative "not at all" scored more than 25%. But the cumulative score in the three alternatives "to

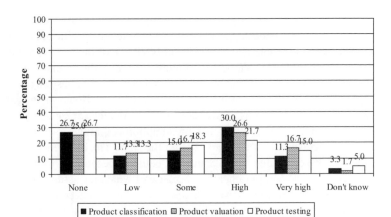

Figure 6.15: Connection to bureaucrats — product regulations.

some extent," "high," and "very high" was also quite high. The values for these three alternatives were 58.3, 60, and 55%, respectively, showing that almost 60% of the firms recognized that they had a negative connection with the bureaucrats. The alternatives "do not know" and "low" scored about 4 and 12%, respectively.

The results also show that the impact from the three bureaucratic areas of product classification, product valuation, and product testing is similar. This can also be verified by the values given to the first two alternatives of "not at all" and "low" in the answers to these three questions. However, in product testing, the bureaucratic procedure had a lower influence than in product evaluation and classification. This is because the exchanged products are simple raw materials.

The similarities in values may have been because the bureaucrats had taken opportunistic positions. No matter what the content of the rules, they may have tried to create obstacles which would strengthen their power against the Iranian firms. It can be concluded that bureaucrats amplify the coercive actions of the political actors and strengthen the negative connection.

In further examining the bureaucrats' behavior towards the Iranian firms, the next two questions evaluated respondents' views on the two areas of customs documentation and inspection time (Figure 6.16). For the first three alternatives, values were very similar, although there were some differences. One difference was in the values given to the first alternative "not at all." Here, the scores were 28.3 and 35%. The first related to the question on documentation and the second to inspection time. Another difference can be seen in the cumulative value of the three alternatives "very high," "high," and "to some extent." In relation to the first question, the score was 61.7%, and in relation to the second, 43.3%.

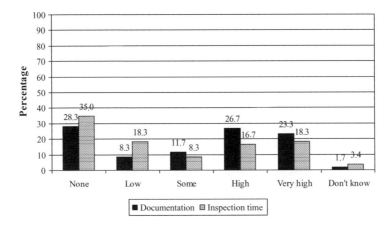

Figure 6.16: Relationship with bureaucrats for inspection and customs.

The comparison shows a difference of 18.4%. This means that the firms are constrained by a higher level of influence from the bureaucratic requirement of documentation records than from the time that the bureaucrats require to inspect the products. The difference could be because the inspection task is carried out by technical people, whereas documentation duties solely involve bureaucrats. No matter what the source of the differences is, the two questions confirm the conclusion that bureaucrats exercise their power to affect the focal exchange relationships via these two areas. The critical problem is the management of bureaucrats or administrators. The influence through political rules can be difficult because, as has been discussed earlier, rules have a general nature. This group, in similar cases, could translate and execute the rules according to their individual means and goals. The general management strategy, as introduced in marketing studies, covers tactics such as negotiation and manipulation.

The answers to the five questions illustrated in Figures 6.15 and 6.16 show that bureaucrats use their position to affect the business exchanges between Iranian and foreign firms. These questions considered five different bonds through which actors could have had interactive exchanges, but in these cases, the political actors have constructed a strong negative connection. In the case that bureaucrats are just following the political rules, the answers have a different structure. The alternatives "not at all" and "low," for example, may have gained much higher values. In such a case, bureaucrats do not impose such a high degree of negative impact on the business firms' operations. Reflecting on the results to these questions, it can be concluded that bureaucrats exercise their power through different connecting ties. All five of the ties examined, with minor differences for product testing and inspection time, have strong negative connections to the focal business relationships. This could be for two fundamental reasons. One is because of the negative connection to the political actors. Iranian managers observe bureaucrats as an extension of the government, even if the bureaucrats just execute the political rules and do not play a political game. The other reason is the translation of the political rules to gain a position of power. In this study, as presented earlier, there are substantial facts that confirm the second hypothesis. Bureaucrats exercise power beyond the formal position authorized by their political power. Their coercive actions explain the high degree of strength in the negative connection and the uncertainty that emerged towards bureaucratic behavior.

7. Managing Political Connections

The results in the earlier section showed the degree of negative influence as well as the areas that are preferred by the firms for building positive and supportive relationships. The results presented are the outcomes of the management activities of the firms. The negative connection could have been stronger, but the firms, as several managers stated, "have done what they could to reduce the negative influence of the government and bureaucrats" in their relationship with their foreign partners.

The next group of questions was focused on the management of the political connection. The questions, which were related to the activities of management, can be divided into three areas: (1) the influence and cooperation of management behavior; (2) management by connection; and finally (3) adapting the internal organization.

7.1. Influence

In this group, two of the questions were simply concerned with the exchange of political knowledge between the Iranian government and Iranian firms. The first reflects the exchange of information about the consequence of the government's political decisions. The next examines the knowledge of the politicians about the consequences of their actions on the Iranian firms' foreign relationships. In the first question concerning contacts with decision-makers, as Figure 6.17 shows, it seems that the majority of the managers had tried to establish contact with the government. Ten percent of the firms reported no effort to build even a simple relationship. In this question, the cumulative value for the first two alternatives of

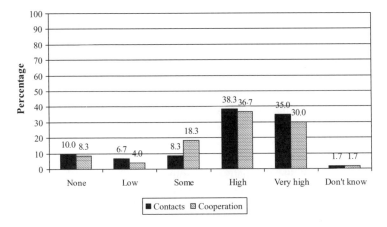

Figure 6.17: Management by exchange of information.

"not at all" and "low" was 16.7%. In contrast, more than 81% selected the three alternatives of "very high," "high," and "to some extent." This implies that most of the Iranian firms intensively discuss the political decisions that concern them. The high intensity in the exchange of information reflects the seriousness of the political issues. This can also be verified by the fact that not more than 1.7% chose the alternative "I do not know," although, the Iranian firms were more certain about the content of this question when evaluating the alternatives. As compared with several other questions examining the focal business interaction, this value is very low.

The cumulative value of 73.3% for the alternatives "high" and "very high" shows the general tendency in the Iranian firms' political behavior. In a sense, the firms did not just accept political decisions but also made an effort to contact the political actors. Surprisingly, when the question becomes more specific (see the next question in Figure 6.17), the cumulative value for the alternatives "high" and "very high" reduces a little to 67.7%.

In the first question, adding these two alternatives to the alternative "to some extent" produced a score of 83.6%, and in the second question, the score reached was 85%. This means that in these two questions, the Iranian firms behaved very similarly. The only major difference in the scores reflects the alternative "to some extent."

The essential aim in these questions was to understand how the Iranian firms manage the interaction and exercise influence on the Iranian government. In this section, two questions are presented. In these questions, the extent of influence of the firms beyond normal communication is examined. One considers the modification of the political decisions on foreign trade through contacts with the government, and the other considers avoidance behavior when facing the impact of the interactions.

The answers to the question on cooperation with government provide more detailed information (see Figure 6.17) and have almost the same structure as above. The scores in the categories of "not at all" and "low" were 8.3 and 5%, respectively. Compared with the first question (contacts with decision-makers), fewer respondents selected the last two alternatives "very high" and "high." The score in the category "very high" was 36.7% and in "high" 30% (with a cumulative value of 66.7%). If the alternative "to some extent" were to be included, the score would be 84.9%. This value shows a slightly higher level of input into the relationship to communicate with political actors. The aim of the firms is to convince the political actors by reasoning about the consequence of their actions. In spite of these differences, these questions together manifest a high degree of investment by the firms in influencing the government through the exchange of information. This score also signifies another fact: that even the state-owned firms are obliged to employ the same management strategy as the private firms.

7.2. Cooperation

As discussed earlier, very few Iranian firms seem to enjoy the specific support they gain from the government. For the other firms, a crucial area in managing political activities is to influence the political actors. The two earlier questions examined the actions undertaken by the Iranian firms, but the questions did not explore how effective their activities were. In the case of influence, the management aims to convert coercive to supportive behavior or, at least, to reduce the degree of impact of coercive behavior.

In the first question ("To what extent can you modify trade policy by contacting decision-makers?"), displayed in Figure 6.18, a few firms (16.6%) selected the alternatives "high" and "very high." These firms are state-owned firms that exercise their legitimate position to affect the political actors. However, the influence of these firms comprises simple relationship areas. Considering the alternatives "not at all" and "low" in the first question, the score was 36.7%. A comparison of the score in the first two and last two choices (see above) shows that twice as many firms cannot exercise influence on the government as can. However, 45% of the firms selected the alternative "to some extent." This is quite a high score. It means that almost half of the Iranian firms can, to some extent, interact with the government to modify their decisions.

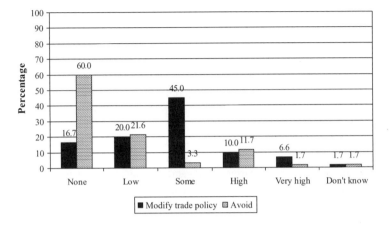

Figure 6.18: Avoidance and negotiation strategy.

In keeping with this hard line of influence, the second question (try to exit) tried to measure whether the Iranian firms could avoid the impact of political connections; in other words, whether they could disconnect themselves from the relationship with the political actors. As Figure 6.18 makes clear, more than 60% selected the alternative "not at all." If this value is combined with the score on the second alternative "low," it produces a score of 81.7%. These firms circumscribe the political control via avoidance strategy. Again, a special group (11.7%) selected the alternative "high." According to previous studies, these firms employ a variety of management tactics to disconnect themselves from political rules. These are "home-made" tactics, indigenous actions adapted to specificity in the circumstances (Hadjikhani 1996).

However, the majority of the Iranian firms have a high dependency on the government. The government uses its coercive power to such a degree that the firms cannot even use avoidance strategies. This means that the elaborated control system has restricted the firms into specific and given positions. Their relationships with their foreign partners have to follow a specific track dictated by the connected political actors. The majority of the firms seem to be unable to manage the political connection through avoidance or negotiation.

7.3. Managing Connections

As concluded above, the Iranian government is the major source of uncertainty in the relationship between Iranian firms and their foreign partners. Given that negative impact, an important aspect is what effort the Iranian managers made to challenge this uncertainty. It should be recalled that the values given to influence and uncertainties are the results of management activities. In understanding the management behavior of the Iranian firms, it is interesting to study which actors in the surrounding environment have assisted the Iranian firms. In the section above, besides the source and types of impact, the ultimate management strategy, namely avoidance, was also discussed. The following presentation covers management by the mobilization of other actors.

The survey included several questions to measure the utility of other actors in this task. Four of these actors — trading partner, local customer, branch industry, and local supplier — manifesting weak and strong connections are presented. The scores for the influence of these four actors are depicted in Figure 6.19. The responses display an interesting aspect concerning the structure of the answers. As illustrated in Figure 6.19, no one selected the alternative "I do not know." It seems that all the managers knew which actors had assisted the firms in their mission.

Among these actors, the highest value for the alternative "very high" was 18.3%. This was given to the organization responsible for the branch industry and shows that this was the most powerful and positively connected actor. More than 41% of the managers supported the alternative "high" and 25% the alternative "to some extent." Combining these three alternatives produces a value of 85%. This verifies the conclusion that there is a strong general and positive connection between Iranian firms and the branch industry. This relationship is not specific, since the branch industry includes a large number of firms from a variety of industries with different demands and questions.

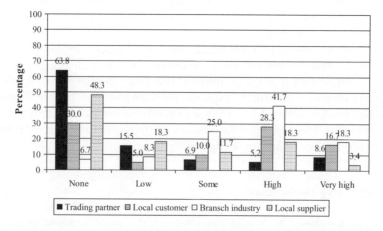

Figure 6.19: Influence of the other connected groups.

The next strong connection was that to the local customer. With a score of 16.7% for the alternative "very high," the local customer's value was not much less than that of the branch industry. The values given to the alternatives "rather much" and "to some extent" were 28.3 and 10%, respectively. These values are much lower than the values given to branch organizations. The cumulative value for the three alternatives ("very high," "high," and "to some extent") is 55%, which is much lower than the 85% in the question on foreign trading partners. However, the values of 45% for the first two alternatives and 55% for all three were quite high, compared with the results on the questions concerning local suppliers and foreign trading partners. In the first question, the value for the alternative "not at all" was 63.8%, and for the alternative "low," it was 15.5%. The cumulative value for the first three alternatives is more than 86%, an indication of the almost total lack of influence of the foreign partners on the Iranian government. This fact may also be true for the industrialized countries, and it would not have been surprising, therefore, if the value had been even higher than 86%. Consequently, the values 8.6 and 5.2% for the alternatives "very high" and "high" become interesting. The Iranian government has always spoken in favor of local sovereignty, independence, and religious values. These scores show the influence of the foreign partners on the Iranian government. One explanation for the influence could be that these foreign firms are involved in a specific type of industry. Project-selling mode, for example, in most cases involved both focal firms and governments. Foreign partners can interfere when decisions relate to aspects such as technical specifications and terms of payments.

For the question on local suppliers, the values for the alternatives "very high" and "high" were 3.4 and 18.4%. Less than half of the interviewees, 48.3%, selected the alternative "not at all," and more than 18% selected "low" in relation to the influence of the local supplier. The cumulative value for the first three alternatives is 78.3%. This is much higher than the cumulative value for the local customer (55%) and branch industry (40%) for the same alternatives. These values show that local suppliers have a weak connection to the Iranian firms and government.

The results show the strength and weakness of the four actors in influencing the government for the sake of this specific dyadic relationship. Comparatively, the branch industry, with its general relationship, has the strongest degree of influence, and foreign firms, with their specific demands, have the weakest relationship with the Iranian government. The values given in these four questions show that the local connections assist the Iranian firms in challenging a negative political connection. Among the locally connected actors, some customers had a stronger positive connection than the suppliers did. This conclusion can be verified by the results introduced in the section on business connections, where there was a strong connection between the Iranian firms and the local customers. It seems that the specific positive connection with local customers has strengthened the Iranian firms' position towards the negative political connection with the government. In other words, they have reduced the strength of the negative connections with the political actors.

7.4. Internal Adaptation

There are conditions when firms, in spite of assistance from other groups, still have strong negative connections to the political actors, and they, necessarily, resort to other alternatives to challenge the uncertainty. They can select from or combine a variety of alternatives, such as negotiation, adaptation, and exit from the market. The exit strategy contains two options. One is to move to another industry; another option is to leave the country, as firms in industrialized countries can. In the first option, as the political impacts have a general nature, as discussed above, the strategy of changing industry does not reduce the level of uncertainty. Further, entering into new markets requires new knowledge and additional resources. Thus, the Iranian firms do not stand to make any gains from the alternative of changing industry. The second option, exit to another country, requires a completely new capability and marketing ability, to which these firms do not have access. These implications leave no space to select an exit strategy. As has been mentioned, Iranian firms have a local market orientation. They have neither the financial resources nor the market and technological capability to penetrate into a stable market in industrialized countries. These factors limit their exit behavior. However, some firms have entered into neighboring countries that require low market and technological knowledge, as well as a low level of capital resources.

In the absence of an exit strategy, the other two strategies require internal structural changes. Some strategies, like negotiation, have a simple nature, and others are much more complex and require adaptation. The latter strategies can force firms into a large investment within the organization. In the earlier section, the study introduced the negotiation and avoidance strategies of the Iranian firms. In this section, facts about four questions will be presented regarding the adaptation strategies. The following two questions evaluate the management in terms of: (1) general adaptation and specific changes in production and the production process; and (2) political units which have evolved to handle the political connection.

For the first area, two questions are introduced. One is about the organizational structure, and the second considers the production process. As Figure 6.20 shows, the values given to the alternative "not at all" in relation to the structure of the organization were 13.3%, and in relation to the production process 22%. The cumulative value for the first two alternatives "not at all" and "low" in question

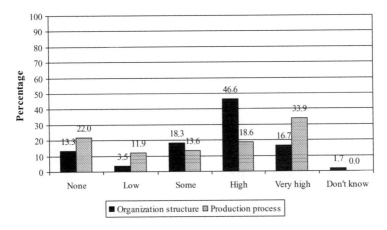

Figure 6.20: Management adaptation.

(1), which dealt with "organization structure," is 16.8%. In question (2), on the "production process," it is 33.9%. This meant that comparatively, the firms had done less adaptation in the production process. A similar outcome could be observed when the three alternatives "to some extent," "very high," and "high" are combined. Values in relation to question (1) were 81.6, and 66.1% in relation to question (2).

These values contain several interesting results. First, as mentioned above, the management of uncertainty required substantial change in the organizational structure. Second, the majority of the firms changed both the organizational structure and production process to deal with the negative connection to the political actors (for example, about 34% of the firms had highly adapted the production process). This value increases to 52.5% if the values for "very high" and "high" are combined. There is such a degree of strength in the political connection that more than 50% of the Iranian firms have made large investments to adapt the production process. This is a significant aspect, as the adaptation in the production process necessarily has to follow the technological interdependency, and not the political or bureaucratic connections. This discloses an important fact about the content of the focal exchange. Technologically, the exchanged products have such a simple nature that the production process can easily be adapted to the demands of the political actors. In other cases, the firms do not have an advanced production process. They have externalized the process to foreign suppliers or local customers.

Another important aspect is the adaptation towards the source of uncertainty. The structural changes presented in the above two questions are not directly related

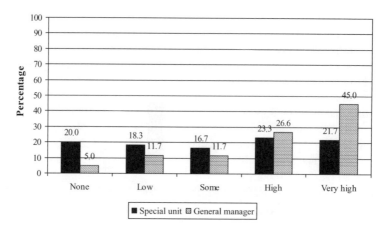

Figure 6.21: Internal task change.

to the flow of financial resources or foreign transactions that have been the main source of uncertainty. The adaptations are the outcome of the negative impacts from regulations such as import quotas, product standards, and so on. This conclusion reveals another serious problem in the political connection. Despite the regulations having a much lower impact than the uncertainty from financial transactions, these factors have created a large investment to change the structure of the organizations. As financial flow does not require high structural changes, the question is what types and how large are the visible and invisible investments to challenge the emerged uncertainty for the sake of foreign exchange. The question above, adapting the organization structure, implied changes in different units of the Iranian firms' organization. In the following section, the questions are more specific and measure adaptation at the middle-management and strategic apex levels. Figure 6.21 shows that the value for "very high" is 45%. If the value for "high" (26.6%) is included, this creates a total of 71.1%. The implication is that in the majority of cases, the general managers undertake the responsibility of challenging the political connection. The value for the alternative "not at all" is very low, only 5%. The result in this question makes clear the critical nature of the political issue. It is at such a level that very few general managers are not engaged in political affairs. The next question measures whether the firms have established specific units to handle their political connection. The value given for the alternative "very high" was 21.7%, and for "high" 23.3%. The cumulative value for the three alternatives of "very high," "high," and "to some extent" is 61.7%. This means that more than 60% of the firms have, to some extent, established specific units to challenge the political uncertainty. Moreover, the degree of uncertainty is at such a level that more than 83.3% (the cumulative values for the alternatives "very high," "high," and "to some extent") of the general managers undertake the management tasks concerned with the political issues. It can also be concluded that most of the managers' time is devoted to managing the uncertainty from the political connection.

The results from the four questions above show that the Iranian managers, in attempting to reduce the impact of government actions, have resorted to adaptation strategies to deal with the major uncertainty in technological and financial areas. The high level of impact because of these negative ties has forced the firms to change their organization at different levels. Adaptations have reflected: (1) the firm's organizational structure in general (such as its stockholding); (2) change in the units' tasks (such as their headquarters); and (3) adaptation in the production process. These structural changes correspond with the different types of influence and uncertainty introduced in this part of the book.

8. Summary

The earlier chapters focused attention on studying the content of the focal exchange relationships, whereas this chapter has covered the influence of the embedded actors on the focal relationships between Iranian customers and foreign suppliers. The earlier chapters left some unanswered questions. Questions such as what keeps the relationships alive or how the low degree of strength in the focal relationships has influenced, or continues to influence, the focal relationship were untouched.

To this aim, the chapter begins with a short conceptual discussion on connections between business and non-business actors, and proceeds with the presentation of four major sections. The first section considered the general views of the Iranian managers about the political and business actors in the environment. The second and third sections dealt with specific business and non-business actors, and their impacts on the focal relationships. The evaluation aimed at constructing a picture of the degree, and negative or positive influence, of these two connection types. Finally, the chapter presented the management actions of the Iranian firms in challenging the uncertainty that emerged from the negative connections. Considering the political actions, the fundamental factor examined in all the questions is trade policy, as the aim of the research was to study the relationships between Iranian and foreign firms.

When evaluating the general views on political and business embeddedness, the three questions evaluated the impact of political actors, competitors, and customers on the focal exchange. The value of the alternative "no importance," in the question on trade policy, was about 1.7%, competitors were considered of no importance by

28.8% of the respondents, and customers by 23.7%. In the alternative "important," the largest impact was ascribed to the political actors' decisions on trade policy. The value for trade policy decisions was 93%, for customers 66%, and for competitors 54%. The question about customers evaluated a positive connection, whereas the other two were considered negative connections. Thus, the highest value was given to a negative connection. This value was confirmed with a question that evaluated the private and political actors comparatively. The impact value for the political actors was 81%, and for the business actors 18%. In another question, the firms were asked to rank all actors, including the foreign suppliers. The ranking was constructed to evaluate the degree of the negative and positive impact of each factor on the Iranian firms. The value for the negative influences of the government was 39%, and for the competitors 3%, whereas the positive value for the foreign suppliers was 19% (although the impact of the government had a higher degree than the focal partner and competitors). In the study of business connections, several actors were examined. For the three positively connected actors, suppliers to the Iranian firms, suppliers to the foreign firms, and suppliers' competitors, the degree of influence is generally low. Among these three, the lowest degree of impact on the focal relationship was allocated to suppliers of foreign firms, and the highest to the suppliers' competitors. The other actor examined was the financial actor and his influence on the focal relationship. The degree of impact from financial actors is even higher than from the suppliers' competitors, but in general, about 50% perceive financial actors as having a very small impact.

In studying political embeddedness, two major decision fields, tariff and non-tariff, were examined. For tariff decisions, areas such as import and export tariffs, consumption of final products, and specific duties were considered. The study shows a large variation in the values given to these different areas. The highest negative impact was in the political rules on the consumption of final products. However, the most supportive influence came from government subsidies, although the degree of intense dependency on financial subsidies was not very high at 30%. This rate is even lower than the rate (33%) for those who proclaim a high level of independence of the subsidies (see Figure 6.12).

The first three questions in the field of non-tariff political actions concerned product standards, product specification, and import quotas. In all three, coercive actions elaborating negative connections had a high degree of support. In product specification, for example, the value for the very high impact on the focal relationship was more than 63%. In product standards, the score given to the coercive impact of the government on the focal relationship was almost 80%.

The areas reflecting the factor of non-tariff coercive actions show much higher degrees. For example, the negative ties for the control measures of the government on foreign financial transactions scored more than 80%. The Iranian government uses its power via the exchange rate, exchange control, and prior import deposits, to create obstacles for Iranian and foreign firms. Among these areas, the strength in the negative bonds varied. Some, such as the deposit required prior to importing, have a weaker impact than credit restrictions.

In one of the questions, the Iranian managers were asked to rank 12 areas in which the government exercises its coercive and supportive actions towards the focal relationship. Strangely, only 36% of the firms gave a very high evaluation of subsidies. This implies that the other firms see subsidies as a negative connection to the government. Similar to this result, the negative bonds were strongest for the foreign exchange transactions. In this and in other questions, evaluations showed a very low impact for export tariffs. This verifies the earlier conclusion that the Iranian firms are not very dependent on the export market but are completely dependent on the local Iranian market.

In another question, the group evaluated the strength of the negative or positive connection with the bureaucrats. Factors, such as customs for product classification, valuation, and testing, were evaluated. Surprisingly, the bureaucrats, similarly to the government, have elaborated a negative connection with a coercive nature. Gradually, bureaucrats have strengthened the impact from the actors that have negative connections. Naturally, the areas in which the exchanges occur have different strengths. Negative connections such as product classifications gained 60% for their high impact, and others, such as product valuation, scored 43%. Bureaucrats create more uncertainty about documentation for customs than for product testing.

The study presented different types of influence and adaptation actions by Iranian managers for the management of the political actors. One interesting finding was that, despite the authority and power of the government, the managers had undertaken actions to influence decisions. The study showed that the actions had different degrees of strength. Questions measuring weak ties, such as simple information exchange to cooperation, were discussed. While the simple actions of information exchange had a very high level of influence on political actors, the cooperation alternatives were ranked very low. This means that political actors, in keeping with their political authority, are not willing to come close to business actors. The political actors prefer to maintain their distance, with a very weak relationship with the local actors.

Management also considered the involvement of other actors affecting the political actors. Several connected actors, among them local suppliers, branch organizations, and foreign suppliers, were observed. Generally, the values show a low degree of influence from these actors. The highest degree for the alternative "very high" was 18%, which was given to the branch industry. The lowest degree (8%) was awarded to foreign partners. However, the combination of the alternatives "high" and "to some extent" showed that the branch industry and customers have the strongest positive connections to the focal firms.

When the uncertainty could not be challenged by the influential activities of the Iranian firms and connected actors, adaptation of the internal structure was a necessity. In two questions, the study measured the extent of change in the organizational structure and production process. The results show a drastic adaptation change in both areas. More than 81% of the firms have adapted their administrative units, and 66% had changed the production process to challenge the uncertainty that emerged from the political connection. In other questions that examined the importance of the political issues, the firms were asked to state who undertakes the task of dealing with the political actors and matters of adaptation. It seems that the tasks were mainly handled by the general managers because of the strategic impacts of political decisions.

Part 3

Synopsis

The previous part was devoted to a presentation of facts about the purchasing behavior of the Iranian firms when interacting with the MNCs. In further understanding the behavior of these firms, the study compared the Iranian case with the IMP2 case. Their relationships were studied in terms of strength and weakness, for example. In order to understand the exchanges between the Iranian and foreign firms, the study focused on the concept of embeddedness. The aim was to conceptualize the content of the focal and connected actors. Since the political actors are important in the business market, the effort was to explore how the politically connected actors contribute their supportive or coercive actions towards the relationship between Iranian and foreign firms.

In the empirical part, some analytical notes are debated to enhance an understanding of the facts. Some of the measures in Chapters 3–5 may have been confusing. A problem was that the strengths and weaknesses in some of the relationships were difficult to analyze. Doubts about the validity of the facts forced the study to check and recheck the measures and carefully compare them. In order to improve understanding of the firms' behavior, the research continued to study the embedded actors in Chapter 6.

Naturally, the answers do not indicate support from all the firms (i.e. the answers were not completely homogeneous). A small group of firms, about 10–20%, had a different view from the mainstream. When discussing the facts, the research presented some explanations about the behavior of the mainstream of firms, as well as those outside the mainstream.

The following three chapters are devoted to an analysis of the facts and findings. In the first chapter, the empirical results will be compared to highlight the similarities and differences, not only among the questions in this study, but also with the results from the IMP2 study. The driving force in the analysis is the strength and weakness in the relationships. The aim is also to find conceptual elements that can describe the behavior in a more consistent way. In the second chapter the results from the empirical evidence become connected to the theoretical foundations introduced in Chapter 2. The specific aim of the final chapter is to present the outcomes that enlarge our conceptual understanding of the firms' behavior in a context that includes non-business actors.

Chapter 7

Relationship and Embeddedness

In this chapter, the study will present an analysis of the measures offered in the earlier chapters. Following the order in the earlier chapters, this chapter is divided into four sections. The first three sections are composed of resolutions that cover the focal actors' relationships, adaptation, and social relationships. The fourth section is devoted to an analysis of embeddedness. In the first three sections, the outcome in the Iranian study is compared with the results reached in the study of IMP2. The comparison is not aimed at an analysis of the purchasing behavior of the MNCs in industrialized countries. Rather, it has the projected aim of supporting or rejecting the measures of the behavior of the Iranian firms when interacting with MNCs. In all these sections, the facts are interwoven with concepts such as interdependency, uncertainty, and trust, which are used to assist in the analysis of the strength and weakness of the relationships.

1. Major Results on Relationships

1.1. Relationship Development

In studying the relationships, the two dimensions of (1) relationship development and (2) relationship extent are explored, in order to understand the content of the relationship between the Iranian customers and foreign suppliers. The first dimensions were examined through questions on the history and expectations of the relationship. Two interesting findings apply to: (1) the development of new relationships; and (2) the connection between development of the relationships and sociopolitical development in Iran. It was surprising to observe how the rate of intensity in the relationships sharply decreases and increases in different periods. Further, these drastic changes coincided with sociopolitical changes. Between the years 1970 and 1998, the number of new relationships decreased sharply, at least six times. In these periods, Iran was faced with increasing oil prices, mass demonstrations, revolution, the initiation and termination of a war with Iraq, and drastic financial crises. These measures are very different from the results obtained in the IMP2. First, the year in which relationships were initiated in the IMP2 cases was much earlier than was the case in Iran. Relationships between firms in the IMP2 study had already begun in the 1920s. In the Iranian case, very few relationships had started by the 1970s. Second, the development process in the IMP2 was not subject to such drastic changes, as the socioeconomic environment of these firms had a higher level of stability. In the IMP2 study, the relationships were of a successive and incremental nature. The principle of long-term relationship and mutual interdependency can easily be observed. Third, with the increasing globalization of the market in industrialized countries, MNCs have extensively elaborated new relationships. In the IMP2 study, the trend shows a sharp increase after the 1960s. Despite the fact that the development trend between the years 1970 and 1997 was also positive in the Iranian case, there were a much smaller number of extensive relationships than was found in the IMP2.

Considering the types of products exchanged, the results in the Iranian and IMP2 surveys showed that the scores for each product type were similar (i.e. in both studies, similar product types gained similar values). This naturally increases the validity in the comparison of the two studies. Almost half of the purchased products were raw materials, and the rest consisted of industrial components and equipment.

One crucial aspect in the existing relationship is the development pattern. The sediment left from past relationships affects the strength of existing relationships. Past relationships leave experiences that create trust or mistrust in the partnerships. In this context, several measures pinpoint the specific role of the past dimension in the Iranian case. One of the questions reflected the development of the relationship over the previous five years. It was interesting to know if the exchanges, like the historical background, had altered dramatically during recent years. The results were enlightening. They showed that more than 46% of the firms, despite the uncertainty in the socioeconomic conditions, had increased the amount of exchanges. (This rate is much lower than the rate given in the IMP2.) If the value for the alternative "unchanged relationship" is included, then the score is more than 81%. In fact, very few (only 15%) of the firms reported a low increase in the number of their relationships during the last five years. This positive development indicates a degree of interdependency and trust, as otherwise the partnerships would have been broken or weakened.

The analysis above is still of a general nature. More specific information about the content of the relationship development was necessary. In another question, the study measured mutuality and profitability. The results show that the firms realized that the mutuality in gains would continue in the future. The answers indicated a high degree of profitability for both actors in the following five years. Very few, little more than 3%, had a pessimistic view about the future and expected poor profitability.

In all the measures on past and future expectations, the Iranian firms identified mutuality and equality in profitability. These are important values because they reject the opportunistic behavior of the actors. Further, they elevate the fact that the Iranian customers and foreign suppliers are bound together and are not merely in a short-term exchange relationship. It is true that the relationships are not as longstanding as those in the IMP2, but they are not short-lived either. This also means that the firms are bound together on grounds other than just the price factor. This conclusion is confirmed by the rate of stability in the exchanges between the Iranian firms and foreign partners. However, the degree of stability is lower than the measures reached in the IMP2. Furthermore, the degree of volatility was much higher in the study of Iranian cases, but in general, the level of instability was low.

Although the previous dimension shows a mutual profitability and a degree of stability in the relationships, it could also be fruitful to study the views of the managers about the future of the relationships. Contrary to the values for the previous dimension and high expectation for profitability, the measures on regularity in the exchange show a lower degree of positive expectation. Here, the degree of irregularity increases to more than 50%. In addition, the firms believed that there would be greater volatility in the future than there had been in the past. Purchasing patterns were three times more stable in the IMP2 case than in the Iranian case. In the Iranian case, the group that expected an increase was two and half times smaller than the group that had increased their exchange in the past. This means that the Iranian customers have a high level of uncertainty regarding the future development of the relationship. This is not simply because of problems between the partners. It may also depend on uncertainty about changes in the environment of the relationships. Despite the fact that the Iranian firms have a lower expectation than the firms in the IMP2, the former are not pessimistic about the future of their partnerships. They recognize the relationship as necessary and essential. There are, however, some firms that expect a weaker exchange development in the future.

1.2. Product and Technological Relationships

The past and future dimensions of the relationship development disclosed some crucial facts about the content of the relationships between the Iranian customers and their foreign suppliers. The study contained questions evaluating the content of the relationships by measuring the strength in the technological and product exchange relationships. One criterion considered the degree of uniqueness of the products. According to the network perspective, a high degree of uniqueness contains an inbuilt strong relationship. This type of product demands technological cooperation and adaptations among the partners. When a supplier provides a unique product to a customer, it generally requires a high level of trust and a long-term relationship. A crucial issue in assessing uniqueness was not only the customers' evaluation of the degree of specificity of a product, but also how unique that product is in the market. A product can be recognized as standardized in one industrialized country but can be seen as unique in a less developed country.

The results are interesting. Almost 60% of the customers specified that the products were of a standardized type. The values given to the "totally new product" were about 13%, with "new in some respect" selected by 10% of the respondents. These last values are much higher than the values in the study of the IMP2. This means that the novelty of the products was higher in the Iranian case. The novelty requires technological competency, specifically for firms from developing countries. The small group of Iranian firms purchasing unique products has to develop technological and organizational abilities that allow them to manage the interaction with their suppliers. These naturally bind the suppliers and customers to each other strongly but, as will be discussed, such a structure is absent for a large number of firms. In those cases where Iranian customers supported the value of products' uniqueness, the business relationship can be of a project-selling type. In international business, this mode is very usual among MNCs and purchasers from countries like Iran. It always includes new technologies but does not necessarily bind the actors in the long-term. As the evaluation on profitability and technological interaction shows, the price of the product is an important factor. A long-term relationship indicates that the partners have a mutual understanding about the price. Naturally, this factor creates a weak interrelationship among the actors, as it is easier for competitors to offer a lower price. However, as will be further discussed, it is not only the price mechanism that binds these actors.

Beside the few unique exchanges, the majority of the exchanges involve standardized products. Such a type of product exchange does not require complex cooperation and adaptations. The conclusions of low interdependency, because of the standardized nature of the products, have a low reliability. Further knowledge is needed on the content of the other bonds binding the suppliers and customers. In challenging this problem, the study contained several questions that examined the technological bonds of the relationships. They measured: (1) the role of the Iranian customers and the foreign suppliers; and (2) the degree of cooperation. The questions measured the partners' degree of engagement in specifying the exchanged products. The aim was to understand if there was a balance or mutuality and cooperation. A high level of cooperation for product specification will generate high interdependency in product ties.

Unfortunately, the evaluation displayed a low degree of strength for the product specification. More than 65% of the Iranian customers explained that they alone specified the content of the products. This large group had enough knowledge about the product technology and did not feel dependent on their foreign suppliers, although the Iranian firms had a low level of uncertainty when the exchange considered the technology of the products. This could be because the simple nature of the products did not require cooperation for technical specification. In no more than 23% of the cases did both partners specify the products equally. The comparative value in the IMP2 cases was about 38%. Thus, in the IMP2 study, for a large number of firms, the customers and suppliers together decided on the content of the exchanged products. Further, the other values in the same question showed that there was more interdependence between the supplier and customer firms in the IMP2. The conclusion is that the supplier and customer firms in the IMP2 had a higher degree of cooperation than the firms in the Iranian study. Furthermore, the exchanged products in the IMP2 study were of a more complex nature.

The discussion above is the basis for the conclusion of weakness in the relationships. Moreover, because of the low level of interdependency, the firms have a high degree of potential mobility. In relation to the factor of product novelty, mentioned above, the value in the Iranian case was three times higher than the value in the IMP2 case. Theoretically, novelty requires a high level of technological cooperation and adaptation in the relationships between Iranian and foreign firms, but the facts do not indicate this degree of technological cooperation, adaptation, or interdependency. A low degree of technological cooperation is combined with reasons such as standardized types of products and a low degree of novelty. Theoretically, a low level of technological cooperation can also be reached when the purchasing firms have a high technological competence. The assumption in the last factor, high technological competence, is that the Iranian firms could, for example, undertake further product development themselves. Otherwise, they purchase the products and sell them as they are to the customers in Iran. In any case, the results from several questions display the absence of a strong technological relationship. In a question examining the "new ideas for product technology," only 8% of the Iranian firms saw their foreign suppliers as a very important source, and more than 51% evaluated them as being very unimportant. In the IMP2 study, the measures were twice these.

Following these results, the question then is whether other factors bind the actors. An important area of study is to know the utility of the suppliers. In one question that examined the importance of suppliers as a safeguard, the aim was to learn the Iranian firms' strategy in the relationships. Surprisingly, the values again showed a weakness in the relationships. The strategy for more than 68% of the Iranian firms was to use their suppliers as safeguards. Only 23% of the Iranian firms observed other factors to be important. In the IMP2, the rates were the opposite. Importance as a safeguard was supported by 26% of the firms, whereas 65% reported other factors keeping the actors together. In terms of technological bonds, the interdependency of the suppliers in the Iranian case is weak, as the Iranian customers have a high level of potential mobility. This means that if alternatives appear, the Iranian firms could leave their partners.

In further examining the activities and role of the foreign supplier and Iranian customer, the question was "Who specifies the technology in the products?" The question showed that more than 76% of the Iranian firms specified the details in the exchanged products. The majority of the Iranian firms could themselves undertake the technological part of the production system without technical assistance from the suppliers.

Another question that examined the role of the firms in the exchange was the degree of importance of the customer. This aimed at providing further facts about the degree of interdependency in the bonds surrounding the technological exchange. The questions evaluated two factors: the "amount of the exchanged product" and "market share." The results are interesting, since a large amount of the products purchased by the Iranian firms show the dependency of the foreign firms on the Iranian firms. However, Iranian customers are dependent on the foreign firms, as the majority of the Iranian customers (70%) purchased 50–100% of their needs from their foreign partners. In either case, the interdependency is high inasmuch as it mainly considers the factor of the quantity in the exchange. However, when the question considered technological cooperation — the core ties — the conclusion was different. This is verified by the presentation of the suppliers' importance as a source for technological development. Iranian customers do not agree that the suppliers assist them in their technological tasks. This supports the conclusion that, because of the weak technological ties, there is only a simple cooperation between the firms, covering aspects such as quantity and price. The situation is different in the IMP2 study, where the firms indicated the importance of the suppliers when developing new products.

1.3. Summary

As mentioned above, a relationship contains other ties that surround the core ties, an example being the delivery of products (see Table 7.1). Understanding the content of these ties between Iranian and foreign firms can increase our understanding of the strength of the relationship and level of uncertainty. In general, a strong relationship provides a strong core and surrounding ties. A weak relationship, in contrast, has an inbuilt weak core and surrounding ties. In the Iranian case, the core

Table 7.1: Summary of the focal relationship.

	Brief Summary	Results
Relationship development	Development patterns follow the critical socioeconomic development. The length of life of the relationships is not short, and during the last five years, the relationships have become stronger because: (1) the partners have had a mutual interest and profit in the exchange; (2) the relationships contain a high degree of exchange and development; (3) compared with the IMP2, there is a higher degree of volatility in the exchange; (4) there is a high degree of stability in the relationship; and (5) there is future optimism about the profitability. At the same time there is a pessimistic opinion on the development of the relationships with the foreign suppliers in the future.	• High dependency on socioeconomic changes. • Mutuality and interdependency between the focal actors. Lack of opportunism and partners do not have short-lived relationships. • Stability in the exchange in the past. • Prediction for mutuality in the gains and prolonged relationships. • A degree of optimism towards the future, but uncertainty is higher than in the past dimension.
Product and technological relationships	Standardized products with the exception of a few unique products. In contrast to IMP2, the customers mainly perform the product specifications. Iranian customers have technological knowledge to decide the content of the products. Contrary to the IMP2 case, the foreign suppliers in the Iranian case are not important for technological development. MNCs are recognized mostly as safeguards. The factor of delivery in the Iranian case is very different from the IMP2 case. Contrary to the IMP2 which employs the "just in time" principle, Iranian customers purchase a large amount of the product each time. The delay in delivery has a low impact.	• The exchange relationships contain core bonds and surrounding bonds. • Low interdependency and weak ties for both core and surrounding bonds. • The factor of price is important in the relationship. • Low dependency on the suppliers to specify the content of the products. • Weak technological cooperation. • High potential mobility of the Iranian firms. • Low interdependency to the delivery time. • High interdependency to the suppliers' ability to deliver a large quantity.

ties have a weak nature, but the surrounding ties have different types of strength. While the quantity of the purchase binds the actors strongly to each other, the delivery factor contains a weak level of interdependency. The results show that almost half of the customers received a delivery only once or twice a year. More than 32% received a delivery between three and five times a year. Even if one assumes that customers buying raw materials do not need to buy several times a year (in the pursuit of cost efficiency), the question is why other customers do not have a higher frequency in their deliveries. Furthermore, the impact of the delay of weeks or months is surprisingly low, even though the factor of "just in time," which is an important management criterion for the reduction in costs and price in industrialized countries, is absent in the Iranian market. A high level of market uncertainty could be the reason that the Iranian firms buy a large quantity in each delivery. The conclusion is that there are two reasons for the principle of few deliveries: (1) the type of purchased product; and (2) the high uncertainty in the environment. This uncertainty forces the firms to buy in large quantities and does not allow them to follow business rules such as "just in time."

2. Adaptation

The above study divided the relationship's content into two groups of core and surrounding ties. Despite the difference in the strength of these two groups of ties, the conclusion was that the relationships had a low interdependency. However, the question is still why these actors have continued their relationships for such a long period. Further, despite the fact that the Iranian firms had lower expectations for the future, they still had some optimism in the relationship development. They predicted a high and mutual profit in the future. The fundamental presumption in the network perspective is that, under conditions of weak relationships, the price mechanism constructs instability in the relationships. But the results showed stability in the exchange relationship. Thus, the measures in the relationship did not provide a complete picture of the content of relationships. The relationship measured in Chapter 3 encompasses some of the ties, but measures on other ties are needed. It could be, for example, that these firms have made new adaptations to increase their fitness for future transactions, and, when this study was conducted, the relationships between the Iranian and foreign firms were not developed to an extent that the research could have shown the outcomes from the new adaptations. A study on adaptation to the needs of the firms may open new doors in further understanding the content of the relationship. A high adaptation in the industrial relationship strongly binds the actors to long-term relationships. A low degree of adaptation, in contrast, generates weakness in the relationship, low interdependency, and high mobility in the partnership.

The aim in the study of adaptation was to measure how the firms have adapted their different types of activities to each other. One question that measured an important aspect of the adaptation was about the uniqueness in the adaptations. The question was to evaluate whether the partners had made unique or general adaptations towards their partners. The measure was important, as the degree of originality was an indicator of how far the partners had sacrificed their resources. The cost of being treated as a unique partner took into account not only changes in routines and administration but also other parts of the organization. The exchange partners, foreign and Iranian firms, would adapt units such as R&D and production. Unique technological adaptations brought high interdependency. A high score in uniqueness of adaptation was seen as a measure of a strong and close relationship.

Unfortunately, the scores showed the opposite condition. The adaptation was not specific but had a general nature. The score for general adaptation was about 60%, and unique adaptation was about 3%. In such a condition, mobility is high, and the cost of changing a business partner is low. Complex and unique products and components require specificity in the relationships. When a product is to be tailored for the specific needs of a customer, the relationship is composed of high adaptation costs for both partners. The measured values in adaptations such as product modification and new product development also disclose weak ties, which are simple in nature. It can therefore be concluded that the actors have created a fit with a low level of adaptation. The fit is an outcome of the balance and stability in the exchange. Another question was how these firms have changed their administrations to increase the degree of fit and to guarantee a long-term relationship. This referred to areas such as service, information exchange, and personal training, which surround the core activities. As has been discussed, the strength of these ties is different depending on the nature of the tie. For example, the adaptation for information exchange is much higher than the adaptation for delivery procedures. However, despite the differences between administrative bonds, more than 70% of the firms explained that they had made no or only very small administrative adaptations.

The differences in the scores given to the adaptations to different ties generated some conclusions about the content. One general conclusion was that the adaptive behavior has two dimensions. One dimension refers to the type of adaptation and the other to the degree adaptation (see Table 7.2). Adaptation can reflect areas, such as information, that are broad. It can also contain new product development that is unique. Furthermore, adaptation for each of these two types can be high or low.

Table 7.2: Summary of the social interaction.

Brief Summary	Results
• The majority of firms do not have the feeling of dependency. The grounds for mutual interdependency and balance in the exchange are different for the suppliers and customers. • Mutuality is based on simple grounds, and therefore firms have a high level of ability to change partners, but the majority of the firms do not act opportunistically. The goal of some firms is short-term profit. • The social relationship has a high level of trust. Contrary to other studies, when the interaction is on formalities, the degree of trust is low, and Iranian customers demand written procedures. The level of trust increases when it considers the measures on social interactions. Here, there is a large difference between the two components of personal and functional trust.	• Mutual interdependency on different grounds. • A high potential mobility. • Mutuality and balance. • Interdependency based on an absence of alternatives. • A low level of social mistrust. • A high level of uncertainty in the environment, causing mistrust in the focal relationship. • Distinction between personal trust and sociofunctional trust. • A high level of personal trust. • Low uncertainty because of high trust in the social relationships. • A very low impact from cultural differences.

The study shows that the majority of the Iranian, and even foreign, firms had high adaptive changes in those types, such as information exchange, which are simple in nature. This can be compared with other adaptive types, such as product development, in which the Iranian firms have a low degree of adaptation. In the Iranian case, there was a difference among the simple types of adaptations. The simpler the adaptation type, the higher the degree of adaptation.

As shown in Figure 7.1, the adaptations in the different cells indicate bonds with a variety of strengths. As the scores in the Iranian case unfold, each type of bond is constrained by a change in strength, which is not exactly the same as in the other bonds. But, in general, the adaptations in the Iranian case amplify a low degree of adaptation. Cell 2 shows the adaptation in the core relationships, which considered a low degree of uniqueness and specificity. Cell 4 shows an example

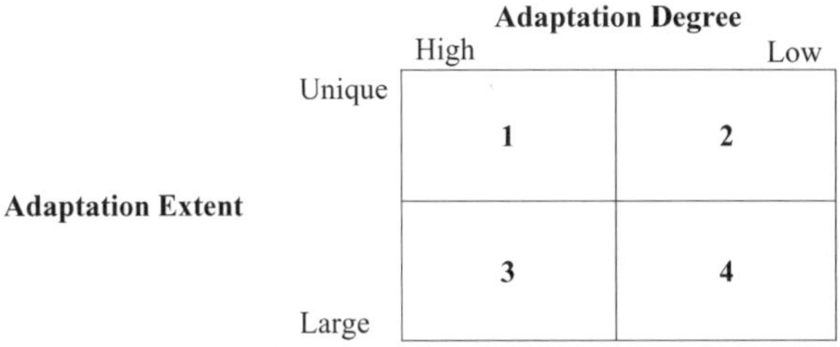

	Adaptation Degree	
	High	Low
Unique	1	2
Large	3	4

Adaptation Extent (row label at left)

Figure 7.1: Adaptation extent.

of a service that involved a large adaptation, but the adaptation itself was of a low degree. Information adaptation, however, gained a slightly higher score and could be placed between cells 2 and 4. Other than this, the different adaptation bonds fall into cells 2 and 4, and show a weak level of adaptation. These cells are composed of values generating a low level of interdependency. Adaptation between the Iranian customers and the foreign suppliers was generally of a low degree and generated a low level of strength.

These factors indicate that the focal firms could change the partnership quite easily (i.e. partners have a high degree of mobility). To provide more evidence on the weakness of the relationship, the values in the frequency of meetings can be mentioned. As discussed above, there was a low frequency of meetings between the Iranian and foreign firms, and the meetings did not involve a large number of people. In particular, the meetings did not involve people from the core task units.

2.1. Summary

An interesting outcome of studying the different types of adaptation was that the measures in the questions complemented each other. Accordingly, it becomes easier to draw conclusions on the content of the adaptive behavior. For example, a conclusion that technological advice does not require a unique adaptation but mainly contains standardized adjustments can easily be verified. The small numbers and low frequency in personal meetings manifest, for example, such a level of adaptation. Verification is also derived from the results of the questions in the earlier chapter. The low degree of delivery adaptation shows an absence of "just-in-time" planning, assisted by the conclusion reached in the question on the amount of purchasing. Thus, the results in the adaptation section complement the results obtained in the earlier chapter. Unanswered questions, such as why these firms have not changed the partnerships, remain. If the conclusion of weak adaptation and interdependency is correct, why then do relationships not have a short life?

3. Social Relationships

While Chapters 3 and 4 attempted to study the hardware field of the relationship, Chapter 5 considered the software field (i.e. the atmosphere). The measure was used to increase understanding of the interdependency and trust between the Iranian customers and foreign suppliers. It first offered measures on the general perception of the social interaction and continued with a presentation of the results for some specific social bonds. In Chapters 3 and 4, the findings showed that the business relationship was weak, and the degree of adaptation to the core ties was low. Accordingly, the expectation was that the answers in relation to social bonds would generate similar values, leading to analogous conclusions. But the values in relation to the social atmosphere disclosed different and interesting results.

In general, the values in the questions show a high degree of mutuality among the actors. The Iranian managers perceived the relationship as containing a balance in the exchange. This implies that the degree of opportunism is low. Despite the balance in the interaction, a large group of the firms in the questions studying the degree of mobility explained that they would not have problems in changing to competitors. This high degree in the ability to change partners is an outcome of the weak interdependency.

A group of firms, about 20%, reported a higher interdependency with their suppliers, despite the fact that their technological interdependency was low. This can be explained by the foreign suppliers' relationship with other firms. As discussed in the chapter on connections, Iranian firms have a very high dependency on suppliers connected with the financing of their activities. Such connections strengthen the dependency of the firms on the foreign suppliers.

In the questions examining the level of cooperation, the values show that the majority of the Iranian firms perceive that their partners could easily switch to others (see Figure 4.4). More than 60% of the firms have no difficulty in changing their partners. At the same time, about 40% have no alternatives and cannot purchase from competitors. Thus, a large group of the Iranian firms that have a low technological interdependency also have a low degree of mobility.

However, for the majority of the Iranian firms, the interesting aspect is that, on the one hand, they have balance and mutuality (see also the results for the degree of profitability in Chapter 3) and, on the other hand, they have a high degree of potential mobility. The question is how this is possible. The only explanation can be that the balance and interdependency can represent different dimensions in the social interaction. Mutuality can be reached with a high level of interdependency but is also possible, as the case in Iran shows, with a low level of interdependency. Thus, each of these dimensions (i.e. mutuality and balance) contains a continuum with a scale from low to high. The degree follows the strength in the interdependency. Thus, the crucial aspect is not the matter of who depends on whom but rather the strength of the interdependency, which affects the degree of mobility.

The study reveals an interesting issue in terms of trust, that is the division of business or functional trust from social or personal trust. The first considers the exchange of, for example, business information or formalities in the agreements; the second reflects areas such as language or personal interactions. Given the high level of ability to change partners, in the Iranian case, the level of mistrust was very low. In a question examining the closeness of the people engaged, the percentage of mistrust was less than 3%. Despite the fact that the degree of mistrust at the organizational level was higher (5%), there was still a high level of trust on the individual and organizational dimensions. On the question concerning closeness in cooperation, the value was more than 87%. A similar value was given to the question of "partners' level of understanding." Contrary to these results, the level was much lower when the question examined the technological cooperation.

The questions above examined general aspects of social trust. When business trust was examined — the functional aspect of social interaction — the results were different. One specific area that was evaluated was the preference of the foreign suppliers for cooperation as opposed to short-term profit. Only 21% of the Iranian firms perceived that the foreign supplier highly preferred cooperation, and 40% agreed partially with this contention. These values can be compared with the score on the question of degree of closeness, which was 87%. The low degree of preference may be because of the uncertainty of the Iranian firms about the strategic purpose of the foreign suppliers in this interaction. A drastic conclusion could be that a large group of the foreign suppliers aimed for short-term profit.

3.1. Summary

The study shows that the Iranian managers distinguished social trust from business-social trust. The first factor was conceived of as a purely personal relationship and understanding. The other, functional trust, considers the formalities and rules of business negotiation. Whereas social trust gained a very high score, sociofunctional trust generated a lower value. The first form of trust exhibited a high level of interdependency and low uncertainty; but the second showed a lower level of interdependency and higher uncertainty. More than 93% of the Iranians did not see cultural difference as a problem. On the other hand, more than 60% of the managers wanted the business to be driven by formal rules. The results are interesting as the Iranian firms, on the one hand, want to build personal relationships and, on the other hand, of necessity, have to rely on written agreements. The high uncertainty did not emerge because of the social setting in the focal relationship but could have been because of environmental factors.

This conclusion has its impact on other studies dealing with cultural differences. The values obtained in the questions (see, for example, Figure 4.8) show facts that are different from the conclusions in earlier studies (see, for example, Hofstede 1983; Usunier 1993). In contrast to those studies that argue that cultural differences between firms from industrialized and developing countries like Iran are a major source of uncertainty, this study presents a different view. The evidence in this chapter indicates that people in these firms have a strong social bond, in spite of the fact that these relationships, as presented in the first question of Chapter 3, do not have a long historical background. The next contradictory and interesting finding concerns the aspect of formality in the interaction. The earlier research emphasized the role of informal relationships when the interaction involves people from developing countries like Iran. This study shows that the Iranian firms rely on formalities and formal business relationships.

4. Embeddedness

In this chapter, the embeddedness of the Iranian and foreign firms is studied by exploring the exchange relationship between the Iranian purchasing firms and the surrounding business and non-business organizations. The question was how the Iranian firms' relationships with their foreign partners affected, and were affected by, the embedded actors. In this section, the empirical findings cover business and non-business connections and their strengths and weaknesses. The analysis also draws conclusions about the management actions of the Iranian firms to challenge the uncertainty created by the embedded actors.

The first group of questions, which examined the strength in the business and non-business actors, concluded with a crucial finding. It was surprising to find that the non-business actors could have such a high level of influence on the focal interaction. The actions of the non-business actors were measured by the decisions and implementation of the trade policy that regulated the behavior of the Iranian customers and their foreign partners. An effective use of the trade policy by the government normally constitutes a structure through which all types of technological, product and financial bonds become affected.

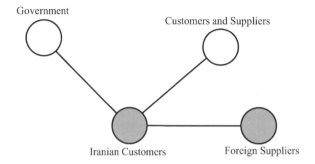

Figure 7.2: Illustration of business-political connections.

In three questions, the Iranian firms were to evaluate the actions of different types of actors. One question was to evaluate the government's trade policy, and the other two reflected the behavior of customers and competitors. The results showed that 93% of the firms selected the alternative "high importance" for the trade policy question. Forty-five percent selected this alternative when considering both customers and competitors, although between the two negative connections (to the government and competitors) the connection to the competitors was weaker. Trade policy has constructed a strong negative connection to the government. In another question that examined the degree of importance of the business and non-business actors, the aim was to compare the strength in the business and non-business connections. The score for the trade policy of the government was 81%, and for the business actors 19%. These values confirm the conclusion that the focal relationship is embedded in a highly negative connection. Figure 7.2 depicts a schematic view of the strength of connections to business and political actors. The political connection is four times stronger than the connection with the business actors. Naturally, the stronger a relationship is, whether negative or positive, the greater the investment made in the relationship will be. Thus, the major attention of the Iranian firms is towards political activities.

The above results expound the general evaluation. A deeper knowledge of the degrees and types of connections was necessary. In one question, the interviewees were asked to compare and evaluate the degree of importance for a large number of business and non-business actors. A very interesting result was that even the score for the foreign partners (19%) was much lower than the rate given to the government (39%). The score for competitors was 3%, which is less than the score given to the banks. Among the business actors, banks were more important in the exchange than any other business actors, but the government remained the major source of uncertainty. Thus, the relationship between the Iranian customers and foreign suppliers was confronted by: (1) a very high power dependency on the political actors. (The Iranian government uses its political legitimacy to control the content of the focal exchange.) Other factors affecting the relationship were: (2) a low degree of negative connections to the competitors; (3) compared with the competitors, a strong connection to intermediary organizations such as a branch organization; and (4) among the business actors, actors with financial resources which have a strong connection.

4.1. Business Connection

When studying each business connection specifically, the results showed that the suppliers of complementary products have the weakest connection to the focal actors. The suppliers' competitors gained a higher score (positive connection). But the critical problem is that the connections to both of the above two actors are not considered to have a high degree of importance. In the IMP2 study, for example, the connection to the complementary products had a higher degree of connection to the focal relationships. The more complex a product is, the higher the interdependence with complementary products will be. In a condition where the producers of complementary products are weakly connected to the focal relationship, the exchanged product has a simple nature. Furthermore, the customer firms do not have a complex technological production process. These results confirm the following conclusions in the above sections:

(1) The focal exchange products are of a simple nature.
(2) In cases where the purchased products are complex, the Iranian firms act in one of two ways. Either they purchase the products in project form, meaning that they do not necessarily hold the technological competency to develop or modify the products, or if they do not have a complex production process, they simply transfer the dependency to the connected actors. For example, dependency on the producers of complementary products would be transferred to the customers' customers. Iranian customers would simply purchase the products from the foreign firms and sell them to the customers without processing them.

The conclusion concerning the weak negative connection to the competitors denotes a weak competitive structure in the Iranian market. However, the financial actors have a higher level of importance than the other business actors. Iranian firms have a higher dependency on the financial actors than on any other business connection. When comparing the importance of the connected business actors, the two highest scores were given to the suppliers' competitors and to banks. However, compared with the non-business actors, the scores for these business actors were very low. Thus, the focal relationship is embedded in a business network context that contains: (1) a weak negative connection to the competitors in the Iranian market; (2) a weak positive connection to the suppliers' competitors; (3) a weak positive connection to the firms producing supplementary products; (4) strong dependency on sources such as banks; and (5) a strong positive connection to the customers. Beside these, as mentioned earlier, the focal relationship itself suffered from weakness in the exchange. This was based on the content of the exchange that did not contain the elements of technological and product development or cooperation.

These measures on the strength in the focal and connected relationships generated a critical conclusion about the nature of the business network context in this study. These relationships construct a business network structure in which actors are weakly bound to each other. That is to say, the Iranian market does not contain a structure through which market mechanisms, as defined in the developing countries, can function properly.

4.2. Political Embeddedness

Political embeddedness was explored by evaluating the connection to the government and bureaucrats. The content of the connection reflects the Iranian government's regulation on foreign trade and the bureaucrats who implement the decisions. In the trade policy, the two major areas examined in relation to non-business actors were the tariff and non-tariff trade policies. In the context of trade policy, the two factors of import and export tariffs were compared in several questions. In all the measures, the import tariff was evaluated as being very important for the Iranian firms' business. If the firms interacted with foreign customers, then the export tariff regulations gained a degree of importance. One may speculate that the low degree for the export regulations was because such regulations are of a supportive nature. Therefore, when examining the coercive actions, the value for the export tariff shows a lower score but, when studying the degree of supportiveness, the Iranian firms did not value the export tariff as an important factor in their businesses. Government subsidies were the supportive tie that had the highest degree of importance.

A comparison of the import and export tariffs generated the important conclusion that Iranian firms' customers are local (i.e. the Iranian firms are dependent on the local market and their foreign partners). This also shows the low degree of internationalization of the firms. This conclusion is verified by several questions measuring the interaction of the Iranian firms with firms in the foreign countries.

In the second area of trade policy, the study examined non-tariff regulations. Regulation of the product and the financial exchange created the bond of influence. The evaluation of these rules showed that the Iranian firms realized that the regulations for the "product standards" constituted the most coercive relationship. The degree of influence for "product standards" was evaluated at more than 80%. However, the bonds through which the government exercised its control over the product exchange had a weaker negative connection than that of the political rules, concerning the foreign financial transactions. It was realized that foreign financial transactions (in the non-tariff trade policy) had had the highest influence. The bonds in the foreign transactions covered, for example, credit restrictions and the exchange rate. The evaluation also leads to another conclusion: that the regulations on foreign financial transactions are different depending on the exchange types. The negative impact of a prior import deposit, for example, is evaluated to be three times less than credit control.

The measures also reveal the effort of the government to control all the areas in foreign financial transactions. The high dependency of the Iranian firms on the Iranian government constructs a weak focal relationship. More than 70% of the Iranian firms observed that the exchange rate was a factor that delimited the extent of the relationship between the Iranian and foreign firms. A comparison of the connections showed that the foreign financial transactions had a much higher degree of strength than the government subsidies.

Beside the government, the bureaucrats are the next group of non-business actors that implement the authorized political rules. The connected bonds between the Iranian firms and the bureaucrats contain an exchange. On the one side, the bureaucrats act to execute the political rules; on the other side, Iranian firms try to find standardized or specific solutions to manage the bureaucrats. The coercive actions of the bureaucrats are exercised in areas such as product documentation in customs, product testing, product evaluation, and classification. The Iranian firms realize that the relationship with the bureaucrats creates a negative impact on their relationships with the foreign suppliers. These bonds are stronger than the connections to market actors like competitors. In all of these areas, only 20% of the firms held the opinion that the interaction with the bureaucrats had not created critical problems. Otherwise, the majority observe the connection to contain a strong negative nature.

4.3. The Challenge

The discussion above shows how a high level of uncertainties that emerged from the connected actors. These uncertainties were transferred to the focal relationships and produced critical problems for the Iranian firms. Of necessity, the firms employed management tools to eliminate or reduce the impact, thus preventing inordinate expenditure in time and resources that the firms could otherwise have invested in the business relationships. In a case such as having a product import certified, the Iranian firms are obliged to collect more than 10 certifications from different bureaucratic organizations. The Iranian managers explained that merely to know how and where to collect such documents requires good political knowledge. Besides the knowledge competency, each certificate demands a great deal of time and work, and occupies a number of people. The other problem is that the rules are always changing. The political competency that is most appreciated, as discussed in other studies (see, for example, Boddewyn 1988; Hadjikhani 1996), is the ability to find specific solutions for each specific case. In order to reduce the uncertainty that emerges from the bureaucrats, the managers use indigenous solutions. These strategies are necessary as the degree of negative connectivity to the bureaucrats is stronger than the strength in the business connections. No matter whether it is of a negative or positive nature, the business connections have a lower impact on the focal exchange relationships.

The measures achieved for the supportive and coercive influences are outcomes from the management activities of the Iranian firms towards the political actors. Iranian managers undertook a number of actions to reduce the impact of coercive actions and increase the support obtained from the government. The management behavior comprises both influential and adaptive actions. When examining the exchange of information, some surprising results were reached. With reference to the earlier results, it was expected that the firms would not have made any effort to influence the government because of the latter's superior role in society. But, when simple management behavior was examined, the scores showed the firms' high degree of political activity. In questions concerning whether the firms had discussed the political issues with government agencies, more than 85% gave a positive answer.

When studying the expectation, the values for future development contained a higher degree of uncertainty. Analyzing the embeddedness provides tools for finding some explanation. The high dependency on the political actors and instability in the political rules naturally generates future uncertainty. This future mistrust affects the management of the political relationships. They imply that:

(1) The challenge has a time dimension. Instability in the political rules is a major source of uncertainty. When firms do not know the future development of the political rules, the solutions are to wait until the new uncertainty arises.
(2) The large variation in the types of coercive actions demands genuine solutions for each type of political action.

(3) Irrespective of the types of uncertainty in the future, one important factor is the stability in the relationships with the bureaucratic organizations. While political formalities reduce the power of the firms to influence political actors, the firms can exercise their influence on the bureaucratic organizations.

In further examining the interaction between the political and business actors, some questions specifically considered the extent of the influence. In one question, the aim was to examine whether the firms have succeeded in convincing the political actors to modify the regulations. The score for the alternatives "high" and "very high" was about 16%. Thus, the results revealed that the cooperation strategy has not been successful. The conclusion is that when the exchange has a simple content without the exercise of influence, the relationship has a positive and strong nature, but when the relationship is more specific and contains a dimension of high influence, it has a weak nature.

In such a condition, the study aimed to establish whether the firms could strengthen their relationships with other connected actors to reduce the uncertainty and strength in the negative connection with the government. The focus was also on examining the utility of the other connected actors. Among these actors, surprisingly, the branch industry had the highest influence. This verifies the conclusion that there is a strong general bond with a positive connection to the branch industry. Furthermore, the result indicates the high influence of the final customer on the government, when deciding on the content of the regulations.

Adaptation has also resulted in internal changes in the organization of the Iranian firms. The firms have been obliged to make comprehensive changes at all levels. Changes in the production process and the centralization of decisions are among those adaptive actions that the firms have instituted to reduce the uncertainty from the surrounding political environment.

Paradoxically, the management of the relationships with the bureaucrats has strengthened the position in the market of the Iranian firms and even of the foreign firms. Since the connection to the bureaucrats is very strong, the competency of the firms to manage the bureaucrats has limited the territory of the network context. The complexity of the bureaucratic rules and the competency to elaborate indigenous solutions obstructs the ability of competitors to break into the business. Lack of political knowledge hinders the penetration of new firms, and the network context becomes limited, although the advantage of a complex bureaucratic rule is that it strengthens the focal relationship. This is also true for the connection with the government. As will be discussed, Iranian firms use their political competency to delimit penetration of others into the market. The strong negative connections to the government have promoted the political competence of the Iranian firms. This has become an advantage that has constrained newcomers in the market.

Thus, the interesting finding is the high level of the managers' knowledge about the embedded actors, specifically the government. This conclusion is based on the answers to the alternative "I do not know" in all of the questions in the Iranian study. The comparison of the answers to the alternative "I do not know" in different chapters shows large differences. The scores given to this alternative are much lower in the questions examining embeddedness than in those examining relationship aspects. While the scores in the other questions hold values at between 3 and 10%, the scores on the question for embeddedness are below 3% and in most cases zero. The reliability could have been questioned if the interviews had not included others besides the general managers.

This produces a condition, as mentioned earlier, of a high degree of potential mobility because of the low degree of technological and product interdependency. This means that the competitors can easily enter or exit from the market. With such a presumption, the question then is why the negative connection to the competitors is so low. One explanation could have its source in the market uncertainty driven by the political actors. The conclusion is that the management of the connection to the government requires a high political competency. The absence of high local political competencies has become a factor that hinders competitors from entering the market. Beside this, the competitors have to find MNCs that are willing to accept the risk and operate in the Iranian market. Political and business relationships, together with knowledge about these actors, are specific competencies that create a barricade against potential competitors. The political and market competencies eventually generate a monopoly position for these firms in the Iranian market. The political competency of the firms is composed of two interconnected factors. One is political knowledge, and the other is the personal relationship with political actors, specifically with bureaucrats.

5. Summary

This research studies the relationships between Iranian firms and foreign MNCs. The study compares the results from some of the IMP2 studies with the Iranian study. The comparison, as has been discussed, does not involve the political connection because the IMP2 study did not contain questions about the relationships between business and non-business actors.

The study of relationship, adaptation, and social exchange revealed how the relationship bonds are structured. The content of the bonds exposed the degree of strength coupling the Iranian purchasers and foreign suppliers. For each type of relationship, several bonds were examined and compared with the results in the IMP2 study, in order to understand the similarities and dissimilarities in the behavior of firms from developing and industrialized societies. The focal actors in the Iranian study encountered a number of sociopolitical impacts, but succeeded in keeping their relationships alive.

The analysis of the relationship showed mutuality and balance in the relationships but was composed of a low level of interdependency. Despite the environmental turbulence, the exchange contains a high level of profitability, and partners have enjoyed stability. The weak ties in the technological exchange, high potential mobility, standardized type of exchanged products, and importance of the price factor, are some of the characteristics in the relationship. The study of IMP2, in contrast, espoused a structure with a lower level of mobility and more complex exchange relationships. The study of adaptation reinforced the belief in this study that the content of the exchange between the Iranians and MNCs has a simple and weak technological structure. The low range of product adaptation, together with insubstantial organizational adaptation, strengthened the findings concerning the weakness of the relationships.

A focal relationship, as has been discussed, is composed of business and social types of exchange relationships. Furthermore, each relationship type consists of several bonds. An important finding in this study is that these bonds can be divided into two groups. One considers the core bonds that reflect core exchanges such as technological adaptation, and the other group considers the bonds surrounding the core bonds. While the core bonds in the Iranian study were weak, the surrounding bonds had a stronger nature. Adaptation of core bonds requires a large investment aimed at a long-term relationship, but adaptation of the surrounding bonds is composed of lower demands. Similarly, in the Iranian case, some surrounding ties are strong, but the focal actors are not strongly interdependent on each other. In such a condition, the question of what keeps these customers and suppliers alive was difficult and remained unanswered. The analysis of the focal relationships and adaptation is not enough to provide the answers.

The purpose of the analysis of the social relationships was to gain a deeper understanding about the atmosphere. On the one hand, the results indicated a high potential mobility and low functional trust. On the other hand, the Iranian and foreign firms had a high social trust, low uncertainty, and low impact from the sociocultural differences. Strangely, and contrary to studies in international marketing that introduce criticality and problems related to the sociocultural differences among MNCs and firms from countries like Iran, this study arrives at completely opposite results. The examination of cultural differences shows a very low impact because of the differences in the country of origin of these firms. Considering functional or informal trust, the conclusion was that the Iranian firms had a high degree of uncertainty, not towards the MNCs, but because of the high uncertainty about the political embedded actors.

In studying embeddedness, the conclusion is simply that the connection to the government contains a very high degree of negative strength. The degree of impact varies depending on the type of political actions. Those coercive actions that had the highest impact considered the areas of foreign exchange, which directly affects the financial exchange between the Iranian and foreign firms. Government subsidies have created positive bonds, which have a positive influence on the interaction between the foreign suppliers and Iranian customers. But the positive value in the subsidies is much lower than the negative values displayed for the coercive actions of the government. An interesting outcome was also that the strength of the relationship between the government and Iranian firms was stronger than the relationship between the Iranian and foreign firms. Furthermore, competitors and producers of the supplementary products are, for example, two of the connected actors that, despite their importance in an industrial network, have, in the Iranian case, a low degree of strength. In a comparison of the negative connections (with government and competitors), the government's link to the focal relationship was much stronger than that of the competitors.

The analysis also covered the management actions of the Iranian firms towards the political actors. As far as the behavior contained simple actions, such as informing the political actors, the values have a high degree. When the questions measured the consequences of more influential activities of the firms, the answers gain lower values. In the context of management, the adaptation of the firms is introduced as a means of reducing the political uncertainty. Organizational adaptations encompass the three areas of:

(1) change in the tasks of the organization units;
(2) adaptation of the production process;
(3) centralization of the decisions.

These challenges are, of necessity, accommodated with a large political investment, which otherwise could have been used in the firms' industrial activities. However, such a condition embodies some advantages for both Iranian and foreign firms. The fundamental factor in the management of the negatively connected actors (comprising political and business actors) is the firms' political competence. Long market experience has generated a market and business knowledge that is interwoven with a well-established market relationship. These have consolidated a monopoly condition for the firms in the market.

Chapter 8

Results

Taking into account the results from the cases, the aim of this chapter is to present results and further develop the notions introduced in Chapter 2. When analyzing the findings, the study presents some provocative comparisons between the Iranian and IMP2 studies, which should highlight the connection to the non-business actors and stimulate new studies. The section begins with the problematic issue of relationship strength. The purpose is to present the problem with weak technological cooperation but containing a large quantity of product exchange. Linked to this, the second issue considers the setting of boundaries. This concept is presented as the fundamental aspect in studying business networks. The premise is that if a specific research is examined with two different boundary settings, the measures on the strength of a relationship will be completely different. Following this presentation, the outcomes from the empirical case that a business network context includes non-business actors will be introduced. This also leads on to another section which contains the interesting issue on purchasing behavior in two different industrial societies.

1. Relationship Strength and Weakness

As Donaldson & Toole (2000) state, the term relationship in industrial marketing can mean a variety of "things" depending on how it is applied. Some studies confer to the economic exchange and view relationship as resource exchange dependency (Wernerfelt 1995), while others concur with the transaction cost. Some research, like this study, adds layers such as social aspects in the relationship. Following the latter line, the theoretical frame presented in Chapter 2 was constructed to present a model on the relationship structure for studying relationship strength and weakness.

A critical issue in studying the weakness/strength structure, even for studies applying social constructions, is that each study envelops a specific combination of variables. Some, like Bradach & Eccles (1989), and Husted (1994), capture the components of trust and price, and combine the social and economic exchange to signify the strength in the relationship. Some authors, like Szymanski & Henard (2001), highlight the factors of expectation and performance, and Hallén *et al.* (1987) recognize the strength in factors such as adaptation, information process. Still others, like Donaldson & Toole (2000), construct a cooperate model on the action and belief components, although, the weakness/strength's structure identifies with the content of a dyadic relationship, and all but Bradach & Eccles (1989), and Husted (1994) stress technological and social criteria. Bradach & Eccles, and Husted (ibid.) stress, more than other researchers, the factors such as price and profit. These factors, which are disclosed as having a significant role in the relationship between the Iranian and foreign firms, will be explored later in this section.

The outcomes of long-/short-term relationships act as antecedents to the social and economic ties in relationships. Against the background of the preceding, the theoretical framework presented in Chapter 2 constructs the network view for studying the weakness/strength structure. The model regards the strength of the relationship as antecedent to the contents in the dyadic bonds and also to the connected relationships. Similar to those authors stressing the role of connection in MNCs-subsidiary relationships, this study recognizes not only the strength of the focal relationship constituted by the content of the dyadic exchange but also the role of the connected relationship on the strength of the focal relationship.

Following the construction above, several researchers identify factors to evaluate the strength that can be considered as synonymous to the length of relationships. A long-term relationship, elaborated by Ford *et al.* (1998), and Håkansson & Snehota (1989), involves strong technological and organizational cooperation and adaptation (Hallén *et al.* 1987). Furthermore, and very importantly, according to the researchers above (ibid.) a requirement for a long-term relationship is exchange complexity. One such criterion which has gained a low value in the Iranian case and a high value in the IMP2 study is product complexity. According to the researchers above, product complexity is the determinant factor that affects the relationship strength and degree of mobility. As discussed in the chapters on empirical study in the Iranian case, the technological and information exchange relationships contain low values. According to the earlier studies (ibid.), these empirical facts have to indicate a weak relationship. The facts manifest that the focal technological and relationship organizational cooperation contained low adaptation and information exchange. The prerequisite for a strong relationship, which purports to be a complex product exchange, is absent in the Iranian case. The exchange products, with some exceptions, have a standardized nature. In addition, as the values for the product delivery indicate, it seems that the Iranian firms have a low interdependency to their foreign partners. Following the rules for deciding the relationships' strength, the values given to these different exchange relationships in Iran construct a low interdependency and weak relationship.

The critical question is why these actors still have a cooperation and why their relationship is not so short-lived. Furthermore, it also seems that the partners are satisfied and have a very positive view of their future relationship, despite the fact that the technological and product exchange have obtained low values of strength. This means that there are other factors beside adaptation, technological cooperation, and information exchange that bind the actors together. The high values for the expectation in the exchange also indicate that the actors are bound very strongly and aim to continue cooperation. In addition, the measures on social atmosphere provide evidence showing mutuality and interdependency, implying a high level of trust in the relationship. Thus, the values in the Iranian case manifest two contradictory facts. While the product and technological cooperation contain a low strength in the bonds, other values provide evidence for strong bonds.

A clear fact is that the quantities measured, such as the amount of financial transaction, have bound the actors strongly to each other. The focal actors have a high mutual economic gain in the interactions. The price has such a level that profit gains in the past and in the future have strongly bound the actors to each other. Furthermore, the product exchange in the Iranian case has a large volume. In network theory, the substantial factor that binds the actors for a long-term relationship is technological cooperation and organizational adaptations (Ford *et al.* 1998; Håkansson & Snehota 1989). According to this view, the economic exchange, in terms of price and quantity, does not have the strength that can bind the actors for a long time period. If we only study the focal relationship, the results in the Iranian relationship with their foreign partners manifest contrary results. In the Iranian case, it seems that the factor binding the actors for a long time is constructed on values other than technological and cooperation. This follows the explanation of Bradach & Eccles (1989), Hadjikhani & Seyed-Mohammad (1997), and Husted (1994), that it is the economic exchange in the relationship which binds the actors. The financial and product volumes, together with economic gains, can tie the actors strongly for a long-term interaction.

Another important result in this study considers the impact of the connected relationships on the strength of the focal ties. Embeddedness injects the negative or positive strength of the connected relationships into the focal relationship. That is to say that the strength in a relationship is constructed not only on the content of the exchange in the focal relationship, but also on the content and influence of the connected relationships. Following the construction of Ford *et al.* (1998), and Håkansson & Snehota (1989), a focal relationship based on financial or product volume will constitute a network, which integrates competitors with strong negative connections, although competitors can easily offer lower prices and break the focal ties. A high degree of mobility indicates a weak focal relationship and strong negative connections to the competitors. However, the presumption in these studies is that a focal relationship constructed by financial exchange and low mutual adaptation, for example, cannot elaborate a long-term relationship. When the economic exchange is the basis of the transactions, the business network contains a strong negative business connection.

The view is built on the construction that the business rules dominate the network's function. The problematic issue in the Iranian study is that the competitors have a weak negative connection, and their impact on the focal relationship has a low value. Furthermore, as mentioned above, despite the fact that the focal technological and product bonds between the Iranian firms and their foreign partners are of a weak nature, the relationship has a high value of strength. We have a low level of mobility, on the one hand, and on the other hand a low level of mutuality and technological interdependency. The critical question is why such a condition can occur. Following the construction in Chapter 2, Table 8.1 illustrates the content of different bonds in the Iranian case.

However, the entire essential bonds in a relationship are not necessarily strong or weak. Some bonds can be strong, whereas others have weak contents. The significant aspect is the accumulation of weak compared to strong bonds, which determines the degree of strength. In the Iranian case, despite a low degree of interdependency in technological and organizational cooperation or adaptation, it seems that the other bonds strongly bound the actors together.

Table 8.1: Weak and strong interdependency.

Weak Ties in the Case	Strong Ties in the Case
Simple product exchange, low technological cooperation	High interdependency for the purchase. Large amount in the purchase. High profit
Few numbers of exchange	Low competition and low degree of mobility
Low technological and organizational adaptation	High social adaptation
Few actors engage	Small number of actors
Economic bases	Exchange combined with large social exchange
Low and simple information exchange	High profit in the past and large future expectation

The critical question is why the network contains such low mobility and low competition. It is difficult to explain the condition by the structure of the "business network." A market network including only business actors has difficulty in defining why, in a condition where the focal actors have high profit gains, the competitors are absent. A high degree of strength in the social bonds between the Iranian and their foreign partners cannot alone constitute a strong relationship. Another problematic issue in the Iranian case is that the social business relationship is highly regulated, despite the fact that the focal actors proclaim a high level of trust. The answer to the questions above does not have its foundation in the content of the exchange relationship; rather, it has its ground in the embedded actors. As the embedded business actors have a low influence while embedded non-business actors have a high influence, the problem lies in the behavior of the political actors or bureaucrats.

One significant aspect in the relationship analysis above is the absence of the connection to the non-business actors. While network studies explore non-business actors as a component of the invisible environment, the aim of this study has been to search and give an identity to the non-business actors, and to measure their influence on the strength of the focal relationship. Considering the values given to the political connection, a clear conclusion is that one main reason competitors have difficulty in penetrating the market is the high political uncertainty. From their experience in Iran, the foreign firms have gained political knowledge that prevents new competitors from penetrating into the Iranian market.

The general conclusion is that the influence from the political actors transfers to the focal relationship and affects its strength. The more specific conclusion concerns the impact on the range of commitment leading to the binding of resources. In other words, the higher the value of the negative connection, the lower will be the commitment that binds the actors for a long period. Technological development or organizational adaptations are among those bonds that bind actors for a long-term relationship, although, a high level of uncertainty in a connected actor possessing a high degree of power affects the nature and strength of the focal relationship. Bonds leading to long-term and high commitment are related to the strength of the negative connections. Where the focal relationship was considered in the case of industrialized countries, the number of competitors were larger, and the degree of mobility was higher. In the Iranian case, the major factor binding actors strongly is knowledge, which will be discussed in the later sections.

2. Boundary of the Industrial Network

Boundary is a perceptual parameter used to surround those issues important for studying a phenomenon. The perspective taken and the objective of the study restrict the setting of boundaries. The content within the boundary must include aspects that are essential for the study. The context beyond the boundary is considered unimportant and is recognized as insignificant to the purpose of the study. The critical question for every study, then, is whether the construction of the boundary is such that the conclusions and results have validity. An essential decision is what is outside and what is inside the context.

The mainstream of industrial network studies only encircles the business actors. The network boundaries delimit the others from the context and position them in the environment. The conceptual framework in Chapter 2 expanded this context to include non-business actors. One may speculate that the reason was exigent to the nature of a study that encompasses a situation highlighting high political impacts, but the theoretical claim of this study has been on the setting of boundaries in the industrial network model in general. The main consideration, as the results in the empirical study show, is the urgent need to include non-business actors in future studies. Boundary expansion can improve our understanding of the industrial network. The conceptual framework used in this study is applicable to different conditions no matter what the level of industrialization (see Hadjikhani & Ghauri 2000).

If the boundary setting in the Iranian case had been similar to that in the IMP2 study, the survey would only have contained questions on the behavior of the business actors. An interesting question then would have been what conclusions could have been drawn and what difference they would have had on the results in this study. The first obvious implication would be the absence of non-business actors and their impact on the Iranian and foreign firms. In such a study, the focal business actors and business connections (Chapters 2–5 and the section on business connection in Chapter 6) would dominate the explanation and analysis. A summary of the results of the impact of relationship and connections is illustrated in Figure 8.1.

As depicted, the importance of the focal relationship with the foreign supplier is only 19%. Contrary to this low value, the political connection to government and bureaucratic organizations has gained 44% impact, more than twice that of the focal relationship. Other non-business actors also have 13% impact (unions 8% and chamber of commerce 5%) on the focal relationship. As has been discussed, the impact of other actors in the value chain, for example, customers (5%) and other producers (3%), is very low. Further, the impact from competitors (3%) is also very low. The figure illustrates the content of the relationships' impacts. While the focal relationship contains a fairly low level of importance, the non-business actors, i.e. government, bureaucrats, unions and chamber of commerce, highly affect the industrial relationships of the focal firms. The focal actors have a weak technological relationship but are highly connected to non-business actors.

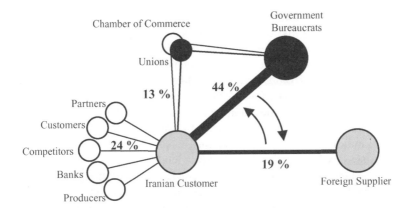

Figure 8.1: Business and non-business network.

Referring to the results illustrated in the Figure 8.1, conclusions such as the following could have been drawn: *The Iranian purchasers and foreign suppliers have weak technological and adaptation ties because of the simple exchange relationship. Consequently, the actors have a high mobility.*

So far so good, but the question is why the firms, despite a high market profit and several years of exchange relationships, still have weak product and technological ties. In searching for the answers, the study could only reflect on the settings of the business actors. The non-business actors that have influenced the construction of the industrial network would be excluded. The factor of political competence that, in reality, has strengthened the focal relationship would be obscured. Another possible conclusion could have been: *There is a difference between the socio-functional and social relationship; or the competitors' position in the market is weak because of the low uncertainty in the focal exchange relationships.*

Simultaneously, these conclusions raise questions such as why and how such a difference in the cultural aspect arises, and why the competitive market does not function properly. Studies that exclude non-business actors, as the IMP2 did, do not contain the substance to provide proper answers for such questions. The low level of competition, for example, is not because of the low business uncertainty. Rather, it is for the cause of political uncertainty and competitors' lack of political knowledge. In line with these results, the study could also have come to such a conclusion as: *The positive future expectation, mutuality, and balance in the exchange have generated a low uncertainty and high level of trust.*

Another example of an incorrect conclusion reflects the delivery frequency. Based on the results in the relationship's adaptation, which illustrates a low frequency and high volume of purchase in each delivery, the conclusion can be that: *The low frequency is because of high uncertainty in the "just-in-time" ability of the suppliers or suppliers' supplier in the delivery of products.*

The conclusion presents the uncertainty in the business interaction to define the behavior of the firms. It omits other sources like political connection. In the Iranian case, the negative connection with government has such a strength that the firms are not able to reduce the production costs by employing the rule of "just-in-time."

Unfortunately, these conclusions are not completely correct. It is true that the measures indicate a high level of social trust, but the Iranian firms want to formalize their business exchange. The degree of relationship formalization in the Iranian study was higher than in IMP2 study. The crucial reason for that is the uncertainty in the connection to the political actors. The political uncertainty transfers to the focal relationship, and the firms challenge it by the formalization of negotiations and details in the contract. This is also relevant for the analysis of the measures concerning the quantity and frequency of a purchase. Without questions on political actors, the analysis may have concluded that "a high uncertainty exists in the focal business relationships."

The discussion above was based on a presumption that the Iranian study had excluded the questions on non-business actors in the survey. It highlights the problems in setting the boundaries of the network. Excluding some actors from the context before any measures are undertaken may raise doubts about the conclusions. Figure 8.1 shows the extent of the relationships and the influence of different actors on the Iranian firms. The political actors' weight in these interactions is about 44%, and compared with each of the business relationships, this value is the highest. The figure exposes the significance of each business and non-business actor in the business network. It is true that in the Iranian case, the extent of uncertainty that non-business actors engender is extreme, but the ultimate goal of the research in this extreme case is to denote the limitations of the industrial network. In line with this track, several researchers have attempted to enlarge our knowledge on political actors. Some researchers, for example, proclaim the influence of business actors on non-business actors (see, for example, Boddewyn & Brewer 1994; Hadjikhani 2000; Hadjikhani & Ghauri 2000). In international marketing, a large number of studies connect the political aspects to the adaptation strategy (Makhija 1993; Miller 1992). Very closely connected to the inquiry of this study is research on lobbying and the influence of business actors and interest groups on political actors and vice versa (Andersen & Eliasson 1996; Potters 1992). There are a large number of studies on pressure groups (Becker 1961; Van Winden 1983), bargaining (Bolton 1991; Crawford 1982), and bribery (Rose Ackerman 1978), all of which are concerned with the subject of influence. This study eventually follows this track, with one exception. It includes not only the dyadic business political interaction but also other actors in the network.

No matter whether the firm influences or is influenced by political actors, the crucial finding is the interdependency among business and non-business actors. Perceptually, a context signifying only business actors leaves others in the environment. The environment beyond the context is a unit in which actors, as Snehota (1990) explained, are not or cannot be identified. This environment is characterized by certain attributes and properties. The actor-environment interaction concerns adaptation that has an internal focus. This one-sided internal focus sees the environment as having factors constraining the behavior of the business actors. Non-business actors, not by definition but for the cause of objects and operationalization, are viewed in the context of the environment. This view leaves no space for elaboration of influence. For example, the political activity of the firms as a marketing tool is not considered. In opposition to this view, political connections and knowledge, as the Iranian case illustrates, are the significant factors by which firms can reduce or eliminate the uncertainty generated by the negative connections. The politically bound specific relationships and knowledge affect the competitive market. On the one hand, political connection can constrain the business firms, and on the other hand, it can become a market advantage.

3. Purchasing Behavior

The analysis of the empirical study discloses the difference between purchasing firms in the developing and industrialized countries. The comparison of the Iranian study with the IMP2 study generates new insights. Long-term relationships are fundamental in industrial networks. In accordance with the rule of incrementality, actors develop their exchange relationships and bonds of mutuality, and the benefits strongly bind the suppliers and customers for a long time. In contrast to this principal, and contrary to the IMP2 study, the majority of the Iranian purchasers explained, for example, that they used their foreign suppliers as safeguards. If competitors appeared, they could change their foreign partners. This, together with several other findings, displayed a weak relationship between the firms. Low levels of technological cooperation and technological adaptation, a low degree of product novelty, and standardized product exchange between Iranian firms and their foreign partners have bound the actors weakly to each other. The consequence was a high level of potential mobility for both Iranian firms and their foreign partners, and, thus, the likelihood of short-term interactions.

A critical question in conducting part of this research was whether traditional marketing or relationship models could have offered a better analytical tool to understand the behavior of the Iranian purchasers. The 4P model (price, product, place, and position), for example, may have been better fitted for the analysis of the firms' behavior. The closest factor, the price, could have been used to explain the purchasing behavior of the Iranian firms, but further analysis of the answers in the survey revealed new facts. The utility of these models for a profound understanding of the firms' purchasing behavior was not high. The driving force in the 4P model, for example, is opportunism. The basic assumptions in these models are based on a highly competitive market, and that the firms can easily change from one partner to another. Furthermore, the presumption for these models is the unidirectional impact of the environment, and that the models do not account for a high impact from the political factor. In all these areas, the facts in the Iranian case disclose different results.

The aspects of length of the interaction and strength in the relationships were more highly valued in the IMP2. This was an outcome of a high level of technological cooperation, and a higher level of adaptation and specificity in the exchanges. Despite the fact that the Iranian purchasing firms have a more stable exchange with their foreign customers, their relationships have a weaker interdependency and high potential mobility. Under such a condition, the study needed a further explanation for questions such as why and how the Iranian firms remain bound to their foreign partners, why the relationships have not developed further, and the nature of the competitors' positions in the Iranian market.

In the analysis, the factors of interdependency and uncertainty are the two dominating concepts. The strength of the interdependency and level of uncertainty are part of the facts needed to understand the content of the relationships. Conceptually, the combination of these two notions generates four different conditions (see Figure 8.2). Cell 1 reflects a condition where the exchange has a simple nature, and actors are linked to each other with few relationship ties. Any change in the terms binding these ties can make the actors break the exchange. The potential mobility is very high, and factors such as price play a significant

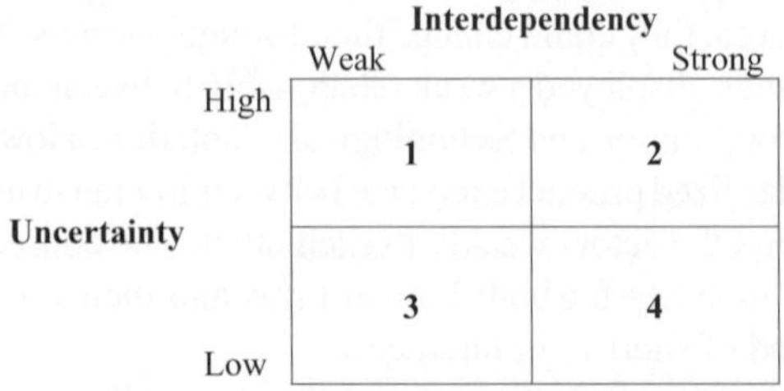

Figure 8.2: Degrees of interdependence and uncertainty in the relationship.

role in the survival of the exchange relationship. Cell 4, in contrast, displays a condition in which actors are bound to each other because of the complexity in the exchange. The industrial relationship for developing new products is an example of this combination. An exclusive technological relationship, high adaptation, and long-term interaction generate high mutuality and fitness. The competitors' power to break such a relationship is limited. Exchange complexity causing strength is not problematic in itself. Complexity is bothersome when an actor cannot select a viable course of action. It becomes a problem when it gives rise to ambiguity and uncertainty, making an actor unable to produce adequate action. This describes the condition in Cell 2. A group of purchasing firms in the IMP2 study have elaborated such a relationship, but there is an absence of such values in the focal relationship in the Iranian case. Cell 3 considers a condition such as the Iranian case. Because of a low technological adaptation, the relationship has a weak interdependency but also a low uncertainty. Adaptation and product exchanges are not unique and are of a standardized nature. Iranian purchasers and foreign suppliers have a similar power position and have preserved mutuality and a trustful relationship.

When the analysis refers to only one specific tie, such as technological exchange, it is not too difficult to position the tie in one of the cells in the matrix illustrated in Figure 8.2. The situation becomes different when a relationship contains a large number of different ties with a variety of strengths. Iranian firms, on the one hand, have technological and product ties that create a weak interdependency and, on the other hand, purchase a large quantity of products that bind the actors more strongly. For a large number of Iranian firms, the size of the exchange is more than two thirds of the suppliers' market share. Moreover, all the surrounding bonds, as discussed in Chapters 3 and 4, are strong, although the relationship contains both weak core ties (e.g. technological, product, and adaptation) and strong surrounding ties (such as delivery and amount of exchanged product, and social interaction). The study, therefore, verifies each conclusion by measuring several questions in the survey.

Since this study examines several exchange ties, positioning the relationship in just one cell is complicated. While the core ties can be placed in Cell 3, the surrounding ties fall into Cell 4. The degree of uncertainty is low mainly because the Iranian and foreign firms have adapted strong administrative routines to deal with the uncertainty. They have reached a stage where both firms gain mutual benefit. They have stability in the exchange and expect an optimistic future development.

The state of interdependency and uncertainty in the focal interaction between the Iranian purchasers and foreign suppliers can be verified by the results reached in the social interaction. A mutual feeling of interdependency and balance in the exchanges relies on a trustful relationship. These results show the atmosphere as it pertains to Cell 4. The high level of social trust signifies that the Iranian firms have a sound knowledge about their foreign partners' behavior. This is due to their relatively long experience in doing business with the same suppliers.

The issue becomes more problematic when the evaluation considers the social-business interactions. The need of Iranian purchasers for certainty has forced them to formalize the social-business interactions. This is completely different from the social-personnel interaction between the purchasers and foreign suppliers. The crucial question is why such a differentiated pattern has arisen. Positioning the social relationship in one of the cells in the matrix becomes difficult, as one social dimension displays a low uncertainty and another a high uncertainty. The above explanation is a simple illustration of the complexity in studying the firms' behavior in such countries.

As discussed, an interesting finding was the diversity in trust. In this case, the evidence is contradictory to the findings in other studies on two different dimensions. The first considers the impact of the cultural differences, and the next comprises the content of the trust. As mentioned in an earlier chapter, while a large number of researchers in the field of business culture have discussed the high complexity in social interaction between international firms and firms from countries like Iran, this study shows an opposite condition. Iranian firms have acknowledged a highly trustful relationship with their foreign partners. None of the variables examined showed a low value. The second finding was that the social relationship needed to be divided into two areas: pure personnel interaction and social-business interaction. The first comprises the social interaction, communication, and the feelings among the individuals coming from different firms. The second refers to the social relationships in formal business activities. The critical issue is that a study that measures the social relationship only in its general sense misses the point. These two dimensions represent different types of trust and have their foundations in different sources. The first relies purely on cultural factors, and the second is based on a combination of cultural, business, and political factors. They contain different degrees of uncertainty and require different types of management action. Further research into different types of social exchange and management is necessary to understand the behavior of the firms coming from countries with different sociocultural environments.

The complexity is aggravated when the analysis incorporates the embedded actors. This research studies the strength of both negative and positive connections. Surprisingly, the business embeddedness that is generally expected to construct a strong context in an industrial network had a weak structure in this study. In industrial network theory, a low degree of negative connection to the competitors, for example, could be explained as being rooted in a high interdependence among focal actors. In this condition (Cell 4), where firms are strongly bound, changing a partner generates costly new adaptations. This exposes a weak negative connection to the competitors. Against this principle in the industrial network, Iranian purchasers and foreign suppliers have a weak technological interdependency (as discussed before, their relationships fall into Cell 3). Apparently, this principle in the industrial network cannot explain the weakness in the connection to competitors. Strangely, this weakness in the connection is verified not only between the Iranian purchasers and their competitors but also between the foreign suppliers and their competitors in the Iranian market. The reason for such a structure could not be found in the industrial context. The weakness in business embeddedness was engendered by other sources. In the Iranian case, even positively connected business actors, such as the supplementary product producers, are evaluated as having a low degree of strength. Another possible speculation is that the market size is not large enough to attract new competitors. However, the size of the purchases shows that there are a few other local purchasers in the market. The low percentage of the impacts from competitors (3%) indicates that each competitor has captured a segment and does not threaten the other. They have to challenge the sources, creating a higher level of uncertainty.

In the cause of simplification, the context can be divided into three zone areas: business, intermediary, and political zones. The intermediary actors, in contrast to the business actors, constitute a stronger relationship (see Figure 8.3). These actors are bound to the purchasing firms and political actors. Their duty is to affiliate with political actors and strengthen the purchasing firms' relationship with the foreign suppliers. A comparison of one individual intermediary with one individual connected business reveals that the intermediary actors do not have a lower strength than the connected business actors. It seems that the role of the intermediary actors is to support the purchasing firms and reduce the uncertainty that emanates from the political actors, although the positive connections to the

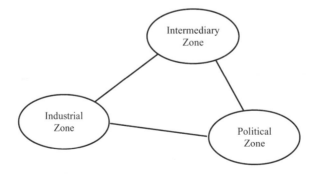

Figure 8.3: Business network conceived as interrelated zones.

intermediary actors place them between Cell 1 and Cell 3 in Figure 8.2. A crucial question is why intermediary actors have gained such a strong position. Perhaps it is because they are among the few organizations that have an influence on the political actors.

Contrary to the business connections, the connection to the political actors has a very high degree of uncertainty. This uncertainty has influenced the focal relationship and generated a low interdependency between the Iranian and foreign firms. The relationship between the Iranian political actors and business firms can be positioned in Cell 2, but we need to note that the Iranian business firms are highly "dependent" on the political actors. To challenge this political uncertainty, the Iranian firms applied adaptation and influence strategies. Adaptation implied changes in the whole organization structure and has been costly. Among influence activities, only the simple information exchange was effective. It seems that the political actors refuse to interact directly with the business actors. The political and ideological values are rigid and dominate the business constructions. Political actors conceive a close cooperation with the business actors as illegitimate and fear that it could divert government policy. One option for the Iranian firms was to reduce the uncertainty indirectly. The firms selected two management strategies. One was the exercise of influence via intermediary actors but this alternative has several shortcomings: (1) it is indirect and less efficient; (2) it is of a general nature, and specific support is absent; (3) the degree of influence is not very high. The other alternative is to influence bureaucrats. Contrary to the first alternative, this alternative is more specific and concrete but is burdensome, with higher costs for the organizations. It also demands indigenous or entrepreneurial actions, as the issues are specific each time.

Naturally, similar to the experience in industrialized countries, a small group of firms have exercised their influence on the political actors and gained specific support, but the majority of the purchasing firms are negatively bound to the political actors. The outcome of this connection is embeddedness in a context structure that is slightly different from what exists in an industrialized country. The industrial network of the Iranian purchasing firms is composed of a very high degree of connection to the political zone. The degree of strength in the industrial zone is low. It is true that the number of ties in the business context is larger, but the strength in each individual business tie, as mentioned earlier, is not much higher than the strength of the ties for the intermediary actors. The purchasing firms are acting in a network where the political zone has the strongest negative structure, and the industrial zone does not contain stronger relationships than those in the intermediary zone.

It also seems that the supportive actions of the political actors are not in balance with the needs of the purchasing firms. Comparison of the positive and negative behavior of the political actors reveals two facts: (1) that the positive actions are general and are perceived by the Iranian firms as inefficient for their real needs; and (2) that the strength in the coercive behavior is much higher than that in the supportive behavior.

Following the structures in the three zone areas, the problematic issue is to consider the influence of the firms' political activities on market activities. It seems that the firms have become political organizations, and management of the political zone has become their crucial and strategic market activity. Consequently, it is not so surprising that the focal dyadic relationship has not been developed.

4. Summary

Following the crucial areas in the theoretical framework presented in Chapter 2, the weakness/strength in the relationships revealed how, specifically in the Iranian case, the partners are related to each other. The interesting issue is that the firms have long-term relationships for the exchange of products and social interactions, but leave aside technological cooperation. Furthermore, the Iranian firms and their foreign partners have trustful relationships. As far as cultural differences are concerned, the psychic distance between the firms is low. But when social interaction considers the business rules, firms have built strong administrative routines. These routines, contrary to the firms in the IMP2, have an impact on the relationships. Moreover, despite the fact that economic transaction between the firms in the Iranian study is the predominant factor, the competitive market does not function properly. The results indicate that the impact from the political actors has such strength that Iranian firms, contrary to the firms in the IMP2, have not succeeded in constructing an effective organization. This conclusion is validated by facts like the low dependency on delays in the product delivery from the foreign suppliers.

Another result considers the boundary settings in the business network. The study of Iran discloses that:

(1) The business network context is composed of different kinds of actors. The context introduced here is composed of three different zones.
(2) Research methods need to be developed further, as non-business actors do not follow the same pattern of behavior and hold different values, and have another basis for their legitimacy.
(3) In studying business networks, the boundary needs to incorporate non-business actors since disconnection of non-business actors may yield unrealistic results.

The final section deals with the behavior of the purchasing firms in the cases. In this section, the strength of different ties and the consequences on the purchasing behavior of the firms has been the focus of attention. The comparison of the Iranian study with the IMP2 study generates new ideas. Long-term relationships are fundamental in industrial networks. In accordance with the rule of incrementality, mutuality and benefit strongly bind the suppliers and customers for a long time. In contrast to this principal, and contrary to the IMP2 study, the majority of the Iranian purchasers explained, for example, that they used their foreign suppliers as safeguards. The study of the behavior shows that the firms have both strong and weak ties. The strong ties are considered to be those exchange ties surrounding the core tie, which encompass adaptation and technological cooperation.

The complexity becomes aggravated when the embedded actors are incorporated into the analysis. Contrary to the study of IMP2, the Iranian firms encounter low competition and a high degree of impact from non-business actors. These conditions have encouraged Iranian firms to adapt themselves to the existing situation. They have incorporated specific market and political knowledge, and have strengthened their market position. This knowledge has lowered the degree of competition and increased the dependency of the foreign firms.

Chapter 9

Concluding Remarks

The study was initiated with the three presumptions of: (1) when doing business, specifically in countries like Iran, political actors exercise their political power on business firms; (2) the political actors are to promote business and preserve business stability, and business actors contribute industrial development and create employment, and that these two are interdependent on each other; (3) network theory is an appropriate analytical tool for studying business relationships. Following the first two presumptions, the theoretical framework in Chapter 2 was adapted, and non-business actors were incorporated into the model. Conclusions were drawn based on the incorporation into the model, and on the outcomes from the Iranian and IMP2 cases.

This chapter concludes the study and aims at pointing out some conceptual areas appropriate not only for Iran but also for other countries. It generates notions like horizontal and vertical connections, political competency and the political market which is aimed at generalization for different types of markets. The generation of a new notion leads on to another concept related to market structure. The large number of firms in the both the Iranian and IMP2 cases have made it possible to draw conclusions on certainties in the business networks. The notion of isolated networks is presented to highlight the situation where firms are obstructed. It is concluded that conditions of high political obstruction transform the business firms to political firms in order to gain business benefit. As the firms in the Iranian case are highly constrained by political and bureaucratic issues, the concept of enfeebled firms and markets is introduced. The essay shows how the resources are committed towards the supplementary and core business. Another conceptual notion under focus is the varieties in market structures for developing and developed countries. With the amplification of business activities in a society and accumulation of industrial consequences, conclusions are drawn on the varieties in the development and types of market structures. The notion is important because it expands the applicability of the business network to the larger society. It connects the development in one country to the construction of a business network structure in a different society.

1. Horizontal and Vertical Dimensions in the Network Context

This research is one of the few in business network studies that includes actors like non-business organizations in the horizontal dimension. The study on the business firms and the impact from the environment can disclose crucial facts on the network boundary. The extension of the boundary and inclusion of actors like government into the network context can increase our understanding. This study explores the view that network context can be divided into horizontal and vertical dimensions. While the vertical context includes business actors which have a value-added business exchange, the horizontal dimension has a non-exchange business relationship. Such a viewpoint will naturally affect the results and conclusions of a research study.

Traditional marketing theories recognize the actors in the horizontal context as environmental constraints (Porter 1986). Political systems are explicitly explained in industrial organization theory as determinants of the firms' success and failure (Egelhoff 1988; Jemison 1981; Porter 1986). The general paradigm is that these structures determine the firms' strategy and performance. As a reflection of this externality, many studies in international business concerned, for example, with the political environment/political environments refer to the hierarchical power of governments. Following this track, marketing mix studies containing economic theory (Norman 1977; Porter 1986) also concur on firms' adaptive and bypass strategies. In a similar vein, elements such as suppliers and customers are treated as environmental components.

The differentiation of actors in the network context into the horizontal and vertical groups is based on types of relationships. Easton (1993) signifies the vital role of the horizontal dimension and elaborates views to divide actors into business or non-business. The approach is grounded on the structural differences in the actors' motives, the nature of the exchanges, and the position of legitimacy. As far as actors in the vertical dimension are engaged in the chain of adding business value and supplementary distributive channels, the horizontal actors can, for example, stand in their regulative position. Contrary to vertical relationships, horizontal relationships are generally indirect and generate conflicts.

Research on industrial networks (Håkansson & Snehota 1995; Hipple 1988), relationship marketing (Bitner 1995; Sheth & Parvatyar 1993), triadic relationships (Hadjikhani & Sharma 1999; Havila 1996), and networks in the context of product and technology development (Håkansson 1987; Wynstra 1997) is limited among the very large number of studies that are pertinent to the knowledge on vertical relationships. Their major contributions reflect the impact of vertical connections. Despite the arguments for the changing role of marketing and need for theories construed by realities, there has been low interest among researchers to develop views that incorporate actors from a horizontal context. The business network in the Iranian case clearly illustrates how the connected actors in the horizontal axel affect the focal business relationships.

A response to this shortcoming was initiated by the study of Easton & Araujo (1992). Their assertion is that business actors also have relationships with non-business actors. An extension of the network context induces complications, as actors in these two dimensions are bound, for example, by different grounds of legitimacy or types of relationships. While, for example, competitors' behavior is constructed on business legitimacy, political actors have political legitimacy. They simply have different functional bases but are all, somehow, interdependent in a complex web of networks.

In relationship theory, the analysis of a relationship ordinarily relies on the behavior of two interdependent actors. In business network theory, the relationship between supplier and customer is embedded in a vertical context. The content of a relationship is an antecedent not only to the focal actors' activities but also to the acts of connected suppliers' supplier or customers' customer. A central theme in long-lasting interdependency is that one relationship has an impact on another relationship. Furthermore, this content is based not only on the partners' actions and sacrifices in the vertical context but also on the actions of actors in the horizontal context. Thus, a dyadic relationship is a part of the "network paradigm" which recognizes interdependency between several types of actors. As illustrated in Figure 9.1, our essential argument is that business networks are composed of vertically and horizontally connected relationships.

The focal relationship is thereby contingent on exchange with both business and non-business environments. The model developed presented in Figure 9.1 explains that a focal relationship can gain support or hindrance/positive or negative (also their strength and degree of impact) from these different sets of connected relationships. They can have positive or negative impacts on the firms. Thus, a network is a set of connected relationships which can support or hamper a focal relationship, depending on whether a dyadic relationship is affected by the connected relationships positively or negatively (Duck 1993). One connected relationship can support, while another can hinder, a dyadic. In this construction, there is reason to expect that the network provides the content of the relationship. Connections can have a business nature for the interdependency in the business and social interactions, and can also meld with relationships of a non-exchange character like political actors. As depicted in Figure 9.1, the content of a dyadic business relationship is determined by: (1) the composition of interactions between two dyadic business partners; (2) the impact of the vertically connected business actors; and also (3) the impact of the horizontally connected relationships. A

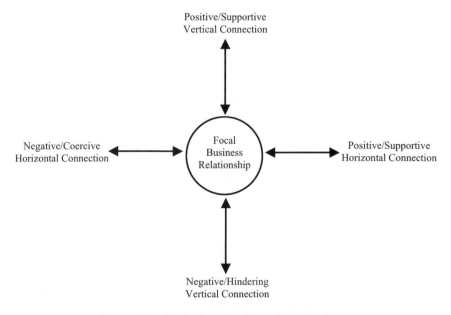

Figure 9.1: Vertical and horizontal connections.

dyadic business relationship is influenced by the support or impediment from the horizontally and vertically connected relationships. In the vertical connection, the main components are suppliers/customers, while in the horizontal context, the relationships are with actors like competitors and political units, because of their importance in the business market.

In studying the positive or negative and also the strength in the impact of, for example, political actors, researchers introduce the two variables of the adaptive and influential activities of the firms. The view is based on relationships due to the indirect interdependency between the political and business units. For the influential actions, strategies like lobbying (Calingaert 1993; Coen 1999), cooperation and partnership (Boddewyn & Brewer 1994), and commitment in social interactions with political actors (Hadjikhani & Ghauri 2001) are ways of gaining some degree of support for the core business. For the adaptive behavior, there are a large number of studies on strategic planning that pose the political factor as a non-controllable (Kotler 1999). In studies on risk management and risk calculation, risk categorization (Friedman & Kim 1988) is presented as a precautionary activity to rationalize business commitment. The political means as a structural constraint leads to the prediction that high impact from the political actors forces business firms to have a low business engagement in a country.

Thus, the political connection is a source of uncertainty which can mean a: (1) positive or negative; (2) strong or weak, impact on business (Hadjikhani 1996). Thus, technological cooperation requires: (1) political stability in the rules; and (2) influential or adaptive strategies interconnected with cooperation activities. Relationships governed by product exchange contain simple adaptive or simpler influential strategies.

The vertical connection is based on resource interdependencies. The connection's property, like low/high interdependencies, determines the nature of impact. Ultimately, the degree of adaptation and mutuality is decisive. The statement confers to the factor of actors' compatibility, i.e. whether the connected and focal actors have supplementary functions or not. Disharmony or conflict between focal and connected relationships generates uncertainty. Business connections to suppliers/customers, which are supposed to supplement the focal relationship, can, in some circumstances, become discordant with the focal relationship and engender conflict affecting commitment in the focal relationship. Problems with such uncertain connections can also germinate distrust. Continuity in the exchange with restrained connected relationships is constructed on a low level of interdependencies. Otherwise, the focal relationship is condemned to dissolution. Low interdependencies and lack of alternative choices will lead to long-term and simple transactions with the connected relationships.

Traditionally, industrial network theory perceives horizontal connections to actors like competitors as having a high negative impact on the focal relationship (Bengtsson & Kock 1999). While cooperative relationships with suppliers and customers are easy to grasp, the relationship with competitors, which lacks direct economic transaction, has been neglected. In advancing knowledge on the relationship with competitors, studies like those of Bengtsson & Kock (1999) and Gynawali & Madhavan (2001) explain the impact of competition on focal firms' relationships. Bengtsson & Kock (1999) and Easton & Araujo (1992), reflecting on the distance between competitors, include two elements of competition/conflict and cooperation/harmony constructed on trust. In the Iranian case, we could illustrate the degree of impact that competitors had on the business relationship. The very low degree of impact manifests two alternative conditions: (1) the lack of competitors and strong market position of the firms; and (2) the cooperative strategy of the competitive firms. Competitive relationships can thus contain elements of negative/positive, constructed on social exchange (conflict and distrust) alone, or together with cooperation and economic exchange relationships, although, a high negative impact of the actors in the horizontal context can have a high impact on the focal exchange relationship. As illustrated in the Iranian case, these actors restricted the cooperative behaviour of the focal actors. Such an impact will be further discussed in Section 4.

2. Political Competency

The network defined for this study is a set of actors — enterprises, competitors, suppliers, governments, unions, and branch industries — linked to one another in various exchange relationships. It seems that the Iranian firms are challenging on two strong fronts, the business and the political. For doing business, the utility of the intermediaries is on the political front. Such an assumption divides the context into two interwoven parts. Similar to other studies, the market activities of the firms can be divided into two distinct activity segments. Figure 8.1 in the earlier chapter, for example, illustrates the fact that there are a larger amount of activities directed at the non-business actors than at the business actors, although firms also devote resources to confronting the political field. Political activities construct a competency that is essential and distinguishable from business competency. At the same time, the political competency subsidizes the business activities. In the Iranian case, it is true that the coercive actions of the political actors have caused a high level of uncertainty, forcing the firms to make large commitments to challenge the burden, but the firms have also accumulated a high level of political knowledge, such as how, when, and where to adapt or influence.

Political competency can be defined as the commitment of resources and knowledge to deal with uncertainty from non-business actors. It includes:

(1) knowledge on positive and negative political decisions,
(2) knowledge on government and bureaucratic agencies,
(3) knowledge on decision and execution processes,
(4) utility of the existing political and business relationships, and consequently,
(5) political ability in terms of mobilizing the resources.

Political competency is attractive to enterprises for several reasons (Etzioni 1988). It creates winners and losers (Alt & Chrystal 1983) and can reduce organizational or marketing costs (Boddewyn 1993). Further, as will be discussed later in the Iranian case, it affects the competitive market. Political competency is a complement to business activities, and its ultimate goal is to strengthen the business relationships.

The notion of political competency has its origin in the recognition of a network arena for political activities. This is an arena where business actors are related to non-business actors in handling political agendas that impede or support the business activities. Firms' relationships with actors will produce reactions that can be grouped into influence and adaptation activities. The reasoning is based on the concept of the network and is similar to Boddewyn & Brewer's (1994) view of the political market, which explains that the political market functions in parallel to the business market. Managing this market recalls the ability in resource mobilization (i.e. political competency). Subdividing the market into two distinct but interrelated political and business markets opens new doors for studying a subject such as political competency. Hopefully, further research can exploit the phenomenon more deeply. Earlier studies, such as those by Boddewyn (1993), Hadjikhani & Sharma (1999), and Ring *et al.* (1990), uncovered political competence by pinpointing only strategically influential activities. In contrast, this study is concerned with both adaptation and influential activities as elements of political competency.

In the Iranian case, the influential activity generated a low degree of output from government, but a higher influence is imposed on bureaucrats and branch organizations. It is fallacious to conclude that because of a low influence, the firms have a low level of political competence. The Iranian firms' earlier experience with different types of adaptation developed their political ability. Since adaptive actions are costly, the selection of appropriate actions is sometimes decisive for the firm's existence in the market. Some enterprises follow the procedures and highly adapt the organization; others can maneuver and find simple bureaucratic adaptive or influential solutions. The latter delimits the negative impact, and the business actors can manage uncertainty with lower costs. Dissimilar to the case with the EU where enterprises lobby the political actors to influence the rules before political decisions are taken (Hadjikhani 2000), in an adaptation case like Iran the enterprises affect the content of the rules after decisions are made. The latter firms exercise their political activities on the bureaucrats.

Political competence is decisive in adaptation outcomes. In a case like Iran, where the political actors control the market activities, the firms have to resort to their ability to maneuver. Otherwise, a high level of control of political actors could force them to exit from the market. In markets with a high level of political uncertainty, the firms, for the sake of their existence, create a competency to avoid confrontation by different untraditional means. These strategies — here called ingenious strategies — are different types of marketing inventions that business actors undertake in order to cut across political barriers. The invention strategy is not a long-term strategy. It is employed until normal conditions return. There are many such strategies. They can mainly be pursued by interaction with intermediaries or political actors. Imagine a case in which an MNC aims to penetrate or expand in such a market. Missing interactions with a local politically competent firm will confront the firm with a condition in which the market uncertainty transfers directly to the MNC. Consequently, the MNC has to undertake all the adaptation costs or leave the market. Apparently, local partners absorb the local uncertainty and create a boundary around the MNCs. This explains why

MNCs always try to find competent partners in foreign countries. With their knowledge of local partners, as well as their networks, local firms have the ability to reduce the uncertainty before it reaches the MNCs.

Ingenious actions or entrepreneurial behavior is specific. In Chapter 6, when discussing the tariff and non-tariff political fields of actions, the study presented at least 12 areas where political actors exercise their power. Each area contains a large number of political issues. Each issue affects specific types of business relationships and requires specific political and business knowledge. Political competency lies in the ability of the firms to accumulate "political resources" and steer them into entrepreneurial actions. While the government in the Iranian case is exercising a high level of power, the firms act via connections with the intermediaries and bureaucrats. The personal interviews disclosed a high input in developing indigenous strategies towards intermediaries and, specifically, bureaucrats. It is because of these indigenous untraditional actions that the firms have survived. The indigenous behaviors reflect political competence, which is an essential component of the political market. No matter what the content of the indigenous strategy, the utility of political competence is to reduce the costs of the impact: the higher the firms' political competence, the more genuine and effective the solution. The connections to unions, the branch industry, and specifically to bureaucrats are strategic means for challenging the uncertainty.

Political competency reflects several complex aspects. Shaap & Twist (1997) stated: "Most network theorists agree that policy network is not easy to manage" (p. 62). There is agreement as to why the options for steering in such networks are limited. Under conditions where the political actors use coercive means to control the business actors, business networks become highly complex. There are five grounds for this complexity. First, there is an imbalance of power. Second, the exercise of authority requires complex bureaucratic procedures for business. Third, the interaction of actors has different grounds for legitimacy, and there are differences in their value systems (Brunsson 1986). Fourth, management of this network is completely dependent on the needs existing in the business context, and finally, firms have to manage two different but interrelated network contexts. These impede interacting firms from developing or integrating actors and resources to build a political competency.

A crucial area, which specifically considers the Iranian case, is the adaptation of the political values prevailing among political and other non-business actors. Political competency is the ability to understand these values and to have resources to undertake appropriate strategic actions. Generation of distinctive and entrepreneurial ideas to integrate business needs with political needs is a determining factor for the survival of the firms. Adapting political values into organizational behavior is a strategy to manifest the closeness to the legitimacy of the political actors. The closer the manifestation is to the political values, the more effective it is to gain support from the political actors.

This also describes the specificity in the political competency. A condition of high political uncertainty requires unique political competency from the firm, which in turn results in a reduced level of threats from possible competitors lacking this competency. Other aspects of complexity, as stated above, are the number of political rules and instability in the political position. Non-business actors in the political context do not hold long-term values or positions (Hadjikhani & Sharma 1999). In the Iranian case, the reasons for the high level of formal agreements or the purchase of large quantities of products rather than adopting a "just in time" approach is a consequence of such uncertainty.

Political competency, similar to business competency, affects the market position of the firms. As discussed in Chapter 7, one reason that Iranian firms have a low level of competition in the market lies in their unique political competence. Firms possess a competence that constrains others. The firms' business and political (institutional) knowledge (Boddewyn 1988; Hadjikhani 2000) and entrepreneurial ability in interaction with non-political actors generate a specific market position. The experiential knowledge of the firms, specifically with the political actors and bureaucrats, gives them a competitive advantage over competitors. An interesting outcome is that this competence also benefits the foreign firms interacting with these purchasers. Foreign suppliers interacting with local purchasers that possess such competence withhold a market advantage from competitive foreign firms in that market. This factor explains the behavior of MNCs in their entrance or expansion in such markets. MNCs' dependency on the local firms is not only because of their shortcomings in the business market, but also mainly because of the burden of political uncertainties and the political competency of the local firms. This keeps MNCs' lacking local partners out of the market. MNCs, for their penetration or expansion strategy, have to "buy themselves in" to the local network via local partners. No matter whether the mode of internationalization is through export or direct investment, interaction with local firms that possess high business and political competencies also constructs a competency for the international firms. In the Iranian case, the strategy of having weak technological relationships, high profitability, and simple product exchange reflects the mutuality in understanding the market uncertainty.

3. Enfeebled Business Market — Bazaar Behavior

Firms can be defined as units interacting with others to exchange resources and gain extra value for their missions. The nature of fundamental exchanges is business. Other exchanges complement the business interactions. Relationships of a troublesome or negative nature call for actions, like elimination, reduction or adaptation, to deal with the high level of uncertainty. In a condition with both high and long-term impacts, the adaptation cost can threaten the firms' business missions. Inasmuch as the nature of the impacts has a general coercive constraining all businesses, we have an enfeebled market.

An enfeebled market is a market condition in which firms divert their core business resources from the industrial activities towards complementary activities. Simply stated, resources that are to be invested in industrial relationships are degraded to upgrade supplementary relationships. Supplementary relationships consist of those, such as social and political, which are necessary for the core relationships. The core relationship is perceived as being composed of industrial and organizational components. Inasmuch as firms have an industrial nature, the resources are primarily to be addressed to the industrial and technological relationships. Technological cooperation, research and development, and organizational adaptations like stock holding, are some of the elements which constitute the content of the core relationships. A large amount of resources put into the supplementary relationships upgrades the supplementary activities at the cost of degrading the core relationships. In terms of relationship investment, industrial activities restrain, and supplementary activities inflate. In markets like Iran, the political connection affects the entire behavior of the firms. The negative impacts are antecedent for a large-scale political commitment. The political commitments are the adaptation investments made to fit the organization and production structure with political rules. Furthermore, the investments committed by firms build and keep the relationships with non-business actors. Other costs, such as bribery, transfer capital resources from the core to supplementary activities. In enfeebled markets, firms are interlocked into a strong contradictory zone of relationships. Firms are simply unable to effectively commit resources to business activities. Their business relationships, for example, incorporate non-business values to a degree that undermines the firms' industrial nature. The peculiarity in a business market like Iran is that the coercive actions of non-business organizations can enrich some of the firms' business activities and become supportive. These firms naturally support the rules and influence non-business organizations to preserve these actions. The distinctive characteristics of markets in which non-business actors have a predominant effect in the business relationships are presented below.

Characteristics of an Enfeebled Market
For Business Relationships
Low capital investment in the industrial relationships.
Weak technological development.

Weak technological and organizational adaptations.
High formality in the business relationships.
Long-term business relationships because of:

> Partners' interdependency due to the large size of the exchange
> Low psychic distance-high trust
> Low competition
> High profitability in the relationships

Low knowledge of and impact on other business actors
Low value added in the production
High level in capital return
High capital liquidity-low interdependency to the financial sources
High level of social interaction with local business firms.

For Non-Business Relationships
High level of corruption
A permanent and high dependency and impact from non-business organizations
Inefficient production and organizational structure
High technological and organizational adaptations toward non-business relationships
High political knowledge.

These characteristics separate the enfeebled markets from the markets in which firms base their activities on industrial attributes. Firms in the enfeebled market avoid large amounts of investment in technological cooperation or research and development, since these investments are built on a long-term return on investment. Instead, firms commit their resources to areas such as bribery in order to influence social relationships and the adaptation of production and delivery to handle the political rules. Efficiency in the business relationship and industrial organizational structure is undermined. Uncertainty from political decisions and bureaucratic procedures restrict long-term investment, and leave no space but for investments with rapid and short-term return. Long-term investment in the production facilities or the relationships' efficiency, like product delivery just in time, is contingent on a business relationship that contains non-business actors with a sound market policy. Limits to the firms' production activity and the low value added in the production process detract from the firms' industrial nature.

Research on firms acting in enfeebled markets like those of Iran, the Middle East, and Central and South America has not been given serious attention. Almost all business studies are concentrated on the behavior of the firms in developed countries. Transaction costs, and relationship or network theories are developed for studying the firms in developing countries. Some general studies on markets in developing countries do exist. But we rarely find studies at the level of the firm. Research that elaborates views on how firms behave in these markets is slim. There has been some research on the interaction of the foreign MNCs with the firms from developing countries. They shed light on aspects such as cultural differences, market risks, etc. and are devised to study the behavior of the MNCs with these firms, but this research neglected the local firms' point of view. However, the studies overlook the contingency elements that block the local firms.

The Iranian exercise shows the serious need for studies that observe the market from the point of view of the firms in developing countries. More research on the behavior of firms in these countries will increase our understanding about these markets. Such studies will also highlight the nature of the cooperation difficulties between MNCs and local firms from developing countries. Recent studies mainly pinpoint the interaction problem but include no deep consideration. It may be that psychic distance has a significant role in the construction of the enfeebled markets. But the case manifesting weak industrial relationships has been mainly antecedent to the general coercive actions from restraining non-business actors. The critical issue did not have a cultural nature.

There are several new studies that reflect on Central and Eastern European (as developing) countries and consider the area of transition. Transition defines the process of transformation from a position of total political constrains towards a democratic and understanding stage, where the business and non-business actors understand their economic and social gains. As the economy in these countries transforms, the researchers introduce concepts such as non-market to market bases demands (Åslund & Layard 1993; Golobeva 2001; Johanson 2001; McCarthy, Pfeffer & Shekshina 1996). The concept of duality in these market systems (Nuti 1996) is introduced to prescribe the process of transformation to a market system. The critical problem in the case of Iran and similar countries is that the markets do not undergo such a transformation process. Every market has an in-built smooth transformation process. Thus, changes in enfeebled markets are not drastic or easily measurable. Firms have been acting under such conditions for decades. Changes or improvements have been within the framework of one specific type of market structure. Improvements do not radically transform the market structure.

There is a large difference between business networks that have business relationships as their primary source of uncertainty and other types of business networks where firms are forced to prioritize the uncertainty from non-business relationships. The Iranian case study contains the basis on which to construct characteristics for firms acting in enfeebled markets. Figure 9.2 is a

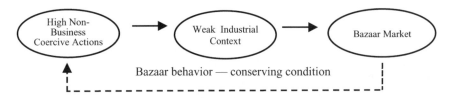

Figure 9.2: Compatibility of the political impact and bazaar market behavior.

simple illustration of the consequence of high coercive impact from non-business organizations.

Business firms are like intelligent organisms. They survive by adapting to a restraining power and use influential activities to gain specific benefits. In an enfeebled market, instead of long-term investment, firms divert long-term business towards short-term investment with a steady and rapid return on investment. This strategy achieves survival and short-term profit. But the consequence is a digression in the technological and industrial activities, which restrains the technological and social development in the country. However, as illustrated in Figure 9.2, we can simply find a business market composed of "bazaar firms." The market can also include frontier firms acting against the bazaar firms' behavior. The frontier group aims to have long-term technological relationships and may also see international orientation as a necessity for their growth. In one instance, the frontier firms challenge the market by building a business network with strong technological relationships with their counterparts. In the other instance, that of the bazaar market, firms have traditionally adapted themselves to the situation and act to preserve the coercive behavior of the non-business organizations. The profit gained with simple exchange relationships is dependent on the coercive behavior of non-business organizations. They commit political investment to influencing political decisions, to preserve their market positions.

Bazaar behavior brings about short-term high profitability in the interactions. The business rules binding these firms' relationships for a long term are, for example:

(1) incorporation of political values to maintain political legitimacy,
(2) strong social interactions,
(3) high delivery capability,
(4) high profitability and rapid capital return,
(5) high political commitment and knowledge, and exercising influence,
(6) other factors, like low competition.

The political interference of governments in business activities affects firms in both frontier and bazaar groups. In a bazaar market structure, resources are not bound for long-term technological development, organizational adaptations, or research and development projects. As elaborated in the earlier section, a large majority of the Iranian firms have developed political knowledge in order to maintain their short-term profit. The conservation of existing political rules preserves the firms' economic benefits. Political and market knowledge prevents the penetration of new players and weakens the frontier firms in the market. For the bazaar group, changes in the behavior of non-business actors can threaten profits and increase the risk for the penetration of new competitors. As far as the bazaar business structure dominates a business society, and the business interactions are constructed on the short-term profit basis, the supplementary relationships are upgraded. The frontier firms' strategic choices are to:

(1) exit from the market,
(2) follow the stream and behave like the bazaar group, and
(3) proceed in a market with high uncertainty and low profit

As long as frontier firms want to commit a high investment in the core industrial activities, they are subject to a high uncertainty. Contrary to the behavior of the bazaar group, the frontier group lobbies for the changes in the political rules. The discussion above about the bazaar group of business firms is not based on a depth of research. However, this is the dominating group of business firms in several developing countries, and future studies on the behavior of this group will increase our understanding about the market in developing countries.

4. Isolation of Networks

No business is an island, but sometimes a network can become an "island." In the Iranian case, a problematic issue was in the setting of boundaries. In an industrial network, with the concentration of activities and resources in a few specific actors, the network has a low density and becomes isolated. An isolated network has weak lines of exchange with its environment. The interaction is with a limited number of actors inside the context. Isolation is a perceptual map of the relationship density and is conceived as a structure coupling a few actors with each other. The more concentrated the density, the more isolated the business network becomes. This study defines isolation in terms of the density of the weak and strong ties. Elliot (1999), when defining isolation, deferred to the explanation offered by Bridges & Villemez (1986) and Granovetter (1985), and connected it to the strength of the ties.

The strength of the ties among the few actors prescribes the type of isolation. Strong ties constitute a strong isolated network and a loosely isolated network involves weak ties. Both types refer to a low density, constructing a limited boundary in the network context.

In a condition where a business network is constrained by some of the actors' coercive actions, regulations, or lack of resources, the relationships constitute a structure in which the numbers of the business actors become delimited. The actors conduct their activities in a limited market space. The business network context of the Iranian firms, for example, is constrained by the political actors. The political actions curtail the territory of the business activities. The firms' resources and activities are concentrated towards the political and a few specific business actors isolated from the Iranian purchasers' network. While the activities in the business context are delimited, the territory of the political context is extended.

Social science studies have shown considerable interest in the subject of the isolated network, among them, Bakkenes *et al.* (1999), on communication networks and isolation, Hill (1996), on sociocultural diversity and isolation, and Lubben (1988), who explored the domains of knowledge on social isolation. Rubenstein & Lubben (1994) developed ideas about well-being and social isolation, and a number of studies have presented evidence on the relationship between social interactions (contra social isolation) and health (House, Landis & Umberson 1988). Researchers in political science, with reference to social networks, present conceptual terms such as closedness in the network (Jordan 1990; Rhodes & March 1992). Closedness is defined as the social dimension that occurs when certain actors are excluded from the interaction, for example, because other actors fail to appropriate their contribution. Some authors have tried to explain such networks by explaining the relativity in the closeness (Hanf & Scharpf 1978). In the context of this study, the concept of closedness is similar to isolation, as both require interactions with few actors, and there are others outside the network that are relatively connected to the actors inside. However, isolation implies a consequence of actions by some actors and not because of, for example, a failure in contributions of certain actors outside the network. The isolation of prisoners, for example, is not the cause of differences in the motivation or values.

While the subject of social network isolation is widely explored in the social sciences, the implication of network isolation is left completely untouched in marketing studies. Industrial and business network studies are always occupied by views on market expansion and development in internationalization. It seems that the phenomenon of isolation does not exist in the market. Further research into industrial network isolation, its advantages and disadvantages, may provide new tools in understanding different network structures.

A secret industrial research project is an example of an isolated network. The members of the network interact only with a small, identified group working together towards a specific mission. Such a highly isolated network is less organic, as the interaction is only with a limited group, but members are more diversified as they all have specific roles. In contrast, in a case like the Iranian study, an isolated network contains two interwoven structures with two completely different sets of goals. They draw the structure and the boundary in different directions.

Weak competition and diffusion are examples of parameters that lie within the interest of studies in isolation (Hill 1996). Apparently, the greater the interdependency between a large number of business actors, such as customers, suppliers, and competitors, the lower the isolation and the higher the diffusion of market knowledge and technology. Isolation with a consensus among actors, in contrast, is the concentration of resources towards a specific goal, but an isolated business network with loosely interrelated members loses its fundamental utility specifically, when its context contains two different structures functioning against each other. In the case of this study, the business context is limited because the purchasing firms only interact with a few business actors. The problematic issue in this study is that the members are not tightly coupled to each other but are strongly related to the regulative behavior of the non-business actors. The values gained in the business interdependencies indicated weakly coupled actors inside the context of an isolated network, or at least, there is a weakness in the industrial context. Isolated networks with loose structures have shortcomings in their ability to develop new products or modify processes. Interactions are few and limited, despite the fact that mutuality and trust can be preserved.

5. Isolation — Internationalization

An industrial network context can be divided into geographical areas, both global and national (Mazet, Spencer & Bocconi 1990). The utility of this spatial perspective is that a researcher can make a distinction between local and international contexts. In industrialized countries, the new marketing process among international companies is through globalization of the firms. The market strategy of these firms is to enlarge the context of the network internationally. Their aim is to capture new foreign markets and spread their networks widely in different countries. The networks are expanded in both local and international dimensions. The results in the Iranian case are completely contrary to this experience. The purchasing firms, beside their foreign partners, have almost no relationship with other foreign firms. These Iranian firms, which belong to some of the largest firms in Iran, have shortcomings in both input and output when considering their interaction with foreign international firms. Internationally, the Iranian firms are isolated. They have no interaction with the suppliers' suppliers, financial sources, or any other foreign business actor. Their products are not exported. Their market activities are aimed towards local customers. The only line relating the firms to the international market is the relationship with the suppliers. In a few cases, there is evidence that the Iranian purchasers, via foreign suppliers, are connected to those who finance projects. While globalization of the firms in industrialized countries is increasing, and their network boundary is expanding, the Iranian firms are addressing the local market. Their networks are isolated and restricted locally. Isolation from the global market inevitably restricts the firms' development and growth.

Another crucial question is how the firms are coupled locally. Based on the evidence in the study, it seems that the Iranian firms are also isolated locally. They have a low level of competition and significant exchange relationships with only a few business firms. This has delimited the network boundary. The firms enjoy interactions with few actors and low competition, and have a low degree of interdependency with the local producers. Evidently, the firms are tied into an isolated and loose local network structure. This, as mentioned above, affects the factor of diffusion of knowledge and technology (Hill 1996). The weaker the ties binding actors in an isolated network, the lower will be the diffusion of the core issues to other network relationships. A weak interdependency in an isolated network leads to lower productivity and innovation. In such a condition, as far as the relationships are not restricted by high competition, the firms can control the market mechanisms. This engenders a self or ego development that can assume two different directions. The first concentrates on short-term interactions and is satisfied with existing conditions for reasons such as a high uncertainty and unpredictability in the future. In the case of Iran, firms are constrained by a high level of uncertainty, and therefore they restrict their market activities towards simple business exchange relationships. Another reason is that behavior is contaminated by cultural factors, meaning that cultural values are the underlying factor for short-term exchange. The strategy of these firms is to gain economic prosperity with simple and short-term business activities. They avoid complex business activities that require long-term investment.

The second direction is that the firms devote resources to developing new ideas or products for their own specific purposes. This signifies the ego development and firms aim to benefit from the outcomes alone. Firms build a very strong boundary, and internal structure and cooperation with external units reflect simple output or input transactions. The Iranian study has an absence of evidence to reject or confirm this development.

The criticality in a loosely isolated network is aggravated if negative connections block the network not only internationally, but also locally. It could also be the case that the loosely isolated structure itself is an outcome of the negative connections. The first condition addresses cultural values. The second condition is engendered by political factors. In this study, the evidence showed that the political connection is the fundamental factor. No matter what the reason is, political actors block the industrial context in the Iranian cases. The political actors, with their legitimate power, generate such a degree of uncertainty that isolation becomes necessary for the survival of the firms. Developing strong relationships becomes problematic because of future uncertainty about the political system. Firms' international business degrades, and local weak business upgrades.

There is a long-standing research tradition in the social and political sciences on the behavior of actors in isolated networks (see, for example, Heath *et al.* 1999; House, Landis & Umberson 1988; Jordan 1990; Rubenstein & Lubben 1994; Swerdlow 1998), but the issue is disregarded in the research on marketing and industrial networks. Research topics, such as why firms are sometimes trapped in a loosely isolated network, can enhance understanding of the firms' behavior and their delimitation in internationalization. It can add new insights to market strategies and their appropriateness in different types of networks. Furthermore, since the diffusion of technology in such a network is delimited, such studies can be related to macro-economic development theories.

6. Market Structures

In concluding this book, the final question is how the results reached in the two cases of the Iranian and IMP2 can be further developed and generalized. The cases covered the behavior of 60 large firms (in each case). They represent two different markets with two extremely different international business environments. The size and amount of firms included in the study represent such a strength that the opportunity is increased to generate conclusions on divergence in market structures for developed and developing countries. The Iranian case is a typical example of the developing countries, and the IMP2 represents a case for developed countries. The firms' major missions (profit and growth) and problems in these different industrial societies are directed towards different structures. Whereas firms in developing countries give priority to the political uncertainty, firms in the developed countries orient the major activities toward business uncertainty. The former commit a large investment to adapt production and administrative routines dictated by political actors, whereas the latter allocate the resources to their cooperation with customers, suppliers and other related firms in the business market. The basis for the difference lies in the fact that non-business actors in developing countries like Iran use their hierarchical power to control the industrial activities. The differences in the major efforts and tasks will consequently create different market structures in developed and developing countries.

As proclaimed earlier, the business market in Iran, similar to many other developing countries, has an isolated business market structure. In contrast, the findings in the IMP2 illustrate a market in industrialized societies which is constructed on an "open" industrial network structure. However, in different market places, for such reasons as the strong impacts from non-business actors or even the willingness of business actors, different market structures appear. The conclusion is that the formation/deformation of a business structure and the utility of analytical concepts to understand these markets are completely contingent on the degree of the values in the elements that firms prioritize and to which they commit their resources. Firms' business capital and knowledge resources are limited. Resources are committed to those elements relating to higher uncertainty. Generally, there are four elements to which firms in every market place commit their resources and direct their activities. The values that firms in different societies give to these elements vary, since they generate different degrees of uncertainties. These elements are:

(1) technological
(2) economical
(3) social
(4) political

Figure 9.3 provides a simple illustration of different market structures. It is the values in the elements (mentioned above) that construct different network structures. These values are gained by the degree of impacts made by these elements on the firms' business activities. The concept of an isolated market

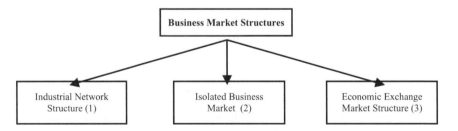

Figure 9.3: Different business structures.

structure that relies on a delimited boundary setting is relevant for societies like Iran, the Middle East countries, and China, which have permanent impacts from non-business actors. In these markets, the power of non-business actors obstructs the natural development of business networks in the country. Firms lack technological cooperation and cannot take advantage of the benefits of expansion and globalization. The term "isolated structures" is even used for the analysis of an industrial group acting towards a specific mission, i.e. project marketing and organizations. These groups act on a "temporary" basis and do not represent the structure of a whole society. The industrial activities of such groups can be confined by the rules of the business network. The political group interference is limited and is generally delimited in the context. These structures are not countrywide.

We assume that firm A, like many other firms in a country, acts in condition 1. The determinant elements for firm A are the industrial and social ones, i.e. strong and long-term technological cooperation combined with long-term and mutual benefit for all engaged. In such a country, the impacts on firm A mainly originate from the relationships with other interdependent business firms. Some firms have strong, and others weak social and industrial relationships. Firm A has low/high adaptations and social interactions to its counter and connected parts. The mission is to develop the relationships, expand the network context, and also gain long-term profit. The firm's context contains a number of negatively/positively connected actors competing with firm A or with its counterparts. For firm A, it is the role of business that dominates the business activities. With adaptive rules like "just in time," firm A saves its capital to invest in technological and marketing areas. Non-business actors stand on the horizon of A's network. The network structure is governed by the principle of industrial relationships, and the political element has a low degree of impact, although, a simple conclusion is that each of the business networks has an in-built ability to promote industrial development in the country. If we now aggregate the business networks in a country and relate them, we will have the business network structure at the country level. The aggregation of the industrial activities of the firms in these networks forms the basis for the industrial development in the country.

The analytical model above used to define the market structure is the business network. Such a condition fits well with the case like IMP2, to which industrial network theory can easily be applied. Contrary to this, the other extreme case is the exchange theory. In such a presumptive society that applies macroeconomic principles for business activities, we find high values in the economic element. Factors such as price, short-term profit, economic exchange, and weak industrial relationships form the foundation of the market principles. This can lead to the hypothesis that the behavior of firms in an isolated market like Iran could have been better understood with conceptual terms borrowed from other theories than the industrial network. Microeconomic theory does not treat and value technological cooperation relationships. This is similar to the Iranian case. In the microeconomic theory, the free enterprise perspective assumes that the market profit balances the market construction. Competition and free entrance carry considerable weight in this market. The Iranian market holds an opposite condition, since the competitors have a low impact in the firms' market operation. In this theory, individual firms or customers have a limited influence on market price. Competition in the market functions to set the market price. In countries like Iran, the firms' competition is not on the business rules or price; rather, it is on the management of political relationships. The presumption in the exchange theory is the availability of market information for all the firms. This is contrary to the experience gained in the Iranian case. One conclusion was that competitors were excluded from the market because of their foible political-market knowledge. The theoretical construction in both business network and macroeconomic theory is grounded on the presumption that the political environment does not interfere in the market space and that the laissez-faire condition prevails. In microeconomic theory, the political actions are limited only to create market equilibrium. In the business network theory, the assumption is not that political actors are to have an affect on the nature of the business activities. In countries like Iran, the condition is completely different as governments control financial and production activities. In macro-economic theory, each business is as an isolated unit. There are no bonds between the firms. The isolated network also holds the view of the separation of firms but with the presumption of a different structure. Separation considers groups of firms, and within each group, firms are interdependent on each other and cannot act in isolation from each other.

When reviewing earlier studies in Chapter 1, two tracks in the research on market and business firms' activities were introduced. The explanation above for firm A is in line with the track on business networks, which implies market activities as the interdependent behavior of industrial firms. But in our Iranian case and in markets in other developing countries, the non-business actors permanently dominate business relationships. The discussions above highlight the fact that firms in these countries have relationships with other firms. However, because of the high power of political actors and the low degree of negative connections to competitors and also weak industrial interactions, the firms remain in an isolated context containing few business actors. Firms are related and bound to specific and limited relationships. The structure has such characteristics that it does not fit with either the macroeconomic or industrial network structure prevailing in developed countries. Isolated network structures stand somewhere in between the exchange market structure and business network structure. Isolated network structures contain strong/weak elements from both structures. On the one hand,

214 Non-Business Actors in a Business Network

the isolated networks have long-term relationships but a weak technological development. On the other hand, the element of price and profit, which is one of the bases in the economic exchange structure, is strong. The conclusion is that the structure envelops firms with long-term relationships constructed on profit and social interactions. This network is delimited to a few business actors that are strongly affected by the political system, which blocks them in an isolated structure. Isolated firms, by definition, are acting in a market composed of strong/weak elements in both exchange, microeconomic, and industrial network perspectives.

In cases where isolated behavior is mainly composed of a strong industrial relationship and weak political element, the firms are acting in an industrial network. There are a large number of secret industrial projects where the actors have a secret mission and are isolated from others in the society. These structures are temporary and constructed on strong industrial relationships, acting towards specific industrial missions. Contrary to this condition, in the cases like Iran and other developing countries, firms are blocked into permanent structures.

Yet, different combinations of the values in the elements (above) can provide different structures. Each condition requires a specific type of analytical concept. Depending upon the strength in the values of these elements, the presumptive structure can hold microeconomic or business network principles. The Iranian and IMP2 cases, for example, construct two different structures. One constructs an industrial network that ultimately creates new business opportunities in the society. The other isolated structure cannot provide new business opportunities and growth to the society because of the firms' industrial isolation. The uncertainty of a long-term investment commitment has forced the firms to adopt another strategy. Firms follow the rule of business networks to keep the relationship alive but with limited numbers. Firms choose simple relationships with a low level of investment. The isolated structure only applies to the strength in the technological development cooperation. Isolated firms have social interactions with a large number of firms in their surrounding environment. But from the technological cooperation point of view, small isolated networks form the business society. Each one derives a business requiring simple technological input. The competition market does not function properly. Firms gain benefits but do not contribute industrial development to their surrounding environments. The capital turnover is high, and resources are not invested in the long-term pay-off industrial activities. Investment in technological research and development is obsolete, as firms do not trust the stability in the political rules. Furthermore, why do firms need to commit large capital resources for long-term industrial gains when the profit gained in simple transactions is high enough? In countries similar to Iran, the business networks' mission is mainly political and does not contribute industrial resources to the economic development of the larger society.

Before closing the book, we need to mention the differences between the isolated structures and the business structures which are completely controlled by governments. The crucial issue is that the isolated structures in societies like Iran and the Middle East countries are not similar to those of the totalitarian systems. In a totalitarian system, the business activities are planned by the political system, and the business firms cannot act as autonomous units. The firms act as political units functioning under hierarchical political decisions. Each firm is like an isolated node related to political system and a few businesses with political power. Instead of an isolated business network, we have isolated firms. The business rules are replaced by planned political decisions, and production units follow procedures for quantity and quality. Business firms, like firms in the isolated structure, are dominated by the political system, but they are more anonymous. Competition is absent not because of market uncertainty but because of political prohibition. While the driving force for the firms in the isolated network is profit, the firms in totalitarian systems have no economic gains. Firms' business knowledge cannot be used for gain and to keep competitors out of the market.

References

Achrol, R. S., Reve, T., & Stern, L. W. (1983). The environment of marketing channel dyads: A framework for comparative analysis. *Journal of Marketing, 47,* 55–67.

Albaum, G., Strandskov, J., Dueer, E., & Down, L. (1989). *International marketing and export management.* Wokingham, UK: Addison-Wesley.

Alt, J. E., & Chrystal, K. A. (1983). *Political economics.* Berkeley: University of California Press.

Andersen, S., & Eliasson, K. A. (1996). *The European Union: How democratic is it?* London: Sage.

Anderson, E., & Weitz, B. (1992). The use of pledge to build and sustain commitment in distribution channels. *Journal of Marketing Research, XXIX,* 18–34.

Anderson, J. C., & Narus, J. A. (1990). A model of distributor firm and manufacturer firm working partnerships. *Journal of Marketing, 42*(1), 71–79.

Andersson, P. (1992). Analysing distribution channel dynamics: Loose and tight coupling in distribution networks. *European Journal of Marketing, 26*(2), 47–68.

Ansoff, H. I. (1979). *Strategic management.* London: Macmillan.

Arrow, K. (1974). *The limits of organization.* New York: W. W. Norton.

Åslund, A., & Layard, R. (Ed.) (1993). *Changing the economic system in Russia.* London: Pinter.

Austen-Smith, D. (1987). Interest groups, campaign contributions, and probabilistic voting. *Public Choices, 54,* 123–139.

Axelsson, B., & Easton, G. (Eds) (1992). *Industrial networks: A new view of reality.* London: Routledge.

Bagozzi, R. (1975). Marketing as exchange. *Journal of Marketing, 39,* 32–39.

Bakkenes, I., de Brabander, C., & Imants, J. (1999). Teacher isolation and communication network analysis in primary schools. *Educational Administration Quarterly, 35*(2), 166–202.

Ballam, D. A. (1994). The evolution of the government–business relationship in the United States: Colonial times to present. *American Business Law Journal, 31*(4), 553–640.

Becker, H. S. (1961). Notes on the commitment. *The American Journal of Sociology, 66,* 32–40.

Bengtsson, M., & Kock, S. (1999). Cooperation and competition in relationships between competitors in business networks. *Journal of Business and Industrial Marketing, 14*(3), 178–193.

Bitner, M. J. (1995). Building service relationships: It's all about promises. *Journal of Academy of Marketing Science, 23*(4), 246–251.

Blance, S. (1980). *Assessing the political environment: An emerging function in international companies*. New York: Conference Board.

Blankenburg Holm, D. (1996). *Business network connections and international business relationships*. Doctoral thesis No. 65, Uppsala University.

Blankenburg Holm, D., Eriksson, K., & Johanson, J. (1997). Business networks and cooperation in international business-relationship. *Journal of International Business Studies, 27*(5), 1033–1053.

Blau, P. M. (1964). *Exchange and power in social life*. New York: Wiley.

Boddewyn, J. J. (1988). Political aspects of MNE theory. *Journal of International Business Studies, XIX*(3), 341–362.

Boddewyn, J. J. (1993). Political resources and markets in international business: Beyond Porter's generic strategies. In: A. Verbeke (Ed.), *Global competition: Beyond three generics* (Vol. 4, pp. 83–89). Greenwich, CT: JAI Press.

Boddewyn, J. J., & Brewer, T. L. (1994). International-business political be-haviour: New theoretical directions. *Academy of Management Review, XIX*(1), 119–143.

Bolton, G. A. (1991). A comparative model of bargaining: Theory and evidence. *American Economic Review, 81*, 1096–1136.

Booth, S. (1993). *Crises management strategies*. London: Routledge.

Bradach, J. L., & Eccles, R. G. (1989). Price authority and trust: From ideal types to plural forms. *Annual Review of Sociology, 15*, 97–115.

Bradley, D. (1977). Managing against expropriation. *Harvard Business Review, July–August*, 75–83.

Bridges, W. P., & Willemez, W. J. (1986). Informal hiring and income in the labour market. *American Sociological Review, 51*, 574–582.

Brunsson, N. (1986). Industrial policy as implementation or legitimation. In: R. Wolf (Ed.), *Organizing industrial development* (pp. 137–156). Berlin: De Gruyter.

Burns, T. R., & Stalker, G. M. (1961). *The management of innovation*. London: Tavistock.

Calingaert, M. (1993). Government business relations in the European Community. *California Management Review, 35*(2), 118–133.

Campa, J. M. (1994). Multinational investment under uncertainty in the chemical processing industries. *Journal of International Business Studies, 25*(3), 557–578.

Cateora, P. R. (1996). *International marketing* (9th ed.). Chicago: Irwin.

Caves, R. (1982). *Multinational enterprise and economic analysis*. Cambridge: Cambridge University Press.

Coen, D. (1999). The impact of U.S. lobbying practice on the European business–government relationship. *California Management Review, 41*(4), 27–44.

Cook, K. S., & Emerson, R. M. (1984). Exchange networks and the analysis of complex organizations. *Research in the sociology of organizations* (Vol. 3, pp. 1–30). Greenwich, CT: JAI Press.

Crawford, V. (1982). A theory of disagreement in bargaining. *Econometrica, 50*, 607–637.

Dasgupta, P. (1988). Trust as a commodity. In: D. Gambetta, (Ed.), *Trust making and breaking cooperative relationships* (pp. 49–72). New York: Basil Blackwell.

Demsetz, H. (1992). *The emerging theory of the firm*. Uppsala: Acta Universitatis Upsaliensis.

DiMaggio, P. J. (1988). Interest and agency in institutional theory. In: L. G. Zucker (Ed.), *Institutional patterns and organizations: Culture and environment* (pp. 3–21). Chicago: University of Chicago Press.

DiMaggio, P. J., & Powell, W. W. (1983). The iron cage revisited: Institutional isomorphism and collective rationality in organizational fields. *American Sociological Review, 48*(2), 147–160.

Donaldson, B., & Toole, T. O. (2000). Classifying relationship structure: Relationship strength in industrial markets. *Journal of Business & Industrial Marketing, 15*(7), 491–506.

Dore, R. (1983). Goodwill and the spirit of capitalism. *British Journal of Sociology, 34*, 459–482.

Doz, Y. (1986). *Strategic management in multinational companies*. New York: Pergamon.

Duck, S. (1993). *Individuals in relationships*. New York: Sage.

Dunning, J. H. (1988). The eclectic paradigm of international production: A restatement and some possible extensions. *Journal of International Business Studies, 19*(1), 1–31.

Dwyer, F. R., Shurr, P. H., & Oh, S. (1987). Developing buyer–seller relationships. *Journal of Marketing, 51*, 11–27.

Dwyer, F. R., & Welsh, M. A. (1985). Environmental relationships of the internal political economy of marketing channels. *Journal of Marketing Research, XXII*, 397–414.

Easton, G., & Araujo, L. (1992). Non-economic exchange in industrial network. In: B. Axelsson, & G. Easton (Eds), *Industrial networks — A new view of reality* (pp. 62–84). London: Routledge.

Easton, G., Burrell, G., Rotschild, R., & Shearmann, C. (1993). *Managers and competition*. Oxford: Blackwell.

Egelhoff, W. G. (1988). Strategy and structure in multinational corporations: A revision of the Stopford and Wells model. *Strategic Management Journal, 9*, 1–14.

Ekeh, P. E. (1974). *Social exchange theory: The two traditions*. Cambridge, MA: Harvard University Press.

Elliot, J. R. (1999). Social isolation and labour market insulation: Network and neighbourhood effects on less-educated urban workers. *The Sociological Quarterly, 40*(2), 199–216.

Esping-Andersen, G. (1985). *Politics against markets: The social democratic road to power*. Princeton: Princeton University Press.

Etzioni, A. (1988). *The moral dimension: Toward a new economics*. New York: Free Press.

Evan, W. M. (Ed.) (1976). *Interorganizational relations*. New York: Penguin Books.

Foord, R., Armandi, B., & Heaton, C. (1988). *Organization theory: An interactive approach.* New York: Harper & Row.

Ford, D. (Ed.) (1990). *Understanding business market: Interaction, relationships, networks.* London: Academic Press.

Ford, D., Gadde, L. E., Håkansson, H., Lundgren, A., Snehota, I., Turnbull, P., & Wilson, D. (1998). *Managing business relationships.* Chichester, UK: Wiley.

Forsgren, M. (1989). *Managing the internalization process. The Swedish case.* London: Routledge.

Friedman, R., & Kim, J. (1988). Political risk and international marketing. *Columbia Journal of World Business, 23,* 63–72.

Galbraith, J. R. (1973). *Designing complex organizations.* Reading, MA: Addison-Wesley.

Ghoshal, S. (1987). Global strategy: An organizing framework. *Strategic Management Journal, 8,* 425–440.

Gnyawali, D. R., & Madhavan, R. (2001). Cooperative networks and competitive dynamics: A structural embeddedness perspective. *Academy of Management Review, 26*(3), 431–445.

Golubeva, O. (2001). *Foreign investment decision-making in transition economies, school of business research reports No. 11.* Edsbruk: Stockholm University, Akademitryck.

Grabher, G. (Ed.) (1993). *The embedded firm. On the socioeconomics of industrial networks.* London: Routledge.

Granovetter, M. (1985). Economic action and social structure: The problem of embeddedness. *American Journal of Sociology, 91,* 481–510.

Hadjikhani, A. (1996). Sleeping relationship and discontinuity in project marketing. *International Business Review, 5*(3), 319–336.

Hadjikhani, A. (1997). A note on the critisism against the internalization process model [Special issue]. *Management International Review, 37,* 43–66.

Hadjikhani, A. (2000). The political behavior of business actors. *International Studies of Management and Organization, 30,* 95–119.

Hadjikhani, A., & Ghauri, P. (2001). The Behaviour of International Firms in Socio-Political Environments in the European Union. *Journal of Business Research, 52*(3), 263–275.

Hadjikhani, A., & Håkansson, H. (1996). Political actions in business networks: The case of Bofors. *International Journal of Research in Marketing, 13,* 431–447.

Hadjikhani, A., & Johanson, J. (1996). Facing market turbulence: Three Swedish multinationals. *Journal of International Marketing, 4,* 53–73.

Hadjikhani, A., & Seyed-Mohammad, N. (1998). Consumer perception and the effect of media — A loosely coupled system: The case of mad-cow syndrome. *Journal of Euromarketing, 8*(4), 69–96.

Hadjikhani, A., & Sharma, D. D. (1993). Political actors in industrial network. Paper presented at the 9th IMP conference, September 1993, Bath, UK.

Hadjikhani, A., & Sharma, D. D. (1999). A view on political and business actions. In: P. Ghauri, & A. Cavosgil (Eds), *Advances in international business and marketing* (Vol. 9, pp. 243–257). New York: JAI Press.

Håkansson, H. (Ed.) (1982). *International marketing and purchasing of industrial goods.* London: Wiley.

Håkansson, H. (Ed.) (1987). *Industrial technological development, adequate approach.* London: Croom Helm.

Håkansson, H., & Johanson, J. (1987). Formal and informal cooperation strategies in international networks. In: F. Contractor, & F. Lorange (Eds), *Cooperative strategies in international business* (pp. 279–379). London: Lexington Books.

Håkansson, H., & Östberg, C. (1975). Industrial marketing — An organizational problem? *Industrial Marketing Management, 4*, 113–123.

Håkansson, H., & Snehota, I. (1989). No business is an island: The network concept of business strategy. *Scandinavian Journal of Management, 5*, 187–200.

Håkansson, H., & Snehota, I. (1995). *Developing relationships in business networks.* London: Routledge.

Hallén, L., Johanson, J., & Seyed-Mohammad, N. (1987). Relationship, strength and stability in international and domestic industrial marketing. *Industrial Marketing and Purchasing, 2*(3), 22–37.

Hallén, L., Johanson, J., & Seyed-Mohammad, N. (1991). Interfirm adaption in business relationships. *Journal of Marketing, 55*, 29–37.

Hanf, K. I., & Scharpf, F. W. (Eds) (1978). *Internationalization policy making, limits to coordination and central control.* London: Sage.

Hannan, M. T., & Freeman, J. H. (1977). The population ecology of organizations. *American Journal of Sociology, 82*, 929–964.

Havila, V. (1996). *International business-relationship triads. A study of the changing role of the intermediating actor.* Doctoral thesis No. 64, Uppsala University.

Hawthorn, G. (1988). Three ironies in trust. In: D. Gambetta (Ed.), *Trust: Making and Breaking Cooperative Relations* (pp. 111–126). New York: Blackwell.

Heath, C., Hindmarsch, J., & Luff, P. (1999). Interaction in isolation: The dissolution world of the London Underground train driver. *Sociology, 33*(3), 555–575.

Hill, J. (1996). Social isolation and sociocultural diversity. *Journal of Social and Evolutionary Systems, 19*(2), 157–170.

Hirschman, A. O. (1970). *Exit, voice and loyalty: Responses to decline in firms, organizations and states.* Cambridge, MA: Harvard University Press.

Hofstede, G. (1991). *Cultures and organizations: Software of the mind.* London: McGraw-Hill.

House, J., Landis, K., & Umberson, D. (1988). Structures and processes of social support. *Annual Review of Sociology, 14*, 293–318.

Hult, K. M., & Walcott, C. (1990). *Governing public organizations: Politics, structure and institutional design.* Pacific Grove, CA: Brooks/Cole.

Husted, B. W. (1994). Transaction costs, norms and social networks. *Business and Society, 33*(1), 30–57.

Jacobson, C. K., Lenway, S. L., & Ring, P. S. (1993). The political embeddedness of private economic transactions. *Journal of Management Studies, 30*(3), 453–478.

Jansson, H., Dagib. M., & Sharma, D. D. (1995). *The state and transitional corporations.* Cheltenham, UK: Edward Elgar.

Jemison, D. B. (1981). The importance of an integrative approach to strategic management research. *Academy of Management Review, 6,* 608–608.

Johanson, J., & Mattsson, L.-G. (1987). Interorganizational relationships in industrial systems: A network approach compared with the transaction-cost approach. *International Studies of Management and Organization* (Vol. XVII, 1, pp. 34–48).

Johanson, J., & Mattsson, L.-G. (1988). Internalization in industrial systems — A network approach. In: N. Hood, & J.-E. Vahlne (Eds), *Strategies in global competition* (pp. 286–314). London: Croom Helm.

Johanson, J., & Mattsson, L.-G. (1994). The market as networks traditions in Sweden. In: G. Laurent, G. L. Lilien, & B. Pras (Eds), *Research traditions in marketing* (pp. 517–524). Boston: Kluwer Academic.

John, G., & Reve, T. (1982). The reliability and validity of key informant data from dyadic relationships in marketing channels. *Journal of Marketing Research, XIX,* 517–524.

Johnson-George, C., & Swap, W. C. (1982). Measurement of specific interpersonal trust: Construction and validation of a scale to assess trust in a specific other. *Journal of Personal and Social Psychology,* 1306–1317.

Jordan, G. (1990). Sub-governments, policy communities and networks: Refilling the old bottles? *Journal of Theoretical Politics, 2*(3), 319–338.

Kagono, T., Nonaka, I., Sakakibara, K., & Okumura, A. (1985). *Strategic vs. evolutionary management: A US–Japan comparison of strategy and organization.* Amsterdam: North-Holland.

Keegan, W. J. (1969). Multinational product planning: Strategic alternatives. *Journal of Marketing, 33*(1), 58–62.

Korbin, S. J. (1982). *Managing political risk assessment: Strategic responses to environmental changes.* Berkeley: University of California Press.

Kotler, P. (1999). *How to create, win and dominate markets.* New York: Free Press.

Kotler, P., Armstrong, G., Saunders, J., & Wong, V. (1996). *Principles of marketing. The European edition.* London: Prentice-Hall.

Larson, A. (1992). Network dyads in entrepreneurial settings: A study of the governance of exchange relationships. *Administrative Science Quarterly, 37,* 76–104.

Lenway, A., & Murtha, T. (1994). Country capabilities and the strategic state: How the national political institutions affect multinational corporations' strategies. *Strategic Management Journal, 15,* 113–129.

Levi-Strauss, C. (1969). *Argonauts of the Western Pacific.* London: Routledge & Keagan, Paul.

Levitt, T. (1983). *The marketing imagination.* New York: Free Press/Macmillan.

Looney, R. (1982). *Economic origins of the Iranian revolution.* New York: Pergamon Policy Studies.

Lubben, J. E. (1988). Assessing social networks among elderly populations. *Family and Community Health, 11,* 42–52.

Lundvall, B.-Å. (1988). Innovation as an interactive process: From user–producer interaction to the national system of innovation. In: G. Dosi, C. Freeman, R. R. Nelson, G. Silverberg, & L. Soete (Eds), *Technical change and economic theory* (pp. 349–369). London: Pinter.

Macaulay, S. (1963). Non-contractual relations in business. *American Sociological Review*, 23, 55–70.

Macneil, I. R. (1980). *The new social contract: An inquiry into modern contractual relations.* New Haven, CT: Yale University Press.

Maddison, A. (1991). *Dynamic forces in capitalist development, a long-run comparative view.* Oxford: Oxford University.

Makhija, M. V. (1993). Government intervention in the Venezuelan petroleum industry: An empirical investigation of political risk. *Journal of International Business Studies*, 24(3), 531–555.

Mazet, F., Spencer, R., & Bocconi, B. (1990, September). Accounting for geographical characteristics in networks: The case of the French supplier in three European markets. Paper presented at 6th IMP Conference in Milan.

McAllister, D. J. (1995). Affect- and cognitive- based trust as foundations for interpersonal cooperation in organizations. *Academy of Management Journal*, 38(1), 24–59.

McCarthy, D. J., Puffer, S. M., & Sheksina, S. V. (1996). The resurgence of an entrepreneurial class. In: S. M. Puffer (Ed.), *Business and management in Russia* (pp. 175–187). Cheltenham, UK: Edward Elgar.

Milbrath, L. (1965). *Political participation: How and why do people get involved in Politics?* Chicago: Rand McNaily.

Miller, K. D. (1992). Industry and country effects on managers' perspective of environmental uncertainties. *Journal of International Business Studies*, 24(1), 693–714.

Moorman, C., Desphande, R., & Zaltman, G. (1993). Factors affecting trust in market research relationships. *Journal of Marketing*, 57, 81–101.

Moran, T. H. (1985). *Multinational corporations: The political economy of foreign direct investment.* Lexington, MA: Lexington Books.

Morgan, R. M., & Hunt, S. D. (1994). The commitment-trust theory of relationship marketing. *Journal of Marketing*, 58, 20–38.

Nordström, K. A. (1990). *The internalization process of the firm in a new perspective.* Stockholm: Institute of International Business.

Norman, R. (1977). *Management for growth.* London: Wiley.

Nowtotny, K., Smith, D. B., & Trebling, H. M. (Eds) (1989). *Public utility regulation: The economic and social control of industry.* Boston: Kluwer.

Nuti, D. M. (1993). Transition or mutation: for a new political economy of post-communist mutations. *EMERGO, Journal of Transforming Economies*, 7, 7–15.

Olson, H. C. (1975). *Studies in export promotion, attempts to evaluate export stimulation measures for the Swedish textile and clothing industries.* Doctoral dissertation, Uppsala University, Uppsala.

Pagden, A. (1988). The destruction of trust and its economic consequences in the case of eighteenth-century Naples. In: D. Gambetta (Ed.), *Trust, making and breaking cooperative relationships* (pp. 127–142). New York: Basil Blackwell.

Peters, T. J., & Waterman, R. H. (1982). *In search of excellence*. New York: Harper & Row.

Pettigrew, A. M. (1979). On studying organizational cultures. *Administrative Science Quarterly, 24,* 570–581.

Pfeffer, J., & Salancik, G. R. (1978). *The external control of organizations*. New York: Harper & Row.

Phillips-Patrick, F. J. (1989). The effects of asset and ownership structure on political risk. *Journal of Banking and Finance, 13,* 651–671.

Porter, M. E. (1986). Competition in global industries: A conceptual framework. In: M. E. Porter (Ed.), *Competition in global industries* (pp. 15–60). Boston, MA: Harvard Business School Press.

Potters, J. (1992). *Lobbying and pressure*. Amsterdam: Tinbergen Institute Research Series.

Poynter, T. A. (1985). *Multinational enterprises and government intervention*. New York: St. Martin's Press.

Reve, T., & Stern, L. W. (1979). Interorganizational relations in marketing channels. *Academy of Management Review, 4*(3), 405–416.

Rhodes, R. A. W., & March, D. (1992). New directions in the study of policy networks. *European Journal of Political Research, 21*(1–2), 181–205.

Ring, P. S., Lenway, S. A., & Govekar, M. (1990). Management of the political imperative in international business. *Strategic Management Journal, 11,* 141–151.

Rose-Ackerman, S. (1978). *Corruption*. New York: Academic Press.

Roth, A. E., & Schoumaker, F. (1983). Expectations and reputations in bargaining: An experimental study. *American Economic Review, 73*(3), 362–372.

Rousseau, D. M., Sitkin, S. B., Burt, R. S., & Camerer, C. (1998). Not so different after all: A cross-discipline view of trust. *Academy of Management. The Academy of Management Review, 23,* 393–404.

Rubenstein, R. L., & Lubben, J. E. (1994). Social isolation and social support: An applied perspective. *Journal of Applied Gerontology, 13*(1), 58–73.

Rugman, A. M., LeCRow, D. J., & Booth, L. D. (1985). *International business, firm and environment*. New York: McGraw-Hill.

Sabel, C. F., & Zeitlin, J. (1985). Historical alternatives to mass production. *Past and Present, 108,* 133–176.

Shaap, L., & van Twist, M. J. W. (1997). The dynamics of closedness in networks. In: W. J. M. Kickert, E.-H. Klijn, & J. F. M. Hoppenjan (Eds), *Managing complex networks: Strategies for the public sector* (pp. 62–76). London: Sage.

Sharma, D. D., & Jansson, H. (1993). Industrial policy liberation and TNCs: The Indian experiences. *Scandinavian Journal of Management, 9,* 129–143.

Sheth J. N., & Parvatiyar, A. (1993). The evolution of relationship marketing. Paper presented at the sixth conference on Historical Thoughts in Marketing, May, Atlanta.

Simon, H. A. (1983). *Reason in human affairs*. Stanford, CA: Stanford University Press.

Snehota, I. (1990). *Notes on a theory of business enterprise*. Doctoral dissertation, Uppsala University, Uppsala.

Stern, L. W., & Reve, T. (1979). Interorganizational relations in marketing channels. *Academy of Management. Academy of Management Review, 4*(3), 405–416.

Swerdlow, M. (1998). *Underground women: My four years as a New York City subway conductor*. Philadelphia, PA: Temple University Press.

Szymanski, D. M., & Henard, D. H. (2001). Customer satisfaction: A meta analysis of the critical evidence. *Academy of Marketing Science, 29*(1), 16–35.

Teece, D. J. (1985). Multinational enterprise, internal governance and industrial organization. *American Economic Review, 75*, 233–238.

Thilenius, P. (1997). *Subsidiary network context in international firms*. Doctoral dissertation, Uppsala University, Uppsala.

Thompson, J. D. (1967). *Organizations in actions*. New York: McGraw-Hill.

Ting, W. (1988). *Multinational risk assessment*. Westport, CT: Greenwood Press.

Tunisini, A. (1997). *The dissolution of channels and hierarchies: An inquiry into the changing customer relationships and organization of the computer corporations*. Doctoral dissertation, No. 69, Uppsala University, Uppsala.

Usunier, J. C. (1993). *International marketing. A cultural approach*. Englewood Cliffs, NJ: Prentice-Hall.

Van Winden, F. (1983). *On the interaction between state and private sector*. Amsterdam: North Holland.

von Hipple, E. (1988). *The sources of innovation*. New York: Oxford University Press.

Weitz, R. (1990). Technology, work, and the organization: The impact of expert systems. *AI Magazine, 11*(2), 50–60.

Wells, L. T. (1977). Negotiating with Third-World governments. *Harvard Business Review, 55*(1), 72–80.

Wernerfelt, B. (1995). The resource-based view of the firm: Ten years after. *Strategic Management Review, 16*(3), 171–174.

Wynstra, J. Y. F. (1997). *Purchasing and the role of suppliers in product development*. Doctoral dissertation, Uppsala University, Uppsala.

Yarbough, B. V., & Yarbough, R. M. (1987). Institutions for the governance of opportunism in international trade. *Journal of Law, Economics and Organization, 3*, 129–139.